SEMIOTICS OF POETRY

ADVANCES IN SEMIOTICS

General Editor, Thomas A. Sebeok

SEMIOTICS
OF POETRY

->>->>->>|<<-<<-<<

Michael Riffaterre

INDIANA UNIVERSITY PRESS
Bloomington & London

Library of Congress Cataloging in Publication Data
Riffaterre, Michael.
Semiotics of poetry.
(Advances in semiotics)
Bibliography: p.
Includes index.
1. Semiotics.   2. Poetry.   I. Title.
II. Series.
P99.R5   808.1   78-3245
ISBN 0-253-35165-0 1 2 3 4 5 82 81 80 79 78

For Hermine

CONTENTS

Preface   ix

1. The Poem's Significance   1
2. Sign Production   23
3. Text Production   47
4. Interpretants   81
5. Textual Semiotics   115

Conclusion   164

Notes   167

Bibliography   202

Index   208

Preface

The theory of poetic semiotics put forward here was first sketched out in a 1971 paper of mine on what makes a literary sentence literary. My previous work had concentrated upon the surface structures of poetic discourse, upon what the reader recognizes and identifies as style. In the 1971 paper I began focussing on the poem as a whole, since it appeared to me that the unit of meaning peculiar to poetry is the finite, closed entity of the text, and that the most profitable approach to an understanding of poetic discourse was semiotic rather than linguistic.

The theoretical aims of this book make it applicable, I believe, to all Western literature, and in all likelihood some of the rules I propose reflect universals of literary language. But I have used only French examples, primarily from nineteenth- and twentieth-century writers (my specialization, aside from poetics). Much space is given to detailed discussion of texts. Nowadays so many literary studies are systems of interpretation wherein symbols, formulas, and the trappings of theory ignore or obfuscate or fall short of the reality of texts. I am more than ever convinced that no theory is worth consideration unless it is solidly grounded upon the phenomena it claims to elucidate. Because my conclusions are generally applicable, I have provided translations of all texts. French specialists may sometimes find these translations awkward or unnecessary; my sole aim is to enable all readers to follow the demonstrations based on texts, and to pass their own judgments. Nowhere do I attempt to "emulate" the original. In addition to pointing up my own shortcomings, any awkwardness will remind readers again that poetry does not translate—not because of certain intangible, quintessential elements usually invoked, but because of a semiotic displacement quite accessible to description.

Most of the text has been tried and tested on various audiences, especially during Visiting Professorships at the University of Toronto (University College), the University of Wisconsin in Madison, and New York University. Some of it also formed part of a series of lectures I delivered at the University of Pennsylvania and at Princeton. This study has greatly benefited from the discussions following such lectures, none more fruitful than those with my students at Columbia.

To no one do I owe more in this endeavor, as indeed in everything, than to Hermine Riffaterre: as a scholar, she was my first and has remained my strictest and soundest critic; as my wife, she is a never-failing source of strength.

⟶≫⟶≫⟶≫ O N E ≪⟵≪⟵≪⟵

THE POEM'S SIGNIFICANCE

The language of poetry differs from common linguistic usage—this much the most unsophisticated reader senses instinctively. Yet, while it is true that poetry often employs words excluded from common usage and has its own special grammar, even a grammar not valid beyond the narrow compass of a given poem, it may also happen that poetry uses the same words and the same grammar as everyday language. In all literatures with a long enough history, we observe that poetry keeps swinging back and forth, tending first one way, then the other. The choice between alternatives is dictated by the evolution of taste and by continually changing esthetic concepts. But whichever of the two trends prevails, one factor remains constant: poetry expresses concepts and things by indirection. To put it simply, a poem says one thing and means another.

I therefore submit that the difference we perceive empirically between poetry and nonpoetry is fully explained by the way a poetic text carries meaning. It is my purpose here to propose a coherent and relatively simple description of the structure of meaning in a poem.

I am aware that many such descriptions, often founded upon rhetoric, have already been put forward, and I do not deny the usefulness of notions like figure and trope. But whether these categories are well defined, like metaphor or metonymy, or are catchalls, like symbol (in the loose sense critics give it—not in the semiotic acceptation), they can be arrived at independently of a theory of reading or the concept of text.

The literary phenomenon, however, is a dialectic between text and reader.[1] If we are to formulate rules governing this dialectic, we shall have to know that what we are describing is actually perceived by the

1

reader; we shall have to know whether he is always obliged to see what he sees, or if he retains a certain freedom; and we shall have to know how perception takes place. Within the wider realm of literature it seems to me that poetry is peculiarly inseparable from the concept of text: if we do not regard the poem as a closed entity, we cannot always differentiate poetic discourse from literary language.

My basic principle will therefore be to take into account only such facts as are accessible to the reader and are perceived in relation to the poem as a special finite context.

Under this twofold restriction, there are three possible ways for semantic indirection to occur. Indirection is produced by displacing, distorting, or creating meaning. Displacing, when the sign shifts from one meaning to another, when one word "stands for" another, as happens with metaphor and metonymy. Distorting, when there is ambiguity, contradiction, or nonsense. Creating, when textual space serves as a principle of organization for making signs out of linguistic items that may not be meaningful otherwise (for instance, symmetry, rhyme, or semantic equivalences between positional homologues in a stanza).

Among these three kinds of indirection signs, one factor recurs: all of them *threaten the literary representation of reality, or mimesis.*[2] Representation may simply be altered visibly and persistently in a manner inconsistent with verisimilitude or with what the context leads the reader to expect. Or it may be distorted by a deviant grammar or lexicon (for instance, contradictory details), which I shall call *ungrammaticality.* Or else it may be cancelled altogether (for instance, nonsense).

Now the basic characteristic of mimesis is that it produces a continuously changing semantic sequence, for representation is founded upon the referentiality of language, that is, upon a direct relationship of words to things. It is immaterial whether or not this relationship is a delusion of those who speak the language or of readers. What matters is that the text multiplies details and continually shifts its focus to achieve an acceptable likeness to reality, since reality is normally complex. Mimesis is thus variation and multiplicity.

Whereas the characteristic feature of the poem is its unity: a unity both formal and semantic. Any component of the poem that points to that "something else" it means will therefore be a constant, and as such it will be sharply distinguishable from the mimesis. This formal and semantic unity, which includes all the indices of indirection, I shall call the *significance.*[3] I shall reserve the term *meaning* for the information conveyed by the text at the mimetic level. From the standpoint of meaning the text is a string of successive information units. From the standpoint of significance the text is one semantic unit.

Any sign[4] within that text will therefore be relevant to its poetic quality, which expresses or reflects a continuing modification of the mimesis. Only thus can unity be discerned behind the multiplicity of representations.[5]

The relevant sign need not be repeated. It suffices that it be perceived as a variant in a paradigm, a variation on an invariant. In either case the perception of the sign follows from its ungrammaticality.

These two lines from a poem by Paul Eluard:

> De tout ce que j'ai dit de moi que reste-t-il
> J'ai conservé de faux trésors dans des armoires vides[6]

Of all I have said about myself, what is left? I have been keeping false treasures in empty wardrobes

owe their unity to the one word left unspoken—a disillusioned "nothing," the answer to the question, an answer that the speaker cannot bring himself to give in its literal form. The distich is built of images that flow logically from the question: "what is left" implies "something that has been saved"; a meliorative or positive version might be "something that was worth saving." In fact the images translate into figurative language a hypothetical and tautological sentence: "keep what's worth keeping [figuratively: *trésors*] in the place where things are kept that are worth keeping [figuratively: *armoires*]." You might expect this tautology to yield "strongbox" rather than "wardrobe," but *armoire* is much more than just another piece of bedroom furniture. The French sociolect makes it *the* place for hoarding within the privacy of the home. It is the secret glory of the traditional household mistress—linens scented with lavender, lace undies never seen—a metonym for the secrets of the heart. Popular etymology makes the symbolism explicit: Père Goriot mispronounces it *ormoire,* the place for *or,* for *gold,* for treasure. The distressed version we have in Eluard's second line negativizes the predicate, changing not only *trésors* into *faux trésors,* but also *armoires* into *armoires vides.* We are faced with a contradiction, for, in reality, "treasures" of illusory value would fill a closet just as well as genuine ones—witness the table drawers in any home, full of shoddy souvenirs. But of course the text is not referential: the contradiction exists only in the mimesis. The phrases in question are variants of the answer's key word—they repeat "nothing." They are the constant of a periphrastic statement of disillusionment (all these things amount to zero), and as the constant element they convey the significance of the distich.

A lesser case of ungrammaticality—compensated for by a more conspicuous kind of repetition, a more visible paradigm of synonyms—is the mimesis devoid of contradictions but obviously spurious; such are these lines from Baudelaire's "Mort des amants":

> Nos deux cœurs seront deux vastes flambeaux,
> Qui réfléchiront leurs doubles lumières
> Dans nos deux esprits, ces miroirs jumeaux

Our two hearts will be two great torches that reflect their double lights in our two minds, twin mirrors

The context of furniture reinforces the concreteness of the image: these are real mantelpiece candlesticks. The image metaphorizes a torrid love scene, quite obviously, but the significance lies in the insistent variation on *two*. This makes it even more obvious that the description aims only to unfold the duality paradigm, until the duality is resolved in the next stanza by the oneness of sex ("nous échangerons un éclair unique" [we shall exchange a lightning like no other]).[7] The mimesis is only a ghost description, and through the ghost's transparency the lovers are visible.

The ungrammaticalities spotted at the mimetic level are eventually integrated into another system. As the reader perceives what they have in common, as he becomes aware that this common trait forms them into a paradigm, and that this paradigm alters the meaning of the poem, the new function of the ungrammaticalities changes their nature, and now they signify as components of a different network of relationships.[8] This transfer of a sign from one level of discourse to another, this metamorphosis of what was a signifying complex at a lower level of the text into a signifying unit, now a member of a more developed system, at a higher level of the text, this functional shift is the proper domain of semiotics.[9] Everything related to this integration of signs from the mimesis level into the higher level of significance is a manifestation of *semiosis*.[10]

The semiotic process really takes place in the reader's mind, and it results from a second reading. If we are to understand the semiotics of poetry, we must carefully distinguish *two levels or stages of reading*, since before reaching the significance the reader has to hurdle the mimesis. Decoding the poem starts with a first reading stage that goes on from beginning to end of the text, from top to bottom of the page, and follows the syntagmatic unfolding. This first, *heuristic reading* is also where the first interpretation takes place, since it is during this reading that *meaning* is apprehended. The reader's input is his linguistic competence, which includes an assumption that language is referential—and at this stage words do indeed seem to relate first of all to things. It also includes the reader's ability to perceive incompatibilities between words: for instance, to identify tropes and figures, that is, to recognize that a word or phrase does not make literal sense, that it makes sense only if he (and he is the only one around to do it) performs a semantic transfer, only if he reads that word or phrase as a metaphor, for example, or as a metonymy. Again, the reader's perception (or rather production) of irony or humor consists in his double or bilinear deciphering of the single, linear text. But this reader input occurs only because the text is ungrammatical. To put it otherwise, his linguistic competence enables him to perceive ungrammaticalities; but he is not free to bypass them, for it is precisely this perception over which the text's control is absolute. The ungrammaticalities stem from the physical fact that a phrase has been generated by a word that should have excluded it, from the fact that the poetic verbal sequence is characterized by contradictions between a word's presuppositions and its entailments. Nor is linguistic competence the sole factor. Literary competence[11] is also involved: this is the reader's familiarity with the descriptive systems,[12] with themes, with his society's mythologies, and above all with other texts. Wherever there are gaps or compressions in the text—such as incomplete descriptions, or allusions, or quotations —it is this literary competence alone that will enable the reader to respond properly and to complete or fill in according to the hypogrammatic model. It is at this first stage of reading that mimesis is fully apprehended, or rather, as I said before, is hurdled: there is no reason to believe that text perception during the second stage necessarily involves a realization that the mimesis is based upon the referential fallacy.

The second stage is that of *retroactive reading*. This is the time for a second interpretation, for the truly *hermeneutic* reading. As he progresses through the text, the reader remembers what he has just read and modifies his understanding of it in the light of what he is now decoding. As he works forward from start to finish, he is reviewing, revising, comparing backwards. He is in effect performing a structural decoding:[13] as he moves through the text he comes to recognize, by dint of comparisons or simply because he is now able to put them together, that successive and differing statements, first noticed as mere ungrammaticalities, are in fact equivalent, for they now appear as variants of the same structural matrix. The text is in effect a variation or modulation of one structure—thematic, symbolic, or whatever— and this sustained relation to one structure constitutes the significance. The maximal effect of retroactive reading, the climax of its function as generator of significance, naturally comes at the end of the poem; poeticalness is thus a function coextensive with the text, linked to a limited realization of discourse, bounded by clausula *and* beginning (which in retrospect we perceive as related). This is why, whereas units of meaning may be words or phrases or sentences, *the unit of signifi-cance is the text*. To discover the significance at last, the reader must surmount the mimesis hurdle: in fact this hurdle is essential to the reader's change of mind. The reader's acceptance of the mimesis[14] sets up the grammar as the background from which the ungrammati-calities will thrust themselves forward as stumbling blocks, to be under-stood eventually on a second level. I cannot emphasize strongly enough that the obstacle that threatens meaning when seen in isolation at first reading is also the guideline to semiosis, the key to significance in the higher system, where the reader perceives it as part of a complex network.

A tendency toward polarization (more of this anon) makes the guide-lines for reader interpretation more obvious: it is when the description is most precise that the departures from acceptable representation induced by structures make the shift toward symbolism more con-spicuous. Where the reader most expects words to toe the line of non-verbal reality, things are made to serve as signs, and the text proclaims the dominion of semiosis. It would be hard to find French descriptive poetry more representative than Théophile Gautier's *España* (1845), a collection of poems written after a journey through Spain. The trav-eler translated his trip into prose reports for the newspaper financing the adventure, and into verse vignettes, like the poem "In Deserto," composed after he had crossed Spain's lonely, arid *sierras*. A village with a demonstrably exotic name is given as the place of composition: this must refer to actual experience and is thus a way of labeling the poem "descriptive." In fact the learned editor of the one and only critical edition that we have finds nothing better to do than compare the verse with the prose version, and the prose with other travelers' accounts of the sierra. He comes to the conclusion that Gautier is fairly accurate, although he does seem to have made the sierra more of a desert than it really is.[15]

This is puzzling. However verifiable the text's mimetic accuracy by comparison with other writers' observations, it also consistently distorts facts or at least shows a bias in favor of details able to converge metonymically on a single concept: pessimism. Gautier makes this unmistakable with bold statements of equivalence; first when he actually speaks of despair as a landscape: "Ce grand jour frappant sur ce grand désespoir" [line 14: daylight striking upon this vast expanse of despair]. Just before this the desert was used as an illustration of the traveler's own lonely life, but the simile structure necessarily kept the setting separate from the character, the one reflecting the other. Now this separateness is cancelled, and the metaphor mingles the traveler's inner with the world's outer barrenness. In spite of this, our scholar, a seasoned student of literature, pursues his habit of checking language against reality. He seems little concerned about what language does *to* reality. This is proof at least that no matter what the poem ultimately tells us that may be quite different from ordinary ideas about the real, the message has been so constructed that the reader has to leap the hurdle of reality. He is first sent off in the wrong direction, he gets lost in his surroundings, so to speak, before he finds out that the landscape here, or the description in general, is a stage set for special effects.

In the Gautier poem the desert is there, of course, but only as long as it can be used as a realistic code for representing loneliness and its attendant aridity of heart—as opposed to the generous overflowing that comes of love. The first, naturally enough, is represented by a plain, direct, almost simplistic comparison with the desert itself; the second by a hypothetical description of what an oasis would be like, combined with a variation on the theme of Moses striking the rock. Thus we have an opposition, but still within natural climatic and geographic circumstances, or within the logic or verisimilitude of desert discourse.

The first pole of the opposition appears to rest upon straightforward mimesis:

IN DESERTO

Les pitons des sierras, les dunes du désert,
Où ne pousse jamais un seul brin d'herbe vert;

Les monts aux flancs zébrés de tuf, d'ocre et de marne,
Et que l'éboulement de jour en jour décharne;
5 Le grès plein de micas papillotant aux yeux,
Le sable sans profit buvant les pleurs des cieux,
Le rocher refrogné dans sa barbe de ronce,
L'ardente solfatare avec la pierre-ponce,
Sont moins secs et moins morts aux végétations
10 Que le roc de mon cœur ne l'est aux passions.

The pitons of the sierras, the desert dunes, where never a single blade of green grass grows; the mountainsides striped with tufa, ochre, and marl [literally: with chalky, rusty, and yellowish stripes; but the code is entirely geological], daily stripped of flesh by landslides; sandstone studded with mica glittering before your eyes; sand vainly drinking in the tears of heaven; rock scowling into its bramble beard; sulphur spring and pumice stone; these are less dry, less dead to vegetation than the rock of my heart is to passion.

But two factors transform this step-by-step scanning of a landscape into an iterative paradigm of synonyms that points insistently to barrenness (both figurative and physical). The transformation is especially obvious when this part of the text is looked at in retrospect, from the vantage point of the opposition's second pole—the last section of the poem. The first factor is the selection of visual details with disagreeable connotations not necessarily typical of the sierra (in any case readers may not recognize their aptness unless they know Spain). They make up a catalogue of hostile connotations: the sulphur spring, for instance, more "fire and brimstone" in landscape lexicon than a clear, apt, or visualizable depiction for most readers, even if it happens to be an accurate detail; or the earth's skeleton, a traditional literary motif in descriptions of rock formation; or the three specialists' words (*tuf, ocre, marne*), doubly technical as names of painter's colors and of soil types, but above all three words any French speaker will find cacophonic; or *zébré*, which does describe stripes and is presumably correct for strata, but also—and perhaps better—fits the stripes left by a whiplash.

The second factor of semiosis that slants representation toward another, symbolic meaning is the way the text is built: we do not know this is all a simile until the last two lines, when everything suddenly changes its function and calls for a moral, human interpretation. The suspense and the semantic overturn are space- or sequence-induced phenomena, inseparable from the physical substance of the text or from its paradoxical retroversion—the end regulating the reader's grasp of the beginning.

The second pole of the opposition is where the semiosis takes over (lines 29–44). In between there are eighteen entirely descriptive, seemingly objective lines, resuming the enumeration of the physical features of aridity. But of course this objectivity, unchallengeable as it may be within its own domain (lines 11–28), is now cancelled or made subservient to another representation, because the reader now knows that the whole sequence is not an independent description allegiant only to the truth of the outside world, but is the constituent of a trope. All the realism depends grammatically upon an unreality and develops not the desert we were initially invited to think real (before we discovered it was the first leg of a simile), but a desert conjured up to confirm contextually the metaphor prepared by the simile: *le roc de mon coeur* [the rock of my heart]. Everything is now ostensibly derived from an exclusively verbal given, the cliché *a heart of stone*. In line 29 an explicit allusion is made to the latent verbal association that has overdetermined, in desert context, the rock-of-the-heart image: a simile brings the rock Moses struck to the surface of the text, and this simile now triggers the unfolding of a new code for reverie about what love could do for this parched heart, and how it could make this desert bloom:

> Tel était le rocher que Moïse, au désert,
> 30 Toucha de sa baguette, et dont le flanc ouvert,
> Tressaillant tout à coup, fit jaillir en arcade
> Sur les lèvres du peuple une fraîche cascade.
> Ah! s'il venait à moi, dans mon aridité,
> Quelque reine des cœurs, quelque divinité,
> 35 Une magicienne, un Moïse femelle,
> Traînant dans le désert les peuples après elle,
> Qui frappât le rocher dans mon cœur endurci,
> Comme de l'autre roche, on en verrait aussi
> Sortir en jets d'argent des eaux étincelantes,
> 40 Où viendraient s'abreuver les racines des plantes;
> Où les pâtres errants conduiraient leurs troupeaux,
> Pour se coucher à l'ombre et prendre le repos;
> Où, comme en un vivier, les cigognes fidèles
> Plongeraient leurs grands becs et laveraient leurs ailes.

Such was the rock that Moses touched in the desert with his rod. And the rock's open flank shuddered all at once and sent an arc of water gushing to the people's lips in a cool cascade. If only some queen of hearts would come to me in my aridness, some divinity, a sorceress, a female Moses, dragging the peoples through the desert after her; if she would only strike the rock in my hardened heart, you would see leaping up, as from that other rock, silver jets of sparkling water; there the roots of plants would come to slake their thirst; there wandering shepherds would lead their flocks, to lie down in the shade and take their rest; there, as in a fishpond, the faithful storks would plunge their long beaks and wash their wings.

Now the semiosis triumphs completely over mimesis, for the text is no longer attempting to establish the credibility of a description. Any allusion to the desert landscape, or to the oasis born of the miraculous fountain, is derived entirely from the name *Moïse*, taken less as an actual wanderer who crossed the Sinai than as a literary theme, or derived from the female variant of *Moïse*, which is of course a metaphor in desert code for *Woman as a fountain of life*. The code itself is not a metaphor: we cannot assign a literal tenor to the *fountain* vehicle; even less can we find a term-for-term relationship between the descriptive vignettes about the drinkers at that spring (roots, shepherds, storks) and certain tenors that would be metonymic of the revived and transfigured speaker.

We must therefore see the code of the poem as symbolic. It definitely represents something that is not the desert to which the description is still referring. Everything points to a hidden meaning, one evidently derived from a key word—*fecundity*—which is the exact opposite of the first key word, *barrenness*. But there is no similarity, even partial, between fecundity, even in the moral sense, and the speaker as the text enables us to imagine him. If the reader simply assumes (since this is the chief rationalization in any reading experience) that the first-person narrator, so long as he remains unnamed, must be the poet himself, *fecundity* will refer to poetic inspiration, indeed often associated with love at last requited. But the description of the oasis still does not match any of the traits, real or imaginary, of a creative writer.

All we can say, then, is that the text's final passage symbolizes the miraculous effects of love on life. The selection of *fertility* as the key to that symbol is determined by the reversal of the symbol used to describe life before the miracle. The last part of the poem is a reverse version of the forms actualized in the first part. The positive "conversion" that accomplishes this affects every textual component regardless of its previous marking or meaning. This is why contradictions or incompatibilities or nonsense abound in the description: such details as *flanc ouvert* or *flanc . . . tressaillant* (lines 30–31), phrases properly applied only to a pregnant woman who feels the child move in her womb for the first time, bring to the fore the repressed sexual implications of the Moses-rod story, as do the storks (43), flown out of nowhere (out of the implied womb, that is)—for, without this displaced determination, why not just any bird, so long as it is a positive sign? These details do not fit the male character who has now slipped into the metaphoric rock. Yet they are contradictory only as descriptions, only if we keep trying to interpret them as mimesis; they cease to be unacceptable when we see them as the logical and cogent consequences of the positivization of desert code.

Other ungrammaticalities are simply the mimetic face of the semiotic grammaticality; the astonishing *Moïse femelle,* the nonsense of vegetable roots endowed with animal mobility, the *Et in Arcadia ego* connotations of the scene around the spring, after the manner of Poussin—all these conform to the conversion according to an indirect, implicit, but continuously present love code. The amplification of *Moïse femelle* as a sexual pied piper—"Traînant dans le désert les peuples après elle"—is intertextually determined by a line from Racine, Phèdre's amorous description of her lover's seductive power: "Traînant tous les cœurs après soi" [dragging all hearts after him]. It translates into a phrase an essential seme of love—its irresistible magnetism—and the same applies to the miracle of the roots, this time overdetermined by another association intersecting the first chain: the hyperbolic positive fountain also involves the cliché of the spot that irresistibly draws every living creature. Upon the oasis oxymorically derived from "aridity," love symbolism superimposes its own theme of the *locus amoenus.*

We cannot, however, understand the semiosis until we have ascertained the place of the text now perceived as one sign within a system (a sign formally complex but monosemic), for by definition a sign cannot be isolated. A sign is only a relationship to something else. It will not make sense without a continuous translatability from component to component of a network. A consequence of the system's latent existence is that every signifying feature of the poem must be relatable to that system. Here everything the text says must be fitted back into the initial code, into the *desert* code, even though it is represented in the end only conversely. Failing this we cannot relate the end and the beginning, we cannot recognize that text and significance are coextensive, we cannot discover that the clausula dovetails with the title.

The one feature pervading the whole clausula (from line 33 on) is grammatical: every verb is in the conditional mood; that is, it expresses an action or state of things not yet realized, a wish unfulfilled, a hope frustrated, a dream dreamt in vain—in short, life still the desert of life, a familiar theme. But this verbal mood's being the grammatical icon of unfulfillment raises the question of the speaker's voice. For the poem is spoken in the first person, and we do not know where from. Then suddenly the puzzle is solved, everything falls into place, indeed the whole poem ceases to be descriptive, ceases to be a sequence of mimetic signs, and becomes but a single sign, perceived from the end back to its given as a harmonious whole, wherein nothing is loose, wherein every word refers to one symbolic focus.

This epiphany of the semiosis occurs when the lost voice is found again, thanks to the hint signalled by the title, misunderstood until the end: this signal is the title's language. In French, *Dans le désert* would be a self-sufficient title and perfectly appropriate for a mere travelogue. The Latin *In deserto* does not make sense unless read, as it must be, as an incomplete quotation. *In deserto* is only the second half of the familiar phrase for words shouted in vain, the voice crying in the wilderness: *vox clamans in deserto*. From this repressed, despairing voice the whole poem is derived; from this bereft speaker issues the dream's unreality. This one conventional symbol, erased from the title, founds a whole new symbolism defining only *this* work of art; and the text, raised from the ashes of familiar description, is made into a novel and unique significance.

Significance, and let me insist on this, now appears to be more than or something other than the total meaning deducible from a comparison between variants of the given. That would only bring us back to the given, and it would be a reductionist procedure. Significance is, rather, the reader's praxis of the transformation, a realization that it is akin to playing, to acting out the liturgy of a ritual—the experience of a circuitous sequence, a way of speaking that keeps revolving around a key word or matrix reduced to a marker (the negative orientation whose semiotic index is the frustration implied by *vox clamans in deserto*). It is a hierarchy of representations imposed upon the reader, despite his personal preferences, by the greater or lesser expansion of the matrix's components, an orientation imposed upon the reader despite his linguistic habits, a bouncing from reference to reference that keeps on pushing the meaning over to a text not present in the linearity, to a paragram or hypogram[16]—a dead landscape that refers to a live character, a desert traveled through that represents the traveler rather than itself, an oasis that is the monument of a negated or nonexistent future. The significance is shaped like a doughnut, the hole being either the matrix of the hypogram or the hypogram as matrix.

The effect of this disappearing act is that the reader feels he is in the presence of true originality, or of what he believes to be a feature of poetic language, a typical case of obscurity. This is when he starts rationalizing, finds himself unable to bridge the semantic gap inside the text's linearity, and so tries to bridge it outside of the text by completing the verbal sequence. He resorts to nonverbal items, such as details from the author's life, or to verbal items, such as preset emblems or lore that is well established but not pertinent to the poem. All this just misguides the reader and compounds his difficulties. Thus, what makes the poem, what constitutes its message, has little to do with what it tells us or with the language it employs. It has everything to do with the way the given twists the mimetic codes out of shape by substituting its own structure for their structures.

The structure of the given (from now on I shall refer to it as the *matrix*), like all structures, is an abstract concept never actualized per se: it becomes visible only in its variants, the ungrammaticalities. The greater the distance between the inherently simple matrix and the inherently complex mimesis, the greater the incompatibility between ungrammaticalities and mimesis. This was already obvious, I think, in the discrepancy between "nothing" and Eluard's thesaurization sequence, between "couple" or "lovers" and Baudelaire's furniture sequence. In all these cases the discrepancy is made graphic by the fact that the mimesis occupies a lot of space while the matrix structure can be summed up in a single word.

This basic conflict, the locus of literariness (at least as literariness manifests itself in poetry) may reach a point where the poem is a form totally empty of "message" in the usual sense, that is, without content —emotional, moral, or philosophical. At this point the poem is a construct that does nothing more than experiment, as it were, with the grammar of the text, or, perhaps a better image, a construct that is nothing more than a calisthenics of words, a verbal setting-up exercise. The mimesis is now quite spurious and illusory, realized only for the sake of the semiosis; and conversely, the semiosis is a reference to the word *nothing* (the word, since the concept "nothingness" would be heavy metaphysical stuffing indeed).

This is an extreme case but exemplary, for it may tell us much about poetry's being more of a game than anything else. I shall use three short texts as illustrations, all of them about paintings or scenes, all three pictorial descriptions, all three reading like picture plaques in a parodic museum. The first is supposedly a "Combat de Sénégalais la nuit dans un tunnel" [Night combat of Senegalese tribesmen inside a tunnel]. The second: "Récolte de la tomate par des cardinaux apoplectiques au bord de la Mer Rouge" [Apoplectic cardinals picking tomatoes on the shores of the Red Sea]. The third: "Perdu dans une exposition de blanc encadrée de momies" [Lost at a white sale surrounded by Egyptian mummies].[17] The first one is a joke familiar in relatively intellectual French circles; it is usually rationalized as a satire on certain monochromatic modern paintings. Every character, every scenic detail being black, you see nothing. The second is from a humorous piece by Alphonse Allais, a minor writer not unlike Alfred Jarry, his contemporary, but without Jarry's genius. Allais is generally credited with being one of the creators of humor as a genre in French literature. Here again: red-faced, red-robed princes of the church, their red harvest, the red locale—redness cancels all the shape, line, and contrast that must set the cardinals off from their surroundings, if they are to be seen. There is nothing here but a one-color continuum.

True, the red of the Red Sea is only a convention, not a real color mimesis; still, it purports to refer to a geographical reality, so that the principle of mimesis, the differentiation, is at work, and it is indeed cancelled here. In the third quotation, from a poem by the surrealist Benjamin Péret, the *white sale* again is more metaphorically than literally white; yet once more the effect is to blend all representation into a uniform whiteness.

One may wonder why I have chosen these three examples to prove a point about poetic discourse. I reply that these and others like them are commonplaces; that the durability of even the oral joke, the first, unsigned text, reminds us that a mere joke is an elementary form of literature, since it is as lasting, and as protected against tampering when quoted, as a more highbrow text. The fact that these lines are intended, or perceived, as jokes reflects only their obviousness of purpose (they are so obviously a game); and the cancellation of mimetic features leads to a pointless semiosis: we do not see where generalized blackness, redness, or whiteness can possibly be taking us. But of course the significance really lies in the gratuitousness of the transformation: it exemplifies that process itself, the artifact per se. It also demonstrates the essential conflict that makes a literary text: no variation-cancelling conversion, no direct decoding of the invariant (here the color) can take place until the representing, mimetic variants to be cancelled have first been stated. No breaking of the rule without a rule.

I am quite sure that even if they agree these jokes may in fact possess the features of literariness, most readers will be unable to resist the temptation to jump from a negative value judgment (these are examples of lowbrow literature or bad literature) to a complete denial that they are literature at all. But other texts evidence the very same "weaknesses" and no doubt is cast on their poetic status, so long as our attention is diverted from circularity, so long as we are able to spot in the text something we recognize as a commonly accepted literary feature—be it a stylistic form, or a form of content like, say, a theme. The text then "passes" unscathed, and yet the formal alteration of the mimesis is no less drastic than that of our jokes, and the semiosis is just as pointless. Take for example this blackness sequence in a Robert Desnos poem, the cause of much emotional upset among critics. It is a portrait of the speaker, head, heart, thoughts, waking moments, and now sleep:

> Un bon sommeil de boue
> Né du café et de la nuit et du charbon et
> du crêpe des veuves
> Et de cent millions de nègres
> Et de l'étreinte de deux nègres dans une
> ombre de sapins
> Et de l'ébène et des multitudes de cor-
> beaux sur les carnages[18]

A good muddy sleep born of coffee and night and coal and ink and widow's weeds and of a hundred million negroes and of two negroes embracing in the shade of fir trees, and of ebony and multitudes of ravens hovering over fields of carnage

Or again (since I have no "redness" example at hand, and for officially poetic "whiteness" Gautier's "Symphonie en blanc majeur" would be too long to quote), let us take this "transparency" text, a passage from André Breton's *Revolver à cheveux blancs:*

On vient de mourir mais je suis vivant et cependant je n'ai plus d'âme. Je n'ai plus qu'un corps transparent à l'intérieur duquel des colombes transparentes se jettent sur un poignard transparent tenu par une main transparente.[19]

> There has just been a death, but I am alive, and yet I no longer have a soul. All I have left is a transparent body with transparent doves inside throwing themselves on a transparent dagger held by a transparent hand.

Here we are ready to pass over the representational nonsense because death is eminently literary. We have no trouble rationalizing that this disembodiment is a legitimate way of representing the afterlife. And of course the question of genuine literariness will not be raised with Mallarmé: for instance the sonnet beginning "Ses purs ongles très haut dédiant leur onyx." The question does not arise, first, because the challenge to mimesis is not so complete that the reader has no chance at all to read the poem as a representation. The lofty language makes up for the circularity. And the obscurity makes less glaring the absence of the symbolism that should compensate us for accepting such detours from straightforward referentiality. Or better, the obscurity hides the fact that the text's implications are just as short range, just as slight, as in a joke. The tone, the style make the difference. But that difference lies in the reader's attitude, in his greater willingness to accept a suspension of mimesis when he thinks no one is trying to pull his leg. Actually there is no difference in the text, for the structure of Mallarmé's sonnet is the same conversion found in all three jokes and in Breton and Desnos.

In the joke subgenre there is no way for the reader to get beyond the laugh, once it has been laughed, any more than he can get beyond the solution once he has solved a riddle. Such forms self-destruct immediately after consumption. The sonnet, on the contrary, leaves the reader free to keep on building, so long as his constructs are not wholly incompatible with the text. The first stanza, "L'Angoisse, ce minuit" [anguish at midnight], seems to adumbrate a meditation upon the problems of life or upon artistic creation. This looks so serious that the reader expects the poem to be about reality, physical or conceptual, especially when the second quatrain presents the familiar livingroom interior:

> Sur les crédences, au salon vide: nul ptyx,
> Aboli bibelot d'inanité sonore,
> (Car le Maître est allé puiser des pleurs au Styx
> Avec ce seul objet dont le Néant s'honore.)

> On the sideboards, in the empty livingroom: no ptyx, abolished bibelot of sonorous inanity (for the Master has gone to draw tears from the Styx, bearing with him this only curio that Nothingness takes pride in).

The mimesis has hardly been offered, however, when reference is withdrawn, so that the structure is a polar opposition of *representation* vs. *nothing*. The text first sets up a particularly tangible kind of reality: the pride of bourgeois life, the ultimate actualization of presence in a house, of its completeness as social status symbol, the furniture. But at the same time the text, an Indian giver, snatches back this reality by repeating Nothingness with each descriptive item. The resulting polarization is the poem's significance, aptly described by Mallarmé himself: "une eau-forte pleine de rêve et de vide" [an etching full of dream and emptiness].[20] That phrase itself is a variant of the significance structure, since *eau-forte* in its telling technicality expresses the mimesis hyperbolically, and *full of emptiness* actualizes the other pole, the cancellation of mimesis. (This other pole is, as it should be, equally hyperbolic, because "full of emptiness" is an oxymoron, and as such repeats and integrates the whole of the opposition over again—*fullness* vs. *emptiness*.) I need not underline that this commentary on the sonnet —*eau-forte pleine de vide*—fits equally well as metalanguage for my three comedy paintings of nothing, and for André Breton's pseudo-representation of afterlife invisibility. Such, then, is the semiosis of the poem, and by happy coincidence it exemplifies the rule that literature, by saying something, says something else. The rule in its *reductio ad aburdum:* by saying something literature can say nothing (or, if I may once more indulge in my irreverent simile: no longer the dough-nut around its hole, but the doughnut as a hole).

The mechanism of mimesis cancellation in Mallarmé's sonnet calls for close scrutiny, being comparable to that of Eluard's *armoires vides,* and susceptible of generalization (later it will be recognized as obeying the rule of conversion):[21] that is, every mention of a thing is marked with a zero index. *Salon* modified by *vide* serves as a model for a striking series of synonymous assertions of void. Within the narrow compass of a quatrain *salon vide* is repeated five times: once through the symbolic disappearance of its owner, who is dead or gone to Hell, an eminently dramatic way of not being around,[22] and then through a fourfold variation on the nonexistence of a knickknack. The *bibelot* is a nonfunctional object, at most a conversation piece, and yet the ultimate filler of emptiness during periods like Mallarmé's, when household esthetics prescribe that every nook and cranny be stuffed with ornaments, that every bit of space be crammed with the shapes of things. But this object is named only to be cancelled as a sign, not just mentioned as a thing gone. The equivalence of *vide* and *bibelot* is insured the first time by *nul ptyx*. Not only because *nul* annuls *ptyx*, but because *ptyx* is a nonobject, a word unknown in any language, as Mallarmé himself boasted,[23] a pure ad hoc product of the sonnet's rhyming constraints. Having imposed upon himself a difficult rhyme, /*iks*/,[24] the poet patently runs out of words. With its outlandish spelling and its boldly non-French initial consonantal cluster, *ptyx*, like everything else in the sonnet, combines high visibility, an almost obtrusive physical presence as a form, and an equally obtrusive absence as meaning. The second equivalence of presence and absence is *aboli bibelot*, as meaning, as the French variant of the semi-Greek *nul ptyx*, and as paronomasia, making *bibelot* an approximate phonetic mirror image of *aboli*, thus a reflection of absence.[25] The third equivalence: *inanité sonore*, a phrase made the more effective by being a cliché or literary quotation about empty words going back to Latin: *inania verba*. The fourth equivalence: the semiotic nonexistence of the object whose existence is asserted by description is translated into a mimesis of philosophical Nothingness itself (*dont le Néant s'honore*), with a pun to top it off, since *Néant s'honore* sounds like *néant sonore*, "sonorous nothingness." Finally, this emptiness, these nonobjects, are paralleled by the graphemic symbolism of the rhyme, since *y* and *x* are the signs of conventional abstractness and of algebraic unknowns.

Such is the force of habit, such the power of the everyday context of cognitive language, that commentators have unanimously endeavored to connect the quatrain with actual representation. Even though it should be impossible to miss the meaning—an exercise in verbal exercise[26]—we find at work here a nostalgia for referentiality that promises us no reader will ever get used to nonlanguage. The efforts of scholars to palliate it only enflame the outrage of words cancelling themselves. The vase *dont le Néant s'honore* has been interpreted as a vial of poison, thus a vial of death, or a vessel of Nothingness as a tangible, physical cause of death. And *ptyx*, despite Mallarmé's own statement, has been forcibly twisted into a full-fledged representation, by way of a Greek word meaning, supposedly, a "fold" or "shell shaped like a fold." The trouble is that the word *ptyx* itself is a hypothesis of lexicographers, deduced from a rare Greek word found only in the plural or in oblique-declension cases, *ptykhes;* Mallarmé could not have known of this. His *ptyx* does have a model: a word Hugo had used a few years earlier for the sake of strangeness per se, since in *his* poem it is supposed to be the name of an actual mountain translated into the language of the Gods—neat proof that *ptyx* has no meaning in any human language.[27] Turn where we may, the picture of reality is erased, so that these varied but repetitious cancellations add up to the one significance so ringingly proclaimed by the title of the sonnet's first version: "Sonnet allégorique de soi-même" [Sonnet allegoric of itself], a text referring to its own shape, absolute form. It takes the whole sonnet to unroll the description and to annul it, point by point. The destruction of the mimesis, or its obverse, the creation of the semiosis, is thus exactly coextensive with the text: it is the text.

An extreme example, obviously, and most poems are closer to the model of Eluard's distich, but the principle is, I believe, the same in all cases. From this principle I shall now try to deduce the fundamentals of my interpretation of poetry's semiotic system.

/*Postulates and Definitions*/

Poetic discourse is the equivalence established between a word and a text, or a text and another text.

The poem results from the transformation of the *matrix,* a minimal and literal sentence, into a longer, complex, and nonliteral periphrasis. The matrix is hypothetical, being only the grammatical and lexical actualization of a structure. The matrix may be epitomized in one word, in which case the word will not appear in the text.[28] It is always actualized in successive variants; the form of these variants is governed by the first or primary actualization, the *model.* Matrix, model, and text are variants of the same structure.

The poem's significance, both as a principle of unity and as the agent of semantic indirection, is produced by the *detour* the text makes as it runs the gauntlet of mimesis, moving from representation to representation (for example, from metonym to metonym within a descriptive system), with the aim of exhausting the paradigm of all possible variations on the matrix. The harder it is to force the reader to notice the indirection and to lead him step by step through distortion, away from mimesis, the longer the detour must be and the more developed the text. The text functions something like a neurosis: as the matrix is repressed, the displacement produces variants all through the text, just as suppressed symptoms break out somewhere else in the body.

To clarify *matrix* and *model* further, I shall use an example of limited relevance to poetry; its very limitations, however, make its me-

chanics more obvious and practical for the purposes of my preliminary
definitions. This is an echoing sequence in a Latin verse by the seven-
teenth-century Jesuit Athanasius Kircher:[29]

> Tibi vero gratias agam quo clamore? Amore more ore re.

> How shall I cry out my thanks to Thee? [the question being addressed to
> the Almighty, who replies:] With thy love, thy wont, thy words, thy deeds.

Each word in the answer accords with the model provided by the pre-
ceding word, so that every component is repeated several times over.
For each member of the paradigm, it would be easy to imagine a de-
velopment wholly regulated by the nuclear word of the one preceding.
The question *clamore* serves as a model for the reply *amore,* and *amore*
serves as a model for the entire sequence—it is the seed of the text, so to
speak, and summarizes it in advance. The matrix here is *thanksgiving,*
a verbal statement that presupposes a divine Providence (as benefactor),
a believer (as beneficiary), and the gratefulness of the latter to the
former. The model is *crying out (to),* not a random choice, but one
already determined by a literary theme: the outcry, the spontaneous
outburst, is a common sign of sincerity and open-heartedness in moral-
istic text, especially in meditations or essays on prayer. The model
generates the text by formal derivation affecting both syntax and
morphology; every word of the text is in the same case, the abla-
tive; every word of it is contained in the first variant of the model
(*clamore*). The conformity of the text to the generating model makes
it a unique artifact, in terms of language, since the associative chain
issuing from *clamore* does not work as do normal associations, play-
ing out a string of semantically related words. Instead it functions
as if it were creating a special lexicon of cognates of *clamor.* The lin-
guistic anomaly is thus the means of transforming the semantic unity
of the statement into a formal unity, of transforming a string of words
into a network of related and unified shapes, into a "monument" of
verbal art. This formal monumentality entails changes of meaning.
Independent of their respective senses, the ways of giving thanks here
enumerated appear to be subsumed under love, since the word for love
contains them and love appears as the essence of prayer, since prayer
is contained in the word for love. In both cases these verbal relations
reflect the principles of Christian living as taught by the Church, so
that the very fact of the derivation is a semiotic system created ad hoc
for these principles: the way the sentence functions is their icon.

The matrix alone would not suffice to explain textual derivation, nor would the model taken separately, since only the two in combination create the special language wherein everything the believer does that is pertinent to what defines him as a believer is expressed in *love* code. Hence the text as a whole is indeed a variant of the verb for the activity typical of the faithful (*to give thanks*). The text in its complexity does no more than modulate the matrix. The matrix is thus the motor, the generator of the textual derivation, while the model determines the manner of that derivation.

The Kircher example is of course highly exceptional, since the paronomasia, like an extended pun, might be said to extract the significant variation from the mimesis itself: the ungrammaticality consists in the dispersion of one descriptive word, in the building of the paradigm out of the pieces of that one lexeme drawn and quartered. Paronomasia, when it does occur, is rarely so pervasive. The usual detour around the repressed matrix, being made of separate, distinct ungrammaticalities, looks like a series of inappropriate, twisted wordings, so that the poem may be regarded as a generalized, all-encompassing, all-contaminating catachresis.

This catachresis has *overdetermination* as its corollary. It is a fact that no matter how strange a departure from usage a poem may seem to be, its deviant phraseology keeps its hold on the reader and appears not gratuitous but in fact strongly motivated; discourse seems to have its own imperative truth; the arbitrariness of language conventions seems to diminish as the text becomes more deviant and ungrammatical, rather than the other way around. This overdetermination is the other face of the text's derivation from one matrix: the relationship between generator and transforms adds its own powerful connection to the normal links between words—grammar and lexical distribution. The functions of overdetermination are three: to make mimesis possible; to make literary discourse exemplary[30] by lending it the authority of multiple motivations for each word used; and to compensate for the catachresis. The first two functions are observable in literature in general, the last only in poetic discourse. The three together confer upon the literary text its monumentality: it is so well built and rests upon so many intricate relationships that it is relatively impervious to change and deterioration of the linguistic code. Because of the complexity of its structures and the multiple motivations of its words, the text's hold on the reader's attention is so strong that even his absentmindedness or, in later eras, his estrangement from the esthetic reflected in the poem or its genre, cannot quite obliterate the poem's features or their power to control his decoding.

I shall distinguish between two different semiotic operations: the transformation of mimetic signs into words or phrases relevant to significance, and the transformation from matrix to text. The rules governing these operations may work together or separately in overdetermining the verbal sequences from the incipit to the clausula of the poem.

For describing the verbal mechanisms of sign integration from mimesis to significance level, I shall propose a single *hypogrammatic rule* telling us under what conditions the lexical actualization of semic features, stereotypes, or descriptive systems produces poetic words or phrases whose poeticity is either limited to one poem or is conventional and therefore a literary marker in any context.

Two rules apply to production of the text: *conversion* and *expansion* (chapter 3). The texts overdetermined according to these rules may be integrated into larger ones by embedding. The components of the significance-bearing paradigm may therefore be such embedded texts. The signs of specialized poetic usage (conventional poetic words) and perhaps others as well may be said to stand for texts: their significance issues from this vicarious textuality.

In all cases the concept of poeticity is inseparable from that of the text. And the reader's perception of what is poetic is based wholly upon reference to texts.

SIGN PRODUCTION

The poetic sign is a word or a phrase pertinent to the poem's significance. This pertinence is either an idiolectic factor or a class factor. It is idiolectic if the poetic quality of the sign is peculiar to the poem in which it is observed. The poetic sign is a classeme if its poeticity is recognized by the reader, no matter what the context (provided, of course, that the context is a poem): that is, if the selection of poeticity markers is regulated by esthetic conventions outside of and in addition to the intrinsic individual features of a word or phrase.

In either case the production of the poetic sign is determined by *hypogrammatic derivation: a word or phrase is poeticized when it refers to (and, if a phrase, patterns itself upon) a preexistent word group.* The hypogram is already a system of signs comprising at least a predication, and it may be as large as a text. The hypogram may be potential, therefore observable in language, or actual, therefore observable in a previous text. For the poeticity to be activated in the text, the sign referring to a hypogram must also be a variant of that text's matrix. Otherwise the poetic sign will function only as a stylistically marked lexeme or syntagm.

If the sign referring to a hypogram is made of several words, it is their common relationship to the hypogram that defines these words as components of one single significance unit.

It will perhaps be useful to observe various types of hypogrammatic derivation yoked together in an example where overdetermination is maximal: a famous line of Baudelaire's in "Hymne à la Beauté" [Hymn to Beauty], one of the most celebrated *Fleurs du Mal* poems. In the Romantic manner, the line conjures up an ideal of the Beautiful both infernal and celestial—this esthetic is aptly summarized by the very

23

title of the collection. *Flowers,* but *of evil,* serves as a model generating every single poem in the book. Or else the phrase is the verbal reference of all Baudelairean narratives, descriptions, images, and symbols. The line goes:

> O Beauté! monstre énorme, effrayant, ingénu

Oh Beauty, enormous monster, horrendous, innocent

There must be a reason why this line is so often quoted, why it is so easy to remember, why it stands out in a long poem overloaded with a mixture of Gothic horror and rhetorical bombast. The reason for the line's "monumentality" is, first, that it is made of pure, unalloyed metal and yet reflects another literary monument. Is is made out of unalloyed metal or, if you like, out of a perfect lexical pertinence, for every word is linked to the nuclear word *beauté* not just grammatically but also by a deeper, semantic relationship. On the one hand, *monstre* stands in direct contrast to *beauté:* the inappropriateness is exact, not random, since two of *monstre*'s basic semes, "horror," or perhaps "repellence," and "disproportion" are the precise contraries of two of *beauté*'s basic semes, "attractiveness" and "symmetry." The basic semes of *monstre* are actualized by the first two adjectives; or, if you prefer, these adjectives, in the guise of modifying or qualifying *monstre,* repeat it, somewhat like a musical variation on the monstrosity motif. Yet at the same time another seme of *monstre,* or simply its etymology, "what is held up as an example, as especially worthy of attention," makes it a devious or paradoxical but true synonym of *beauté.* Now the final shocker in the line, *ingénu,* "innocent" or "artless," almost "naïve" in a virginal way, is diametrically opposed to the allegorical female figure in the poem embodying the Beautiful and represented as a sort of she-devil—trampling upon corpses, adorned with gaudy trinkets (*breloques*), Horror and Murder. But this adjective *ingénu,* punlike, also evokes the noun *ingénue,* a positive word connoting the youthful feminine beauty we enjoy in a *young thing.* More important, *ingénu* is semically related to *beauté* as *énorme* or *effrayant* is to *monstre,* since *ingénu*'s basic seme, "purity," is one of *beauté*'s possible semes. And *ingénu,* meaning first of all "natural," is the contrary of the seme "anomaly," which forms part of the "monstrousness" semantic complex: thus *ingénu* duplicates the adversary relationship of the *beauté/monstre* predication.

Regarded as forms, then, the relationships among the line's lexical

components are all extreme, absolute, or exemplary. From the stand-
point of meaning, the whole line merely develops simultaneously two
opposite semantic potentialities of its nuclear word; the line is simply
the transformation of that word into a sentence that is *about* the word,
and is made entirely out of the *stuff* of the word. Nor is this all; the
verbal sequence is further determined and turned into a remarkable
object worthy of contemplation by the fact that the Baudelairean mon-
ster is superimposed upon a Vergilian monster, the Cyclops, as he ap-
pears in a familiar line, a monster who was part of the cultural code
of the Frenchmen to whom literature was directed. So true was this
that until the years just before World War II the line persisted in
Latin grammar books as an example of spondaic heaviness: "mon-
strum horrendum, informe, ingens, cui lumen ademptum" [a monster
horrendous, misshapen, gigantic, one deprived of light]. *Ingens* in
particular—pronounced in the French fashion—dictated the choice,
from among the suitable synonyms of *innocent* as well as from the anto-
nyms of *monstrous,* of the word most resembling it, *ingénu.*

The most extended hypogram is Vergil's entire line, and it makes
Baudelaire's whole line into one poetic sign. In this role it will neces-
sarily be one of the most effective variants of the poem's matrix, for
it adds to the denotation of monstrousness the connotations of the
Cyclops—since classical times one of the great traditional examples (on
a par with Laocoon's serpents and the hybrid Siren) of an object re-
pellent in reality paradoxically turned into an object of admiration,
solely by transposition into the medium of an art—painting, sculpture,
or poetry.

The grouping of *monstre, énorme,* and *effrayant* has for its hypo-
gram the presuppositions of the nuclear or kernel word, *monstre.* The
grouping of *monstre* and *beauté* is derived from a cliché or set of
clichés built on the linking of polar opposites, Beauty and the Beast
being the most famous example. Here they are rolled into one, so to
speak, but the point is that a polar opposition creates an exceptionally
powerful link and one that produces exciting images.

I shall now discuss the various types of hypogram—semes and presup-
positions, clichés (or quotations), and descriptive systems.

Semes and Presuppositions

The hypogram is formed out of a word's semes and/or its presuppo-
sitions. The poetic sign actualizes some of these; the hypogram's nu-
clear word itself may or may not be actualized.

The sememe of the kernel word functions like an encyclopedia of representations related to the meaning of that word.[1] Their actualization has the effect of saturating the derivative verbal sequence with that meaning, overtly confirming what could have been gathered from a single word. Hence emphasis, visualization, and the need for the reader to decode connotations as well as denotation. A *flute*, for instance, presupposes a flutist, entails an audience, contains semes such as "melodiousness," but also "rusticity," since one kind of flute is Pan's, etc.

A neologism of Hugo's actualizes part of a hypogram in precisely this way. New coinages have this in common with ungrammaticality: wherever the existing lexicons impose limits upon derivation, they allow extension of the derivative sequence. This extension of language potentialities is necessarily conspicuous and effective, for a neologism is perceived like any other word, save for its function as a new coinage, a function perceived because the neologism is in this case opposed to a non-neological homologue or synonym. This opposition has the advantage of compelling the reader to decode the word quite consciously, and even to memorize it, and the inescapability of the word contributes further to make it exemplary and a verbal "monument." Thus the neologism, like the archaism, is not a word per se, or isolated in context, but is a relationship between two equivalent forms, one marked and one unmarked. The unmarked form antedates the text, the marked one does not. Finally, neological derivation has the capacity to represent the seme or sememe whose lexical variants it enumerates in "pure" form (since existing words entering a paradigm can be no more than partial, approximating synonyms).

The word created ad hoc to repeat another or to actualize part of its semic setup therefore offers perfect tautology. The following example is taken from a Hugo collection of pastoral poetry in modern adaptation: the tautology lies in an adjective ostentatiously formed on a Latin word.

> Comme Properce, j'entends
> Une flute tibicine
> Dans les branches du printemps[2]

Like Propertius, I hear a tibicine flute on the branches of Spring

Because of its Latinate form, the new fangled adjective has a tautological link of sorts with *Properce,* the exemplar of the lyric poet in ancient Rome, and here a first symbol of the genre Hugo is imitating. Second, thanks to its etymology, the adjective reflects or reproduces exactly the noun it should modify, since it is formed on the Latin *tibicen*, "flutist," and this circularity works much like emphasis by repetition: this flute-truly-flute is therefore exemplary. First of pastoral poetry, because it relates to Properce. Second of a poetic diction, because of the way the Latin ending is Frenchified; it is replaced by a quasi-homophone, the *-in* suffix, no longer active but found in adjectives considered pertinent only to literary discourse: *adamantin* "diamondlike," "hard and pure as diamond"; *ivoirin* "ivory-white," "made of ivory," etc. Paradoxically (though this is not unusual), the new coinage thus has an archaic flavor—another index of poetic quality in the lexicon. Hence the group *flute tibicine,* as one tautological sign, literally means the poetic Latin flute, since Hugo, who describes himself as an imitator of Propertius and an heir to Latin, is a modern poet. For him the Latin flute he is listening to can be no antique instrument, but must be a compound symbol: by referring to a thematic text (the scene of a shepherd playing at dusk in springtime), the tautological group becomes a marker of the bucolic genre, where a setting like this is a strict requirement for any action. In context the flute is stated to be real, it is actually heard by the narrator, but the tautological adjective transfers the statement from the mimesis (at which level it functions as a constituent of the bucolic picturesque) to a semiotic system: every apparent detail of the scene and the setting is but the figurative equivalent of a pastoral marker.

Except that it is so blatantly new—even a *hapax* formation—*tibicine* would traditionally be interpreted as a *stock epithet,* that is, a permanently or conventionally poetic word that can be analyzed as a hypogrammatic derivative, e.g., *fleet-footed* Achilles or *rosy-fingered* Dawn. The selection of such words is regulated by tradition, by a historically definable esthetic system; that same system dictates the words' interpretations (especially their perception as signs of values). Conventional though they are, stock epithets survive the death of the esthetics that begat them. They continue to be effective mainly because the reader is under stronger compulsion to perceive them as poetic, for they are the more conspicuous the more and more remote they seem, with the passage of time, from everyday speech.[3]

Stock epithets have always been studied from the viewpoint of the nouns they modify. One or more stock epithets conventionally marked a given noun as poetic: *cimes vaporeuses,* for instance, instead of *cimes couvertes de nuages* for cloud-covered mountaintops. Such epithets do not necessarily remain poetic conventions attached to just any noun. But if we look at the epithet per se—which is the normal procedure in actual reading, when our attention is drawn first to the convention—we find that certain epithets feel poetic no matter what noun they modify. Such is the French *agile*, "agile," "nimble," for instance: (1) "fleur pure, alouette agile" (Hugo); (2) "le soleil agile et rayonnant monta dans les cieux" (Chateaubriand); (3) "les navettes agiles des années tissent des fils entre . . . nos souvenirs" (Proust); (4) "Puis j'étalais mon savoir enfantin, / Mes jeux, la balle et la toupie agile" (Hugo); (5) "Qui a tracé en vermillon le plan de mes colonnettes agiles?" (Quinet)[4] [pure flower, nimble lark; the sun climbed up the heavens, agile and radiant; the agile shuttles of the years weave the fabric of our memories; I was showing off all my childish knowledge, my games, my ball, and my nimble top; who traced in red the blueprint of my nimble columns?]

Any native reader will recognize all these lines as poetic utterances; but we cannot explain this by the presence of a trope. Examples (2) and (5) are indeed metaphors, and (3) extends the metaphor Loom of Time. But (1) and (4) are literal statements, not figures of speech. On the other hand, their poetic quality would vanish, were the sentences to read: "l'alouette (le soleil, la toupie, etc.) est agile" or "je vis une alouette agile" or "l'alouette si agile." It would vanish even if the metaphor remained intact, as in "les navettes des années sont agiles." Thus poeticity disappears when the adjective is modified or qualified or enters into a predicative relationship—in short, when it ceases to be an epithet.

We must therefore conclude that the agent of poeticity is a specific relationship between epithet and noun, which designates a quality of the noun's referent, or a seme of that signifier, as characteristic or basic. So that the poetic is born where an adjective's meaning, normally contingent, accessory, in any case context-determined, is represented *a priori* as a permanent feature. This permanent or context-free factor is evidenced by the practice, widespread from the seventeenth to the nineteenth century, of compiling dictionaries for the use of would-be poets and students of literature. These tomes contained long lists of epithets matched up with the nouns they should legally modify, in either their literal or figurative senses.

This permanence is the variant in the adjective class of an invariant of literary esthetics embracing all lexemes, namely, in one way or another they must be *exemplary*, strikingly representative. As Abbé Batteux wrote in his 1747 treatise on *Les Beaux Arts réduits à un même principe:* "Si les Arts sont imitateurs de la Nature, ce doit être une imitation sage et éclairée, qui ne la copie pas servilement; mais qui choisissant les objets et les traits, les présente avec toute la perfection dont ils sont susceptibles."[5] [If art must imitate nature, it has to be a wise and enlightened imitation. Not a servile copy, but a copy that selects objects and features and represents them in the most perfect state attainable.]

It must be understood, however, that this exemplariness is not referential and is not to be seen as an aspect of the literary mimesis of reality. True, in many cases it seems to be that: the swift vertical flight of example (1) does characterize the skylark; *agile* is the appropriate epithet for *aile, course, esprit, feu, flèche, fuseau,* "spindle," just as prescribed in one of the poetic dictionaries mentioned above.[6] For all of these nouns, swiftness equals effectiveness or full realization of potentialities. But at the same time swiftness is not a simple factor—if it were, *rapide* would do as well. *Agile* is obviously less a mimesis of quickness than a positively marked equivalent of *rapide*. A phrase like "nimble top" (4) suggests this positive nature, because it entails animation. I do not mean that the top is personified; we have here less a sketchy or playful animization of a toy, à la Disney, than a make-believe or symbolic allusion to such animation and to the attendant transformation of the toy's gyroscopic principle of equilibrium, its rapid rotation, into an adroit and willful balancing act. A positive esthetic marking results from this symbolic, empty animation simply because it reflects a scale of values that sets reason above instinct, consciousness above automatism, and so forth—the attitude of those who judge everything in relation to man as sensate being. If this were only a representation, it would be a misleading or figurative one.

On the other hand, the same dictionary links *agile* to words that do not usually make one think of nimbleness: *animal, vaisseau, air,* "atmosphere" (a possible exception if regarded as a metonymy—though an improbable one—for "wind"). Since real animals can be heavy-limbed and ships can plod, we must recognize an embellishing parti-pris, which is prone to ignore other, perhaps incompatible possibilities in the real thing. In (5) this is even more obvious: as mimesis, nimble columns are nonsense, since architecture is the epitome of immobility.

Nonsense only as mimesis, however. For the exemplariness implied by *agile*'s epithet function may look sometimes like mimesis, sometimes like a denial of it, but it always works like an index of beauty, or rather like a coded invitation to the reader to admire. In (1) *agile* is to *alouette* what *pure* is to *fleur,* and the whole analogic combination is an indirect comment on the promise of a spring morning. In (4) the significance resides in a sequence of images synonymous not just with naïve childhood memories (Hugo reminisces about his little-boy crush on a much older girl) but with sweet memories. The context of (2) and (3) clearly indicates, through "free," author-controlled collocations, that a positive marking is needed (*rayonnant* is for glorious suns: *souvenirs* are sought for, not evaded, etc.).

Agile is thus appropriate within a semiotic system of exemplariness. The noun it modifies does not generate the epithet because reality demands a more complete picture, but because the context demands a positive picture.

When we now try to delve deeper into the relationship between epithet as exemplariness-marker and its context, its grammatical definition must remain inadequate. As we just noted in the case of (3) and of *air, animal,* and *vaisseau,* positivization cannot stem from the noun alone. The epithet can have a meaning without the noun, but not a literary function; it therefore falls into the class of *synnomous* lexemes, according to Benveniste's terminology.[7] But it derives its motivation as marker from a sentence rather than from the noun it is tied to. In (5), for instance, *agile* echoes a metaphor that is implicit or perhaps suppressed. This metaphor is a French literary theme depicting pillars —especially Greek-style pillars—as young maidens.[8] Young girls are lithe, hence the indirect appropriateness of *agile* for "column," detoured through an image kept in an intertextual background. Not kept there entirely, perhaps, since the frisky young thing also surfaces, you might say, in the diminutive form *colonnette.* Since Quinet's text requires no precise or realistic distinction between thick and thin columns, the *-ette* suffix simply reflects another feature of the standard maiden description: svelteness.

Thus the stock epithet presupposes a sentence or even a text already endowed with an ideological *ethos;* the epithet has its place pegged in the sociolect's scale of values. Witness Omphale's spinning wheel in another Hugo poem: symbol of Hercules enslaved by love, his club turned into a distaff, if I may so put it:

> Il est dans l'atrium, le beau rouet d'ivoire.
> La *roue agile* est blanche . . .
> Des aiguilles, du fil, des boîtes demi-closes,

Les laines de Milet, peintes de pourpre et d'or,
Emplissent un panier près du *rouet qui dort*.[9]

The handsome ivory spinning wheel stands in the atrium. The agile wheel is white. Needles, thread, half-closed box, wool of Miletus, all purple and gold, fill a workbasket beside the sleeping spinning wheel.

Note the incompatibility between *roue agile* and *rouet qui dort*. This is a night scene, everyone is sleeping, the spinning wheel is motionless. In fact, *agile* is referring indirectly, and metonymically, to the industry and deftness of certain absent characters, the spinners of thread. Not that the metonymy is truly activated, but quick and hardworking servants are part of a system of positive indices,[10] which comes to the text ready-made and immutable. Because these values are incompatible with the context, they are eliminated as meaning. But they continue to function as meliorative, or perjorative, signs. Halfway between text and reality, there remains only a semic reference to the *hard-work* ideology, a reference irrelevant to the text except insofar as it is a positive marker, in a form appropriate to the context. Appropriate not to the topic but to the language in which the subject is couched.

The stock epithet is thus poetic because it implies a hypogram, usually a descriptive system (here the ensemble of stereotyped commonplaces for the Good Servant) whose nuclear word remains unsaid and appears only in the expanded form of a sentence. This sentence is the word's periphrasis, so that the true referent is not a lexeme in the text but a syntagm in the intertext. That is why the empirical reader bypasses the noun modified by the epithet and focusses on the adjective. That is why he thinks he recognizes the adjective as a borrowing from an intertext.[11]

This displacement of focus depends upon how strong the connections are that hold the hypogram's components together. Obviously they are stronger in the case of words actualizing the semes, rather than the presuppositions, of the nuclear word, since the semes are the very core of a word's meaning. When this *is* the case, the hidden network of the hypogram becomes a means of endowing with poetic quality words conspicuously lacking in the emotional or intellectual connotations expected of poetry. It is quite enough for such words to become poetic signs, if they simultaneously actualize a seme and their relationship with the kernel word. This relationship grammatically expresses the distance or difference from the kernel word; thus is created the semantic "space" required for the development. At the same time the word's actualizing of a seme makes it a metonym of the kernel word, whose connotations it eventually absorbs.

My example is the compound *miroir sans tain,* an important motif in modern French poetry. The mirror theme itself is certainly one of the most fertile in literature. The richness is readily explainable: mirror tolerates easy analogies and lends itself to moral interpretations —mirror as Emblem of Truth or of Deception; the endless variations on reflection as a physical fact or a mental one (most of which are traceable to Plato's analogy between mind and mirror). Yet none of this can explain the sudden popularity among poets at the turn of the century of the image *miroir sans tain.* First the symbolists seem to favor it, then the surrealists.

The explanation is that *glace* or *miroir sans tain* is a compound word. This compound word has a complex meaning, and this meaning submits to word play. Indeed, the compound has three possible referents, all of them natural paradoxes that easily translate into verbal paradoxes. It may refer to the two-way mirror—one side a reflecting surface, the other transparent. Or it may refer to plain plate glass, no mirror at all; or to a mirror whose silvering has been worn off its back. In the last two cases you can see through the mirror, but you still get a reflection: a reflection confused or blurred by the shapes perceived behind the glass. The last two meanings play a significant role in poetry, for when *miroir sans tain* is used in these senses, it becomes a metaphor for sadness, or, more generally, an image with melancholy connotations.

Tain, a technical word to start with, has become a literary one in functioning as a metonym for the mirror itself, or rather as a substitute sign for specularity. And it has ended up as a negative marker in poetic discourse.

There are, to be sure, negative mirrors outside our phrase—especially melancholy reflections, mirrors of distressful memory or bad conscience. These are characterized by a shadowy or dim reflection, or the reflection that lets you see beyond, as in dark stagnant waters—Hérodiade's mirror, for instance:

> Eau froide par l'ennui dans ton cadre gelée
> Que de fois et pendant des heures, désolée
> Des songes et cherchant mes souvenirs qui sont
> Comme des feuilles sous ta glace au trou profond,
> Je m'apparus en toi comme une ombre lointaine[12]

Cold water, frozen with boredom in your frame, how often, and for hours, disconsolate with dreams and looking for my memories that are like

leaves under your ice in the deep hole below, I looked to myself in you
like a distant shadow

Here *reflection* vs. *see-through* is the specular translation, the transla-
tion into *mirror* code of another image-for-the-past or image-for-con-
sciousness-of-the-past: the theme of the palimpsest of memory.

But transparency as a defect in the mirror, or, in semantic terms,
as the cancellation of *mirror*'s basic seme—*reflectivity*—does not seem
enough to justify this particular motif's function, or to explain how
it holds its own in competition with the archetypal magic of water.[13]
For one thing, there is no good reason to think that the mirror's flaw,
its imperfect reflectivity, is enough as concept or as reality to endow
the representation of that defect with a negative symbolism. In point of
fact, the meliorative or pejorative interpretation of this mimesis and
its symbolism must depend upon the context, which will actualize
favorable or unfavorable connotations, as in the phrase *see through
a glass darkly*.[14]

I propose to account for the gloomy or sinister symbolic poten-
tialities of the *miroir sans tain* and the gradual shift of that symbolic
power to *tain* alone by a single factor: the presence in the text of
the word *sans*. It is not so often that an object is referred to by a
phrase stating lack. Hence a compound word containing *sans* is bound
to force the reader to see *miroir sans tain* not just as a reference to a
non-mirror (when it means "plate glass"), or to a negated mirror (when
it means a worn-out old mirror with its backing eroded), but as a
sign of lack or defect per se.

That this semantic shift is indeed taking place is demonstrated by
the elimination from literary texts of the "plate glass" meaning and
its replacement almost exclusively by the "dilapidated mirror" sense,
as in these lines from Desnos:

> Chaque jour de ses dents aiguës
> Le temps déchire un peu le tain
> De ce miroir[15]

Day by day with his sharp teeth Time gnaws away at the silver backing
of the mirror

where the allusion to the cliché *tempus edax* must be taken as a peri-
phrasis of *sans tain*. It reduces the two possible meanings (without
silvering, having *lost* its backing) to one, the second and more dramatic.
Or again, still from Desnos, a stanza where the stereotype for pointless

reminiscing and for the irrevocable past (*un passé de cendres*) generates
an image of resentful, willful blacking out of painful memories:

> Brûlez les vieux billets et puissiez-vous ternir
> A jamais le miroir dont le tain mord la glace[16]

Burn your old letters, and so may you tarnish forever the mirror with
the silvering that eats away the glass

But even if the context does not clearly indicate that the mirror is in
decline, has lost its reflective power, the context reveals the semantic
shift I speak of by its clear negativity. For instance, consider this from
a prose poem of Eluard's:

> Je devins esclave de la faculté pure de voir. . . . Je supprimai le visible
> et l'invisible, je me perdis dans un miroir sans tain

I became a slave to the pure faculty of seeing. I got rid of the difference
between the visible and the invisible. I lost myself in a mirror without
silvering

or these lines from Verlaine's "Le Clown":

> Vides et clairs ainsi que des *miroirs sans tain*
> Ses yeux ne vivent pas dans son masque d'argile.

Empty and clear like mirrors without silvered backs, his eyes are not
living eyes in his mask of clay.

In these examples words like *esclave, se perdre, vide, ne pas vivre,* in-
dependently of their separate meanings, their narrative or descriptive
roles, all have negative markings in common.[17] The simile functions
less as if it were the illustration of a certain type of reflection than as
if it were the visual climax of a *-less* paradigm. This paradigmatic
effect is perhaps even more striking in the following almost ludicrous
poem of Milosz's:

> J'ai senti mon coeur saisi . . . éteint
> Comme un moi-même indistinct
> Au fond d'un miroir sans tain,
> Etrange, secret tintouin
> Intérieur et lointain[18]

I felt my heart stricken, extinguished like a self dimly discerned in the
depths of an unsilvered mirror, strange, secret botheration, inside of me
and far away

A stanza, by the way, that clearly establishes *sans tain* as generator of the negative sequence rather than the other way around; plainly the negative words are derived from *sans tain* rather than from the mirror simile it creates. For the *tin tin tin* jingle would be absolutely pointless and random, and there would be no need to pick mournful words ending with the "tin" sound, were it not for the fact that the one word that seems to be here solely for the sake of that sound happens to characterize the gloom-mirror.

No longer does *sans tain* serve as a precise description of a certain sort of mirror, an accurate detail creating the illusion of its reality. Instead, *tain* now functions as the formal rationalization or justification for *sans,* which is the one sign for evil within the descriptive system of the looking glass. *Sans tain* need no longer be used compatibly with the description of a looking glass alone: it may be used anywhere as a pseudoadjective to modify any noun and change its metaphorical value from meliorative to pejorative. For instance, in Michel Leiris's "Les Veilleurs de Londres":

> Ils réclamaient les joies sans lendemain de la vigueur
> . . .
> Le coït en plein ciel illuminé d'ardeur
> Ils ne pouvaient hanter que d'étranges coulisses
> Où les baisers vendus par des lèvres sans tain
> Permettent d'entrevoir triste feu d'artifice
> Les miroirs éclatés au fond des spasmes feints.
> Or nous étions dimanche
> Les plaisirs vrais ou faux dormaient dans les boutiques
> Et tous les coeurs étaient fermés[19]

They demanded vigor's lusty joys without tomorrow, coupling under an open sky alight with passion. They could do no more than haunt the backstage of strange theaters where kisses sold by lips *sans tain* permit a glimpse of dismal fireworks, the broken mirrors at the heart of pretended spasms. Now it was Sunday. Pleasures true or false were sleeping in the shops, and all hearts were closed

The text makes its sexual symbolism clear and explicit with *coït* at the beginning and *plaisirs* in the last stanza, so that there can be no argument as to what the middle, mirror stanza is about. The minute sex is mentioned in an obscure text, we set to work decoding every point of obscurity, hoping for erotic innuendoes. The last three lines make just as clear the rule for proper decoding: the text's idiolectic grammar first posits a semantic transfer—here words associated with the mimesis of an English Sunday are used to represent indirectly the availability (or unavailability) of love or sex. I prefer to speak of semantic transference or transcoding (from Sunday code to love language), rather than of metaphor, since there is no conceivable similitude that could make Sunday stand for coitus. The text's grammar posits that the words of the transferral code are scrambled to the detriment of representation, so that only their marker value is left. Sunday closing slides from *shops* to *hearts*. *Shops* retains only its *venality* seme and business closure only its *interdiction* seme, both playing the role of negative marker to the word *pleasure*. Following the same rule, the descriptive system of *miroir* is scrambled, but without losing the pertinent components: *miroir, sans tain*, and *entrevoir*—fitting verb for the dim perception of something beyond. Within the code it is obvious that *sans tain*, the visual indistinctness, and the splintered mirrors mean no more (and no less) than *étranges, vendus, triste*, and *feints*. They are negative markers for a spectral representation of unsatisfying or venal sex. Or rather, for a textual sign (textual because the whole stanza functions as one sign) for the mirrorlike deceitfulness of love/sex. It is worth noting that *sans tain* operates as if it were self-sufficient, making its appearance in the sentence *before* the kernel word, without hampering the reader. *Tain* comes to annex or absorb the adverse meaning of *sans*, this function being displaced from its carrier (the preposition) to the prop (*tain*) that makes it possible to insert *sans* into the sentence. As usual in poetic discourse, the abstract geometry of meaning is fleshed out, so to speak, with figurative words.[20]

This annexation is demonstrated by the ability of the word *tain*, first, to substitute completely, all by itself, for the group *sans tain;* and, second, the ability of *tain*, again all by itself, to replace, or displace, the word *miroir* and usurp its thematic function.

A Benjamin Péret distich well exemplifies this first type of *tain* self-sufficiency:

> lourd sommeil . . . caverne habitée d'anciennes joies
> à conserver dans l'herbier des miroirs déteints[21]

heavy sleep, cave inhabited by past delights to be conserved in a herbarium made out of tarnished mirrors

A good example, because it is a case of automatic writing verging on nonsense. Nonsense, that is, to the reader who is longing for some sort of reference to reality. But to the analyst, the lines offer proof that verbal collocations have not been tampered with by any intent of the writer—a perfect opportunity to find out which word associates with which, and what function these associations most naturally represent.

Now *miroirs déteints* must mean tarnished mirrors. This is a common stereotype: "tarnishing" translates sadness and old age into mirror language. But in that language the true cliché is *miroir terni:* the verb *ternir* is in fact the proper word for discoloration of polished surfaces, metal or like metal. In short, it is technically the aptest word for describing a mirror's loss of reflecting power. And aside from its association with mirrors, *terni* is a familiar metaphor for moral stain or blemish. *Déteint,* on the other hand—"faded," or better, "washed out," with colors that have run—is used for other materials, not for mirrors—only for painted surfaces or dyed fabrics or colored paper.

Thus we have maximal appropriateness replaced by maximal inappropriateness at the very point of significance, at the very focus of our poetic stereotype. The only explanation is that *déteint* covers a hypogram restoring it to perfect appropriateness—and that hypogram is of course our *tain,* disguised by a pun, but at the same time reinforced by a privative prefix. *Déteint* strikes the reader and makes him pay heed to the text because it is the wrong word for *terni.* But intertextually, by reinjecting *tain,* the pertinent marker, into the tarnish, it remotivates and overdetermines the cliché by translating it into mirror language twice over, at the semantic level (tarnish) and at the lexical level (silvering), where *tain* has become the reverse of the word *miroir* with a plus sign, as it were, instead of being a descriptive detail of *miroir,* indifferent, a mirror with a plus or a minus sign.

As for the second type of substitution, where *tain* entirely displaces *miroir,* my example is Verlaine's poem "Le Rossignol."[22] Here a tree embodies the first-person speaker, the birds in the leaves embody his memories, the nightingale his one happy recollection; a half-implied actualization of the mirror represents his forlornness:

> Comme un vol criard d'oiseaux en émoi,
> Tous mes souvenirs s'abattent sur moi,
> S'abattent parmi le feuillage jaune
> De mon cœur mirant son tronc plié d'aune
> Au tain violet de l'eau des Regrets
> Qui mélancoliquement coule auprès,
> S'abattent, et puis la rumeur mauvaise
> Qu'une brise moite en montant apaise,
> S'éteint par degrés dans l'arbre, si bien

Qu'au bout d'un instant on n'entend plus rien,
Plus rien que la voix célébrant l'Absente,
Plus rien que la voix—ô si languissante!—
De l'oiseau que fut mon Premier Amour,
Et qui chante encor comme au premier jour;
. . .

like a shrill swarm of fluttering birds, all my memories swoop down upon me, swoop down into the yellow foliage of my heart that sees its bent alder-trunk reflected in the violet silvering of the waters of Regret, flowing nearby in its melancholy. They swoop down, then their nasty din, lulled by a moist rising breeze, gradually dies down in the tree, so that after a moment nothing more is heard. Nothing but the voice praising the Absent One, nothing but the voice—ah! so languishing!—of the bird that my First Love was, singing still as he sang the first day

Without *tain* this would be just an example of the reflecting-water-surface theme, hence an indirect variation on the mirror theme; that is, the looking glass would function only as a secondary simile pointing to the water's reflectivity. But with the mention of *tain,* the mirror becomes the primary code—and no wonder, since otherwise the reflecting water could mean sadness only if sadness were spelled out periphrastically. *Tain* suffices to transform the whole looking-glass mimesis into one symbol of sorrow. It may be objected that the water here does reflect images, that the mirror works, that even the word *sans* first negativizing *tain* is absent, that this is in truth a regular mirror *with* silvering. And no doubt these objections would stand up if this were a real landscape, of things. But it is a verbal landscape. We are dealing with words, not with things. And when you *speak* of a real working mirror, you do not mention its silver backing—you do not say *miroir avec tain.* Despite its presence at the level of mimesis, then, at the significance level *tain* is actually the sign of its absence. Which is why it is an image of sorrow—not because water in itself or tinfoil in itself would represent sorrow, but because *water* here is subordinated to a word implying the transparency of memory's palimpsest. And that is why *tain* is violet: no foil or quicksilver or silvering or water is that color, but if *tain* be sadness, purple is a color of bereavement. *Tain* is the sole carrier of significance, the one sign that converts the entire passage from a text about a tree by the river into a text about melancholy, from a variation on specularity to a variety of dirge. Hence there is no direct representation of the whole looking glass. It is displaced by the one metonym that conveys the specular meaning and at the same time the anamnesis significance. This displacement is compensated for by actualization of the presuppositions of the absent word *miroir,* each actualization being appropriately marked negative in obedience to the semantic given, that is, to *tain:* reflection (*mirant*), whose marker is *tain* itself; the reflector, *eau,* flowing with otherwise unaccountable melancholy (a notable case of textual paranoia); and the reflectee (marked by "yellow" and "bent").

To conclude, the *miroir sans tain* is less a subcategory of the mirror theme than a case of poeticization, or rather, of semioticization of a word that would be nothing more than a realistic detail, did it not become a metonymic substitute for the kernel of the theme, and thus for a specific variant of that theme's structure. The functional cancellation denoted by *sans tain* is inserted into the semiotic system of lyricism (as poetry expressing the emotional life of the individual). Its being a metonym of the un-mirror in language in general makes the working mirror that *tain* implies in the text's discourse a metaphor for absence.

It will have been noted that I have resorted to the traditional category of theme: this does not affect my analysis, since the theme is simply a culture-marked hypogram. That it should have become the vehicle of a specific symbolism only testifies to the power packed into a semic derivation. This now stereotyped identification also demonstrates how a sign until recently favored by literary rebels, or at least innovators, can rapidly change into a permanent, conventional poetic sign.

Clichés and Descriptive Systems

These hypograms differ from the preceding category in that they are already actualized in set forms within the reader's mind. They are part of his linguistic competence, and literary connotations are often attached to them (to say nothing of the negative value judgments prevailing against clichés in any period when esthetics puts a premium on originality, inspiration, and the like). But clichés are everywhere, ready-made examples, well-tested images, always the vestiges of particularly felicitous phrases uttered long ago for the first time, and always containing a trope, a canned or preserved stylistic device.[23] Their basic mechanism, however, is also one of seme actualization.

Similarly, the descriptive systems are more complex than the presupposition networks, but in their simpler form they are very close to the dictionary definition of their kernel words. The descriptive system is a network of words associated with one another around a kernel word, in accordance with the sememe of that nucleus.[24] Each component of the system functions as a metonym of the nucleus. So strong are these relationships that any such metonym can serve as metaphor for the ensemble, and at any point in the text where the system is made implict, the reader can fill in gaps in an orderly way and reconstitute the whole representation from that metonym in conformity with the grammar of the pertinent stereotypes.

An especially productive cliché is the hypogram that makes the collocation of *fleur* and *abîme* (sometimes *gouffre*) a poetic sign. Compare the following quotations:

Cette fleur des prés croissant paisiblement et selon la douce loi de la nature . . . au centre de Paris, entre deux rues . . . au milieu des passants, des boutiques, des fiacres, des omnibus . . . cette *fleur* des champs voisine des pavés m'a ouvert un *abîme* de rêverie (Hugo)

Voilà qui est surnaturel, dit le vieillard en voyant une *fleur* éclose en hiver.—Un *abîme!* s'écria Wilfrid exalté par le parfum (Balzac)

ne sera-ce pas te mériter que de me sauver de ce *gouffre de fleurs?* serais-je digne de toi si je profanais un cœur tout à toi? Non, je ne tomberai pas dans le piège vulgaire que me tendent mes sens (Balzac)

Le vice chez lui n'était pas un *abîme,* comme chez certains vieillards, mais une *floraison* naturelle et extérieure (Zola)

De ces grandes feuilles de calcaire, *à fleur d'abîme,* sur des socles: dentelle au masque de la mort (Saint-John Perse)

> Sous les fleurs que je sais il n'est pas de prairie
> mais le lait noir de l'abîme inconnu;
> . . .
> Indolente demoiselle
> qui passes près des fleurs,
> entends tonner l'abîme!
> . . .
> alors ô fleurs en vous-mêmes à son tour
> l'abîme se blottit. (Jean Tardieu)[25]

This meadow flower growing peacefully in obedience to the sweet law of Nature, right in the center of Paris, between two streets in the midst of passersby, shops, cabs, and omnibuses, this flower from the fields growing beside the street cobblestones, opened up an abyss of reverie to me; This is really extraordinary, said the old man when he saw that flower blossoming in wintertime—An abyss! cried Wilfrid; Wouldn't I be worthy of you if I could save myself from this abyss of flowers; Vice in him was not an abyss, as it is in some old men, but rather a blossoming, natural and open for all to see; Like great limestone leaves on pedestals, level with the abyss: lace on Death's domino; Under the flowers I know there

is no meadow but the black milk of the unknown abyss. Indolent young
lady passing by the flowers, listen to the thundering abyss! You, flowers,
now it is the turn of the abyss to nestle into you.

Quite obviously it is not by mere chance that *fleurs, abîme,* and their
synonyms recur here together. The Saint-John Perse example even
demonstrates how well established, well-nigh automatic the linkage is,
since the prepositional phrase *à fleur* has nothing to do with flowers,
except that the compound happens to coincide morphologically with
fleur—yet it is attracted by *abîme* rather than *au ras de,* which is more
common and would mean the same thing. There is beyond doubt a
lexical constant, but finding a semantic justification for it remains
impossible. It is perfectly natural to speak of a mystery or marvel in
terms of depths that neither mind nor imagination can fathom; and
it is not straining things to speak of vice as a falling, hence as an abyss
(compare the falling or sinking imagery of phrases like *tomber dans
la débauche, sombrer dans la folie,* etc.). But there is no logical reason
for constantly linking these chasms with flowers in such widely differ-
ing contexts.

The only explanation for the *fleur-abîme* collocation is that it is
superimposed upon a familiar hypogram, the stereotyped image of the
flower on the edge of the abyss. The literary popularity of this image
peaked during the romantic era, as would be expected of an esthetic
that favors picturesque contrasts and natural or contrived antitheses.
The defining feature of the hypogram is a polarized opposition oxy-
morically uniting these contraries, linking term for term the flower's
fragile littleness with the chasm's awesome immensity, the delicate
with the sublime, beauty with horror, charm with danger, the lure of
the flower with the lure of the abyss.[26] Because of its extreme, even
paradoxical character, this opposition in poetic discourse replaces the
oppositions that prevail in everyday language: defining *fleur,* for in-
stance, by opposition to *feuilles.* It serves as core for two types of meta-
phor representing either beauty doomed to die (the flower on the
brink, its petals drifting down into the void), or beauty masking
peril (the flower concealing the dangerous brink, enticing you toward
it—as in Racine's Machiavellian "Je leur semai de fleurs le bord des
précipices").[27]

All my examples have this in common: nothing is left of the hypo-
gram's fundamental opposition because in each case the polar oppo-
sites have become equivalent. In Hugo and in the first Balzac excerpt,

abîme translates *fleur* into "wonderment" code; in the second Balzac passage, *fleurs* modifies *gouffre* like an adjective; in the Zola, *floraison* and *abîme* are alternate definitions of the same word; and in the last examples, *fleur,* far from opposing *abîme,* expresses a proximity-relation in its own "abyss" code. If we call the hypogram the norm from which my examples are derived, then the derivation process—cancelling the polarity—is a case of ungrammaticality, and this ungrammaticality accounts for the effect of the resulting text. To be sure, the effect here is not so strong as to create obscurity or nonsense, but it is strong enough to make the reader perceive one noun or both as metaphors. In most instances the phenomenon I am describing does more than just force the reader to become aware of tropes, or, if you prefer, to separate form from meaning in his perception of the text. But even in this mild form the semantic transfer makes reading an experience of literariness. To perceive the text as a transform of an intertext is to perceive it as the ultimate word game, that is, as literary.

The phenomenon is indeed intertextual, since the agent of its effect, the ungrammaticality, cannot be seen, let alone defined, without a comparison between the text and its generator, the hypogram. In other words, even though nothing is left of the striking and exemplary opposition that elsewhere made *fleur* and *abîme* inseparable, as polar opposites must be, their collocation or mutual dependence survives. Thus the destroyed model has left enough of a trace imprinted upon the text to create a unit of significance.

Now I shall demonstrate the role of the descriptive system as hypogram, using the case of a word perceived as permanently poetic, even though it is under no dogmatic or normative esthetic constraints such as control stock epithets, and even though it would seem to have no poetic predestination. *Dawn,* for instance, is so predestined—we know instinctively that it is a poetic word; we know that *grove* is more poetic than *clump of trees,* though both may be talking about the same copse. (On the other hand, some words are poetic wherever found, while others are less context-resistant: *crimson* is more poetic than *red,* except when it is the color of the human face, and so on.) The word I have in mind for my demonstration is *soupirail.* Its lexical collocations in everyday language hardly suggest any emotional or conceptual potentialities. The *soupirail* is the opening or vent that lets light and air into a cellar or basement, and more dramatically, into a dungeon. One constant here is that the space opened into must be manmade, not natural, and must be subterranean and confining. The other constant is that the opening must be narrow, flush with the ground, and usually at the foot of a wall. You have to crouch to look down through it, you have to crane your neck to look up through it. Conceivably, an appropriate context could make poetic even a word with such a lowly referent. What is startling is that *soupirail* is permanently poetic in literary discourse, that it is perceived as such without regard to context. And even more surprising is that this poetic aura cannot be accounted for by the existence of a literary theme or motif. "Literary" windows serve as settings for contemplation, as symbols of contact between the inner life and the world of sensation. Their glass panes permit visual communication but prevent direct touch, and so they may also be a metaphor for absence, separation, longing, memory, and so forth. *Soupirail,* however, has neither the pane nor the lofty vantage point that makes windows a locus of poetic feelings or meditation. And finally, *soupirail*'s very specific and inglorious meaning places it among the words most unlikely to fit esthetic norms like those of the French classicism that produced the stock epithet and excluded words representing pedestrian realities. Yet this very esthetic admits such images as:

je ne suis pas surpris que quelques auteurs aient pris les volcans pour les soupiraux d'un feu central, et le peuple pour les bouches de l'enfer (Buffon)

le prince des ténèbres [Satan] achevait . . . la revue des temples de la terre, . . . sanctuaires du mensonge et de l'imposture, l'antre de Trophonius, les soupiraux de la Sibylle, les trépieds de Delphes, . . . les souterrains d'Isis (Chateaubriand)[28]

I am not surprised that writers should call volcanoes the vents of the fire that burns at earth's center, while the common people call them the maws of Hell; Satan was visiting the temples of Earth, sanctuaries of lies and deceit, Trophonius' cave, the Sibyl's *soupiraux,* the Delphic tripod, the crypts of Isis

What gives our word its poetic vitality is the hypogram of which *soupirail* is the surface actualization. This hypogram—the word's descriptive system—happens to have a grammar and a lexical distribution characterized by polar oppositions. I believe polarization is always present in the hypograms of permanently poetic nouns. I believe further that *polarization is responsible for the noun's exemplariness and consequently for its poetic nature.* Polarization begets striking contrasts. Its cancellation (by statement of an equivalence between polar opposites) generates paradoxes, oxymorons, and conceits. Any word that plays a role in a polar opposition is pushed by that role toward the culminating point of the paradigm of its synonyms or analogues: their semantic field becomes a veritable geometry of extremes.[29]

The first polarization in *soupirail's* hypogram is the opposition between the narrowness of the aperture—you cannot squeeze through—and the temptation it offers: an interdiction structure that seems to cancel, and yet maintains, the sort of representation that symbolizes despair, frustration, yearning—the stuff of lyricism. For instance:

> un appel, . . . une prière, . . . un
> cri, . . . un regard du prisonnier
> vers le soupirail (Cocteau)[30]

a call, a prayer, a scream, the gaze of the prisoner toward the dungeon window

A second opposition is that between wall and opening. This certainly derives from the characteristic smallness of the vent, which triggers the maximal (blank wall)/ minimal (vent) polarity: *fenêtre* does not entail *mur*, whereas *soupirail* does. I find my proof in a nonsense sentence, in a surrealist poem, generated by automatic writing—that is, under conditions where the mimesis of reality does not operate and verbal associations are undisguised:

la merveille au mur est un éventail à soupiraux (André Breton)[31]

The marvel on the wall is a lady's fan with cellar vents

Third and last is the opposition between the vent's narrowness and the immensity upon which it opens—an immensity upwards or downwards. The open skies or the abysmal depths—but always a verticality with readily dramatic or metaphysical implications:

un morceau de ciel aperçu par un soupirail . . . donne une idée plus profonde de l'infini qu'un grand panorama vu du haut d'une montagne (Baudelaire)[32]

a patch of sky glimpsed through a cell window gives a deeper sense of infinity than a broad view from a mountaintop

When it owes its poeticalness to such a hypogram, a word has three functions. It functions *first* as a *marker,* quite like stock epithets. In the case of *soupirail,* the first and second polarities just described involve a negative marking. For example:

pourquoi une apparence de soupirail blêmirait-elle au coin de la voûte
(Rimbaud)[33]

why should what looks like my dungeon window be glowing wanly in
the corner of the vault

The pejoration process (*blêmir* instead of the expected *luire*, "shine,"
"light up") provokes an inversion of the traditional symbolism (the
onlooker no longer craves a glimpse of the distant sky; he rather fears
it or is indifferent to it, for the man in the cell is no prisoner, but one
who has chosen to bury himself in a voluntary grave: hence the world
above is evil). Hugo best exemplifies one word's transforming the sig-
nificance of a whole sentence by simultaneous conversion of all its
components from positive to negative:

> [l'homme est une] mouche heurtant de
> l'aile au soupirail du faux (Hugo)[34]

Man is a fly thudding against the dungeon window of falsehood

The reader recognizes the familiar theme of the fly attracted by light
but foiled by glass. It applies perfectly to the quest of Man for Knowl-
edge or Truth; but this text is pessimistic, the quest is a false lure.
Instead of a laborious reversal through the pathos of the toilsome
search, we have a shortcut to a maximal *coup de théâtre*, achieved by
substituting *soupirail* for *vitre:* the representation of Evil, the deceptive
goal, instead of Good, and the complete conversion of the positive
quest theme into a negative image of its converse—all is accomplished
at one stroke by our one word.[35]

The poetic noun's *second* function is that of *generator*. The word is
capable of re-creating, of actualizing in the text, the hypogrammatic
sentence it equals at lexematic level.

> O sainte horreur du mal! devoir funèbre . . .
> Les soupiraux d'en bas teignent de leurs rougeurs
> Le mur sinistre auquel s'adosse Jérémie (Hugo)[36]

sacred dread of Evil! our mournful duty . . . The vents from down below
stain red the sinister wall the prophet Jeremiah is leaning against

Here is a perfect example of a setting, complete with character,
that serves solely to translate into figurative language an abstract re-
lationship: the moral complementary of crime and punishment. A
window on Hell generates light, the light cast entails a reflecting screen,

the negative representation of Evil entails its positive counterpart, the castigating prophet, etc.

The poetic noun's *third* function is the actualizing of the very polarization that organizes its hypogram: in other words, *it symbolizes its own structure.* Neither in Rimbaud, nor indeed in Hugo, do we find *soupirail* used as a metaphor. Nowhere can we say that it stands for something other than itself: that is, *soupirail* does not designate a referent but serves as a kind of lexical shorthand for an abstract dialectic between a *here* and a *beyond,* between oppression here and a fantasy of imagined release elsewhere.[37]

Thanks to these three functions, the permanently poetic word is not simply decoded and understood in the light of its grammatical and semantic relationships with the other words in the text: it is not just *understood* like these other words. The poetic word is also *recognized,* that is, perceived as representing and summing up a sentence whose nucleus it is, a sentence to be found (remembered from) elsewhere, in a place that antedates the text, in the hypogram. The interpretation of the significance depends entirely upon the correct identification of the hypogrammatic sentence for which the prepoeticized word has been substituted. The poetic word thus plays the role of *interpretant*[38] in the reading process, a role the reader rationalizes as a symbol of the writer's intention.

TEXT PRODUCTION

The text as locus of significance is generated by conversion and expansion. Whereas only the presence of stylistic features, such as tropes, differentiates poetic discourse from nonliterary language, conversion and expansion both establish equivalences between a word and a sequence of words: that is, between a lexeme (always rewritable as a matrix sentence) and a syntagm. Thus is created the finite, formally and semantically unified verbal sequence constituting the poem. Expansion establishes this equivalence by transforming one sign into several, which is to say by deriving from one word a verbal sequence with that word's defining features. Conversion lays down the equivalence by transforming several signs into one "collective" sign, that is, by endowing the components of a sequence with the same characteristic features. Conversion particularly affects sequences generated by expansion.

EXPANSION

Expansion integrates the sign-producing actualizations of hypograms, heretofore discussed, and follows the patterns of descriptive systems. Most conspicuous are the periphrasis and the extended metaphor, but expansion is a phenomenon ranging far beyond these tropes. I should say that it is the chief agent in the formation of *textual signs*[1] and *texts,* and is therefore the principal generator of significance, since a constant can be spotted only where the text spreads out into successive variants of its initial given, the more complex issuing from the simpler.

RULE: *Expansion transforms the constituents of the matrix sentence into more complex forms.*

The first example is a portrait of Gérard de Nerval by Théophile Gautier:

> Cet esprit était une hirondelle apode. Il était tout ailes et n'avait pas de pieds, tout au plus une imperceptible griffe pour se suspendre un moment aux choses et reprendre haleine; il allait, venait, faisait de brusques zigzags aux angles imprévus, montait, descendait, montait plutôt, planait et se mouvait dans le milieu fluide avec la joie et la liberté d'un être qui est dans son élément[2]

> This mind was an apodal swallow. He was all wings and had no feet, at most an imperceptible talon for hanging on to things for a moment and catching his breath; he would fly back and forth, make sudden zigzags at unexpected angles, rise, fall, mostly rising, he would hover and move about in the fluid milieu with the joy and liberty of a being who is in his element

Here and elsewhere Gautier depicts Nerval as the dreamer and esoteric writer he was, engrossed in mysticism and an orphic vision of poetry. A recurrent, and predictable, image makes Nerval a "winged spirit," a "pure soul hovering forever above the real world without ever touching down."[3] Thus *esprit pur* (or any of the winged imagery that fills the fantasy heavens of Western literature) is the matrix's key word. A piquant motif provides the model, an *exemplum* from ancient natural history.[4] The apodal swallow, or swift, can be seen flying about—it even has legs, though hardly visible. But what makes it an image is the fancied physical impossibility and the rhetorical *adynaton* translating it. The bird's scientific name, with its Greek adjective, is the contextually abnormal lexeme, the stylistically marked form, which, together with the metaphor itself, gives the model its propulsive power. The model makes explicit those semes of *esprit* that oppose it to matter, the semes that have organized countless representations of elevated spirituality as a soaring upwards. The expansion proper develops the group *hirondelle apode* into phrases or sentences. The adjective generates the explanatory sentence (*il n'avait pas de pieds . . .*), which aggravates the intellectually challenging impossibility, whose explosive force was still relatively defused. Further, the footless bird does not risk the fate of the "exile on the ground," like Baudelaire's *Albatros*, famous symbol of the poet. I am not being too literal, for there is a theme *walk vs. flight* defining the duality of man and poet within the same individual.[5] The bird's name generates the sequence running from *tout ailes* to *allait, venait,* and *allait, venait* in turn serves as a secondary model for the other binary groups (*montait, descendait; planait et se mouvait*), and for translation into a geometric lexicon, a nominal variant: *zigzags* is taken up by *angles,* its metonym, just as *brusques* repeats itself in *imprévus.* Each clause generates its homologue, in order of increasing complexity. The text is clearly perceived as one unit of meaning, first because its repetitiveness so plainly reflects, in enlarged form, the given of the bird that never alights. Second, because the conclusion is not an arbitrary cutoff point: the image of levitation in one's natural element, a commonplace of both bird and fish description,[6] brings the reader back full circle to the initial metaphor. As Eluard neatly put it in one of his early poems: "L'oiseau s'est confondu avec le vent"[7] [You can no longer tell the bird from the wind]. The text is nothing but the metaphor stated over again with emphasis.

In its simplest form the expansion may be made up entirely of repetitive sequences (an ancient rhetorical device aptly labelled *amplificatio*), which serve equally, and often simultaneously, to create rhythm and to insert descriptive discourse into a narrative.[8] Repetition is in itself a sign: depending as it does upon the meaning of the words involved, it may symbolize heightened emotional tension, or it may work as the icon of motion, progress, etc. Both functions are performed in the following Michelet lyric piece on the Northern Lights: the *aurora borealis* theme is exploited in typical romantic fashion for an anthropomorphic representation of pantheistic, or rather animistic, Nature. The initial, objective description of the spectacle plainly presents luminous shapes and electromagnetic movement. These statements are expanded at a level first purely descriptive; Michelet is depicting the aurora's shafts of light as curtains hanging down from the sky: "Ils ondulent. Un flux et reflux de lumière les promène comme une draperie d'or qui va, se plie, se replie" [They undulate. An ebb and flow of light shifts them like a golden curtain moving, twisting into folds, untwisting]. New repetitions transmute the mimesis of motion into that of play or contest: the need to vary the vocabulary forces the writer to run the gamut of animization images, and it is unavoidable that game and contest ultimately end up as an awesome love scene:

Le combat s'harmonise. Les lumières ont lutté assez. Elles s'entendent, se pacifient et s'aiment. Elles montent ensemble dans la gloire. Elles se transfigurent en sublime éventail, en coupole de feu, sont comme la couronne d'un divin hyménée. A l'âme terrestre, magnétique, reine du Nord, l'autre s'est mêlée, l'électrique, la vie de l'Equateur. Elles s'embrassent, et c'est la même âme.[9]

The struggle comes to a harmonious conclusion. The lights have battled long enough. They come to an understanding, are appeased, love one another. Together they arise in glory. They are transfigured into a sublime fan, a cupola of fire, they are like the crown of a celestial marriage. With the terrestrial soul, magnetic, Queen of the North, mingles that other soul, the electric one, the life of the Equator. They embrace, and they are one soul.

Before this climax is attained, the back-and-forth movements of the lights (repeated so often that the entire text looks like a variation on *va-et-vient*) are rewritten in one paragraph: the poem's significance— the erotic cosmos—issues whole from the one variation that translates the *va-et-vient* model into *alternatives*, a word from the animate (or "thinking") code:

Puis des alternatives, des appels, des répliques violentes, des oui, des non, des défis, des combats; des victoires et des défaillances. Parfois des attendrissements, comme ceux de la fille des mers, qui flamboie la nuit, la méduse, quand tour à tour sa lampe rougit, languit, pâlit.

Then alternations, calls, violent rejoinders, yeses, noes, challenges, combats; victories and failings. Sometimes more tender feelings, like those of the sea's daughter who flares up at night, the Medusa [jellyfish], when her lamp by turns reddens, languishes, goes pale.

The highest point of the paradigm of expansion from *alternatives* is *combats,* which in turn acts as secondary model for its own expansion into *victoires* and *défaillances.* The latter word may mean a failure, a defeat, or, in feminine context, a swooning or moment of weakness and consent, that is, erotic surrender. This is the turning point, where the transition from the initial series to the final amplification, the one ending up with a wedding of cosmic souls, is mediated by a variation, this time wholly feminine, disambiguating *défaillances,* that is, selecting the word's strongest connotations: hence *attendrissements,* immediately motivated or developed into a feminine figure.[10] The lamp is a descriptive, allegorical ploy for characterizing the Medusa while maintaining the humanization; it is also one more step up the expansion's ascending scale, for *tour à tour* picks up the alternation thread, while *rougit, languit, pâlit,* still a to-and-fro but on a downbeat, brings *défaillance* and *attendrissement* together in a code of woman succumbing (with an echo of the Foolish Virgins' lamp).

In most cases the expansion involves more than repetition—there are also changes in the grammatical nature of the model sentence's constituents: pronouns turn into nouns, for instance, nouns into groups, adjectives into relative clauses, and so forth. Each group thus produced is also capable of generating another by adjunction or embedding. As for the model's verb, it is transformed so that the state of affairs or the process it describes can be represented in dramatic or at least dynamic form; or else the verb is repeated with or without dramatization, with each repetition generating a whole new sequence of expansion. In such cases, as in that of the repetitive *amplificatio,* the constituents of the expansion sequence grow longer and longer and more and more complex, heading for a spectacular climax. This last makes the reader see clearly that the whole sequence forms a textual unit, and this sense is further confirmed by the retroactive perception of significance.

The stanzas that follow demonstrate how expansion carries meaning both by simple reiteration and by generating increasingly complex forms:

> Les yeux fixés sur moi, comme un tigre dompté,
> D'un air vague et rêveur elle essayait des poses,
> 15 Et la candeur unie à la lubricité
> Donnait un charme neuf à ses métamorphoses;
>
> Et son bras et sa jambe, et sa cuisse et ses reins,
> Polis comme de l'huile, onduleux comme un cygne,
> Passaient devant mes yeux clairvoyants et sereins;
> 20 Et son ventre et ses seins, ces grappes de ma vigne,
>
> S'avançaient, plus câlins que les Anges du mal,
> Pour troubler le repos où mon âme était mise,
> Et pour la déranger du rocher de cristal
> Où calme et solitaire, elle s'était assise.

With her eyes fixed upon me, like a tamed tiger, looking vague and dreamy, she was trying out poses, and her candor combined with lewdness gave a new charm to her metamorphoses; her arms and her legs, her thighs and her buttocks, smooth as oil, sinuous as a swan, passed before my serene, clear-seeing eyes; and her belly and her breasts, grapes of my vineyard, more coaxing than the Angels of Evil, they kept coming closer, to trouble the repose my soul had found, to disturb it from off the rock of crystal where it had settled, calm and solitary.

Baudelaire is here (in *Fleurs du Mal,* "Les Bijoux") recounting a commonplace sexual incident that might be crudely summed up: *she was striking erotic poses to arouse me.* This is the matrix sentence; a fragment of it is actualized in line 14: *elle essayait des poses.*

In the first derivative sentence (lines 17–18), the subject pronoun (*elle*) is transformed into a series of metonymic images of Woman as object of desire: her physical charms. This series is further developed by adjectives, each reinforced by a simile. The similes underscore the transference of *bras, jambe,* etc. from the *body-limb* class to the *erotic-object* class. There is in each simile a meaningful circularity: instead of an adjective's being generated by a noun through actualization of one of that noun's semes, a noun is generated by the adjective—but the noun actualizes a seme of the noun which generated that adjective in the first place. Thus the seme "suppleness" is implicit in both *reins* (a euphemism for *fesses,* "buttocks") and *cygne,* and explicit in *onduleux,* which links the two, thereby actualizing the voluptuous connotations of *reins,* but by displacing them from the body—the movement would be too graphically suggestive—to the bird. This displacement is the more effective, and the indirectness of the description becomes the more suggestive, because the swan itself metaphorizes the undulating movement, but as a simile its neck (*col de cygne*) is a clichéd hyperbole of litheness. The force of the erotic innuendo increases in direct proportion to the distance covered by the expansion, from tenor to adjective to simile proper, and within the simile from the implied pertinent swan-neck to the whole bird, that is, from an implicit simile to a metonym of that simile.

As for the verb of the matrix (*to assume erotic postures*), it is rewritten first in a dynamic variant: *passaient devant mes yeux,* then a second time in the dramatic *s'avançaient,* being thereby transformed from plain exhibitionism into sensual teasing. Here again the expansion process is triggered at the semic level: it literally actualizes the etymological meaning of the now obsolete word best designating woman's physical charms: her *appas,* "bait."

The male partner, temptation's target, is situated in the narrative where two possible sequences fork off: to yield or not to yield. Proairesis follows the rule of polarization: not to yield, which is bound to be the more interesting solution because resistance protracts the erotic game. Hence *yeux clairvoyants et sereins,* the cool, dispassionate gaze of a paradoxical voyeur.

A second derivation (lines 20–24) works like a hyperbolic version of the first, which serves as its model in terms of transformation and as its microcontext in terms of stylistic structure.[11] The paradigm of the sexual "lures" reaches its apex in *ventre* and *seins,* with the ultimate *grappes de ma vigne.* The reader will think this is borrowed from the *Song of Solomon,* of course, and it adds to the seme "femininity" the seme "ownership," which makes the mistress also a possession or slave of love.[12] Metaphorical oppositions now replace the adjectives-cum-similes of the first derivative string. And to cap all this, the *temptress* vs. *temptee* opposition is twice polarized. First, instead of being expressed through adjectives (e.g., *onduleux* vs. *sereins,* that is, "enticing" vs. "cold"), the opposition is now a conflict between two allegorized characters pitted against each other (*Anges* vs. *âme*), a spiritual duel more reminiscent of the Demon tormenting the anchorite with voluptuous visions than of mere amorous combat. On the other hand, expansion has moved on from narrative to description. For the sentence indeed generates an allegory by almost automatically following the lead of a stereotyped hypogram. For one thing, this is a commonplace symbol, the seated figure daydreaming (favorite representative of philosophic contemplation in French romanticist poetry). For another, the symbolic stance presupposes that a sitting character needs a seat to sit on, and this component of the allegory must be as positive as the entire allegory; hence the laudatory *rocher de cristal* (note that even this final image is overdetermined like the rest, since the meliorative representation is a fantastic vision, or at least a patently fanciful figment of imagination; yet it is legitimized or "justified" by its own hypogram—the compound *cristal de roche,* whose component-order it merely reverses).[13]

Such transformation of simple components into complex representations makes literary discourse the grammatical equivalent of the allegorical figure, whose every attribute (clothing, weapons, the scales of Justice, the hourglass of Time, etc.) is in turn a "story," a text within a text.[14]

From Abstract to Figurative Signs

Expansion has another far-reaching effect upon poetic discourse: it transforms the more abstract language forms, especially the grammatical connectives, into images. Signs indicating the functions, the grammatical relationship between full-fledged sememes; adjectives like *all* and *every,* negations, and conjunctives requiring little or no adjustment to the stylistic characteristics of their lexical environment—all these are abstract in that they refer directly to structures and are context-free, thus are conventions like all signs, but are more conspicuously arbitrary. Even more than is the case with the other words, which at least appear to have referents admitting of sensory perception, these abstract words need show no connection between their physical—phonetic and graphemic—shape and their meaning.[15]

It is an accepted dictum that poetic discourse tends to veil or do away with the arbitrariness of signs.[16] Most approaches to the study of the phenomenon have long emphasized sound symbolism almost exclusively. More recently, however, thanks to Genette, attention has been given to what this phenomenon implies for a topology of tropes (diegetic metaphor, for instance), and, finally, the metalinguistic (or sociolectic) aspects of Cratylism, its mythology, and the representations of that mythology. It seems to me that expansion is the principal, perhaps the only, agent operating (apparently) to remove arbitrariness in the extreme and exemplary case of abstract signs, because it substitutes for these symbols icons or "ideograms" that seem to explain or legitimate the relationships they symbolize by rewriting them in the code of the words linked by these relationships.

In a sentence like *I hear (see) nothing,* for instance, the relationship expressed by *nothing* is a cancellation of the fact or action expressed by the verb. *Nothing* is completely arbitrary and conventional in the way it stands for the "absence of perceptible objects" and the way it refers to one particular mode of perception rather than another. Expansion transforms this abstract negation into a topical one by replacing *nothing* with a concrete, less economical and more space-consuming representation of what could have been perceived in the sensory sphere designated by the verb: *I see nothing* becomes **I see a no-sight,* and *I hear nothing* becomes **I hear a no-sound.*[17]

Thus in each of the following examples, we find variants of the matrix I have just posited: the sign of negation, instead of being linked to the verb it modifies by mere contiguity, is that verb's tautological variant with a negative marker, and so is linked to it by semic identity. From a baroque poem:

> J'escoute, à demy transporté,
> Le bruit des ailes du Silence,
> Qui vole dans l'obscurité[18]

I listen, half in rapture, to the noise of the wings of Silence flying through the dark

Here the picture of the allegorical character is nothing but the transference of the negation affecting the sensory-perception verb onto the mimesis level. But this pseudomimesis—a plain negation masquerading in various descriptive disguises—points precisely to a basic condition of contemplation, the poem's subject: the contemplator has to be *à demy transporté,* in a state of abstraction from the sensory world. The key word, developed by the matrix into a first expansion, so to speak, is *silence,* just as Shelley's phrase about the moon derives from *silence* expanded into one of two clichés belonging to the mimesis of night— *silent night* or *silent moon:*

> . . . the beat of her unseen feet,
> Which only the angels hear[19]

This is not to say that the mimetic expansion is nothing more than an enlargement, with the stronger impact due only to sheer volume, to the bigger space-occupancy that goes with transference from lexeme to syntagm. If that were so the mimesis would be merely a mechanical, unavoidable consequence of expansion (since even padding with words, if indeed it is padding, cannot help suggesting representations). Such a reductionist interpretation would betray the most radical misunderstanding of semiosis in general and expansion in particular— a misunderstanding that creeps at regular intervals into critics' and academics' literary evaluations. It takes the form of censorious labelling like "verbalism," "padding," in French *"remplissage,"* and other pejoratives commonly garnered by *amplificatio* techniques. Far from being a mere mechanical result, the mimesis is the visible form of the significance. Not through the agency of constant or repeated distortion, the process we have heretofore observed in various texts, but through the unique, unrepeated ungrammaticality of the self-contained contradiction exemplified above in *I see (hear) a no-sight (no-sound)*—that is, an incompatibility of subject and predicate: the subject entails a predicate that contradicts or cancels its presuppositions. The radical, self-destructive nature of the contradiction makes up for the absence of what normally leads the reader from variant to invariant, that is, repetition: the challenge to common usage is too basic to be missed, even where it occurs only once. This contradiction is perceived thanks to the readers' common knowledge or consensus about things, but as always a selection is made from the vast field of possibles by preexisting commonplaces, and therefore by another level of oral or memorial "texts."

For instance, André Breton, in these two passages from unconnected poems, gives us two variants of the *hear a no-sound* predicative incompatibility:

Mes rêves seront formels et vains comme le bruit de paupières de l'eau dans l'ombre

Les mille paupières de l'eau qui dort[20]

My dreams will be mere empty forms like the noise of the water's eyelids in the dark; the thousand eyelids of the sleeping water

Everyone knows, of course, that fluttering eyelids make no sound, and we understand accordingly. But "eyelids" is a verbal choice, for the expansion works on the model of a wink-as-silent-signal theme.[21] Now, since the blinking eyelids are clearly an image, the reader assumes that at least the dormant water is a reality, for an image implies that the something it is illustrating must be a fact. But the fact too is only apparent, since its true function is to be a synonym for the noiseless eyelids in a silence paradigm: motionless water is here only because there are clichés about the silence of *still* waters in the night. Again, another apparent component of the setting, the mention of night, may look like a statement of reality to be taken literally, but this too is an expansion of "sleeping waters," actualizing as it does a presupposition of *dormant* in any context, literal or metaphorical. As for the second passage, were it not for the primacy of the word—if the reader had to rely upon a "direct" apprehension of reality—the *mille paupières de l'eau* would make no sense.

Thus the verbal structures of incompatibility are not striking examples culled from the common lore of experience, they are themselves the matrices for figurative expansions on the grammatical geometry of language. Expansions of this type will consequently yield as many different variants as there are contexts in which figurative grammar happens to be employed. Another version of *I hear a no-sound* uses as its matrix the proverbial *écouter pousser l'herbe* [listen to the grass growing]: in common parlance this is a joking reference to laziness or idleness, presumably because the slothful person potters about aimlessly, and listening to nonexistent sounds epitomizes his occupations. It is revealing that the matrix is not only a verbal sleight-of-hand about reality, but a humorous one, that is, a verbal construct underlined as such, a twisted way of saying things. Humor vanishes when the phrase actualizes our structure instead of being used for its own sake. Take Valéry's twilight scene:

La voix des sources change, et me parle du soir
. . . .
J'entends l'herbe des nuits croître dans l'ombre sainte,

Et la lune perfide élève son miroir
Jusque dans les secrets de la fontaine éteinte . . .[22]

The voice of the springs is changing, it speaks to me of evening. . . . I hear the grass of the night growing in the holy shadow. And the perfidious moon lifts up her mirror and reaches it into the secrets of the extinguished fountain

Here the expansion is as plainly conformant to the model as it can be, for all that is needed in context is emphasis upon silence (note that the only unusual collocation, aside from the incompatibility structure, is *des nuits* as modifier of *herbe:* the mention of night, ostensibly a mimetic fact, has exactly the same semiotic function as an indirect modifier of *paupières* in the Breton examples). But other variants replace grass with other growths equally denotative of no-sound. These changes are conversions, for they affect every structural constituent, and all of them in the same way, melioratively or pejoratively, modifying the entire expansion to accord with the significance of the poem as a whole. For instance, this "georgic" description by Chateaubriand of the night following Roman Catholic rites of spring:

La lune répand alors les dernières harmonies, sur cette fête . . . On croit entendre de toutes parts les blés germer dans la terre et les plantes croître et se développer[23]

Then the moon pours the last harmonies over the festival. It is as if you could hear the wheat germinating in the earth all over the world, and the plants growing and developing

The no-sounds are dual signs:[24] from the conversion standpoint, since corn and other crops have been described as objects of thanksgiving, their noise still represents sound and symbolizes Providence at work preparing future harvests for the faithful. But the expansion enunciates silence: as no-sounds, then, they represent the holy peace of an orderly Creation, so that silence stands for religious mysteries.

A meditation of Hugo's on precisely this subject predictably follows the same conversive pattern, but it pushes the expansion further (I am quoting only part of it), until the clausula. This comes when the text runs out of descriptive variants (these are all given over to hidden, secret aspects of Nature observed in its tiniest creatures—insect life, the world of flowers, moss, roots, anthills, and the like). The last expansion accordingly returns to the bare matrix, but now that it is actualized after the derivation, its relative abstractness looks like generalization, or like translation into metaphysical discourse. This very appearance is another sign, a stylistic one, of the text's significance:

> le bruit doux et indistinct des végétations, des minéralisations et des fécondations mystérieuses; [. . .] les demi-révélations qui sortaient de tout; le travail calme, harmonieux, lent et continu de tous ces êtres et de toutes ces choses qui vivent en apparence plus près de Dieu que de l'homme; vous dire tout cela [. . .] serait vous exprimer l'ineffable, vous montrer l'invisible, vous peindre l'infini[25]

> the soft, indistinct sound of vegetation growing, of minerals forming, of mysterious fecundations; half-revelations coming out of everything; the calm, harmonious, slow, continued labor of all these beings and of all these things that seem to live closer to God than to Man; to tell you all this would be to speak the ineffable, to show you the invisible, paint you the infinite

Of course, negative conversion works just as well as positive. Witness Rimbaud's vignette on the secret charms of mediocrity: in the daytime a child hides in the outhouse to escape parental surveillance, at night he dreams of freedom in the moonlit *jardinet,* where

> Gisant au pied d'un mur, enterré dans la marne
> Et pour des visions écrasant son oeil darne
> Il écoutait grouiller les galeux espaliers

> Lying at the foot of a wall, buried in the marl, pressing his sullen eye in hard to see visions, he was listening to the mangy espaliers swarming with vermin

Or worse, this repulsive portrait, again by Rimbaud—the title, *Accroupissements,* "squattings" (with implications of privies), converts the nocturnal grass into rank overgrowth:

> L'écœurante chaleur gorge la chambre étroite,
> Le cerveau du bonhomme est bourré de chiffons.
> Il écoute les poils pousser dans sa peau moite.[26]

> Nauseating heat chokes the cramped bedroom. The brain of the old fool is stuffed with rags. He is listening to the hairs sprouting on his clammy skin.

The most common substitute transformation of abstract into figurative signs is the metonym, and it seems to me that nothing better demonstrates to what extent the representation of reality in poetry is used to point indirectly to something else, and to make the reader take a circuitous route.

Let us return to Gautier's "In Deserto," discussed in the first chapter, with its lengthy desert description. We now recognize it for what it is, a perfect example of expansion with negative conversion. From the very beginning the poem keeps repeating in various forms the dryness of the sierra; the sequence culminates in

> Le lézard pâmé bâille, et parmi l'herbe cuite
> On entend résonner les vipères en fuite.
> Là, point de marguerite au coeur étoilé d'or,
> Point de muguet prodigue égrenant son trésor;
> Là, point de violette ignorée et charmante,
> Dans l'ombre se cachant comme une pâle amante

the swooning lizard yawns, and in the baked grass you hear the resonance of vipers fleeing. No daisy there, with her heart of starry gold, no prodigal lily of the valley scattering her treasure, no violet, unknown, charming, hiding in the shade like a pale lover

This paradoxical enumeration of absent flowers is clearly a paradigm of "vegetation" metonyms, each member modified by negation, each therefore acting to develop the poem's second line: "a desert where not a single blade of green grass grows." More simply and schematically, each metonym descriptively develops *nothing* in a matrix *nothing grows there,* which is itself a periphrasis or a possible definition of *desert.* Each flower is a hyperbole of flowery daintiness and dewy charm, and each is connected with love in the traditional discourse of flower symbolism [27] Thus the poem not only expands the abstract *rien* into concrete representations of what it negates, but the expansion selects the representations most diametrically opposed to what is meant. The desert is described in flower code; the epitome of vegetationlessness is described in the code of the epitome of vegetation. I think this underscores the essential role of the detour: its catachresis tends toward extremity, and the detour therefore tends to describe the widest circle around its object.

For maximum reach of the circuitous route, there are two possibilities or two directions. There is aggravated ungrammaticality of the expansion, where the reader is made to feel the distance between the abstract matrix and the transform by the shocking assault upon language. Or, the other way around, the distance will seem greater when the abstract matrix stands low in the stylistic hierarchy of words, is a mere grammatical tool. The two tendencies, one centrifugal, one centripetal, combine to create the same effect.

In Mallarmé's −yx sonnet,[28] the first line describes an allegorical figure lifting a lamp or torch. "Ses purs ongles très haut dédiant leur onyx" cannot mean anything but "sa main levée très haut," or better, "sa main s'élevant, elle (la lampadophore) soutient . . ." [with hand held high, the torchbearer lifts . . .]. Attendant upon the expansion process is an embellishing conversion, possibly suggestive of a hieratic gesture, a ritual offering: *dédiant* [consecrating], and the use of a Greek, hence elevated-style word, *onyx,* the precious stone, a frequent meliorative simile or color metaphor in descriptions of elegant feminine fingernails. But the point is that here the expansion is circular, for *onyx* in its predicative function repeats the object *ongle.* Repeats it not only because it is its metonym, but also because *onyx* is the Greek word for "fingernail." *Leur onyx* is thus really, disguised as a descriptive detail in lofty language, the expansion of the reflexive pronoun *se* in *s'élevant,* "raising itself," the transformation, into a pseudorepresentation, of the sign of a grammatical function, the sign of reciprocity.[29]

To be sure, the ungrammaticality here is only in the transfer of the metonym to a metaphorical role, and in a circularity astride two languages. Below is a more radical departure, taken in a short Eluard poem where the figurative expansion makes the whole text:

UNIS
Une caverne dont l'entrée est au pied d'un rocher plus haut que moi, et qui sert lui-même de base à une montagne plus haute que toi. A quelques pas de l'entrée, on trouve une galerie par laquelle on arrive à une chambre où nous nous unissons, pied à pied, tête à tête.[30]

United. A cave whose entrance is at the foot of a rock taller than I, which in turn forms the base of a mountain taller than you. A few steps from the entrance is a gallery leading to a room where we are united, foot by foot, tête à tête.

The cave-in-the-wilderness as trysting place has a long literary tradition; it goes back to Dido and Aeneas's first night together. But the traditional link between cave and couple remains arbitrary, for the setting is a convention, at both the thematic and the narrative levels. Here, on the contrary, the whole poem is determined by expansion on the verb's reflexive form, as it appears in the clausula: *nous nous unissons.*[31] In a description that respects the stereotypes of speleological discourse (rock, gallery discovered, gallery opening out), the reader finds it absurd to measure the lovers by their surroundings. But then he notices that the relationship of man to rock and woman to mountain is not one of incongruously disproportionate size but is a transference from sex to gender: *rocher,* a masculine word (we could have had *roche*) applies to the man; *montagne,* a feminine word (instead of the possible *mont*) applies to the woman. And the repetition of *plus haut que,* accurate enough in both cases but pointless, performs as repetition a function equivalent to that of the reflexive pronoun in *s'unir,* "unite with each other." We can also draw a parallel between the repetition of *plus haut que* and the first-person plural form of the reflexive pronoun, also repetitive: *nous nous,* an abstract grammatical sign, is picked up by the descriptive repetition. And again by *tête à tête,* and again by *pied à pied,* in both cases through a second revealing ungrammaticality, for in context they mean two bodies welded together from head to toe, the iteration of *tête* and *pied* translating that of *nous* [from (two) heads to (two) feet]; whereas *tête à tête* in ordinary usage simply refers to intimacy, with no particular part of the body specified, and *pied à pied* ordinarily means "foot by foot" in the sense of "inch by inch," applied to ground yielded in a hotly fought last-ditch battle. While separately the two phrases would still describe one erotic togetherness, the other amorous combat, the grammatical structure and the context of the absurd *plus haut que,* make them variants, like the latter phrase, of *nous nous.* The entire poem thus transforms the grammatical symbol of reciprocity into an icon of sexual intercourse.[32]

It stands to reason that this kind of expansion, actualizing as it does only the geometry of language, should be the one device whereby poetic discourse represents nothing but itself, and the poem attains the outermost limits of its potentialities, as an expansion on *rien,* a zero-matrix.

A noteworthy example is Eluard's most famous line (a verbal scandal in the French intellectual sociolect on a par with Chomsky's *green ideas sleep furiously* in our own intellectual circles):

> La terre est bleue comme une orange
> Jamais une erreur les mots ne mentent pas[33]

Earth is blue as an orange. Never a mistake. Words do not lie

There is simply no way for anyone to lessen the absurdity of the simile: at the level of mimesis both sides of the coin are wrong, the earth is not blue, nor is the orange. This two-sided ungrammaticality blocks any possibility of a metaphoric interpretation such as would solve Eluard's own *soleil vert* [green sun],[34] clearly motivated as spring-time sunshine, or Aragon's *soleil bleu*,[35] as clearly the winter sun, in a context where blue stands for blue with cold. Just as it blocks a metonymic interpretation like that for the chiasma or *chassé croisé* of colors in René Char's "Le ciel n'est plus aussi jaune, le soleil aussi bleu" [the sky is not so yellow any more, nor the sun so blue].[36] As Captain Haddock says to Tintin, hero of France's most popular comic strip (a young amateur detective, both Hardy Brothers rolled into one), upon finding a suspicious blue orange-shaped object: "For me, oranges are orange. If an orange happens to be blue, mark my words, Tintin, it is not an orange any more."[37] The reason has little to do with the nature of things and much to do with the shape of words: *orange* is the typical dual sign, since the same word refers to color and to fruit—a rare coincidence—and it is a "circular" sign, since the color is also the fruit's.

Needless to say, this high visibility of the ungrammaticality has opened the sluices to a deluge of ecstatic rationalization. A poet, André Pieyre de Mandiargues, admires Eluard's prescience in discovering, from his *observatoire passionnel,* the true color of Earth before the astronauts. An academic, Jean Onimus: "to say that earth is blue as an orange is to bind the joyous infinity of the azure skies to the density of the sphere, a double shout of joy that ushers in Paradise on earth." Or this attempt at semanalysis, with *terre* and *orange* sharing a "rotundity" (fair enough), and with "an isotopy of sweetness: orange, kisses, mouth, love, smiles, solar delights (?)" derived from "happy" meanings of rotundity: union, harmony.[38] All of which testifies to the fantasizing power unleashed by any threat to mimesis.

But the threat itself is the simplest expansion on the grammar of the simile. Indeed Eluard's verse is built on the model of the simile, well represented in popular parlance; to the ordinary speaker the appeal of semic conversion is irresistible, because it gives birth to witty conceits. I could list quite a few colloquial forms that couple poetry and humor: real ones, like *blanc comme un cygne qui casse des noix* [white as a nutcracking swan = black as a crow];[39] or some invented by writers, like Queneau's *vivant comme un caillou* [as alive as a pebble],[40] or in Balzac's *Cabinet des Antiques: se marier comme Mlle Cormon* [get married like Mademoiselle Cormon = remain single], referring to the perennially engaged old maid. Like these forms, Eluard's verse is positing an impossible simile: *the earth is as blue as an orange is blue,* which is to say *not at all blue.* This does not mean the reader is really expected to see earth and orange as comparable in their common lack. It is simply an expansion that fleshes out a simile structure with words not comparable—and this destroys the mimesis and triggers genuine literary behavior in the reader, as we have seen, even if it is wrong behavior. Observe, however, that this extreme ungrammaticality is as usual the very point where a new aptness of words is perceived, since the incompatible *bleu* and *orange* are oxymorically tied, true in each other's context, being complementary colors, a "harmony" exploited in literature.[41]

In this case, however, mimesis is annihilated and truth is left standing, so that the simile works after all, as Eluard's second verse confidently asserts: *jamais une erreur les mots ne mentent pas.* It works, but at the semiotic level, as a sign unto itself, demonstrating that the structure of comparison itself (all that is left after the defeat of mimesis) is true. Because they are ungrammatical as mimesis, the words actualizing that structure are nothing more than its expansion from morpheme to text. Nothing more, but that is the triumph of literariness—to derive a poem from a zero matrix, to make the text the transform not of a word but of a trope.

CONVERSION

Conversion is most conspicuous when it involves morphology and therefore phonetics, as in paronomasia or anaphora, but it is by no means limited to such figures. It is always, however, the agent that creates a formal unity by an operation that is immediately apparent, indeed seemingly almost mechanical.[42]

RULE: *Conversion transforms the constituents of the matrix sentence by modifying them all with the same factor.*

If he is to perceive the converted verbal sequence, the reader must make a mental comparison between the sequence and a hypogram that is the text imagined by him in its pretransformation state. This hypogram (a single sentence or a string of sentences) may be made out of clichés, or it may be a quotation from another text, or a descriptive system. Since the hypogram always has a positive or a negative "orientation" (the cliché is meliorative or pejorative, the quotation has its position on an esthetic and/or ethical scale, the descriptive system reflects the connotations of its kernel word), <u>the constituents of the</u> <u>conversion always transmute the hypogram's markers—in some cases</u> <u>the conversion consists of nothing more than such a permutation of</u> <u>the markers.</u>[43]

This means that the significance will be a positive valorization of the textual semiotic unit if the hypogram is negative, and a negative valorization if the hypogram is positive.

Take the following sentence: "Silence! il passe un cortège funéraire à côté de vous. Agenouillez-vous et chantez un hymne funèbre" [Silence! a funeral procession is passing. Kneel down and sing a funeral hymn]. Clearly the exhortation to pay respect to the dead belongs to the sociolect of conventional honor and awe in the presence of Death and Eternity. As such it has a positive significance, like any ritualistic gesture of social conformism. Lautréamont rewrites the second sentence by substituting for *s'agenouiller* a periphrasis composed of technical words, and for the *chanter* clause an allusion:

> Inclinez la binarité de vos rotules vers la terre et entonnez un chant d'outre-tombe (si vous considérez mes paroles plutôt comme une simple forme impérative, que comme un ordre formel qui n'est pas à sa place, vous montrerez de l'esprit et du meilleur). Il est possible que vous parveniez de la sorte à réjouir extrêmement l'âme du mort, qui va se reposer de la vie dans la fosse. Même le fait est, pour moi, certain.[44]

> Bend the binarity of your rotulas towards the ground and intone a chant from beyond the grave. (If you take my words as a simple imperative rather than a formal command that is out of place, you will be showing wit of the wittiest.) It is possible you may thereby make the soul of the dead man rejoice exceedingly as he goes to the grave to rest from life. In fact, to my mind it is a certainty.

The irony of the speaker's parenthetical aside confirms that I was not wide of the mark in positing the hypogram I did. It also underscores the comic effect expected of the conversion ("if you insist on taking this technical gibberish as an ordinary imperative, like, say, *agenouillez-vous,* if you pretend not to see my satiric conversion, then you are one up on me").

The literariness of the converted sentence lies in its double nature, which compels the reader to interpret it as a function of its form rather than as content. It conveys at the same time a message (the command) and a comment on that message. The meaning (the series of acts the addressees are to perform) is incompatible with the lexical masquerading,[45] which destroys serious or somber connotations and in fact cancels the symbolism of the acts urged upon the people addressed. This cancellation constitutes the significance: the story is not of funeral rites, nor is it just a bit of farce or gallows humor on the theme. The text's significance resides in its being a formal construct, a verbal artifact created by consistent negativizing (through the whole five-page "stanza" of the canto, in a variety of forms) of literary conventions—here the formal rules of a genre or subgenre, meditation on Man's mortality. Verbal shapes molded on a reverse image of a traditional literary form, much like the plaster cast of a bronze statue—as if the sculptor were to keep the hollow cast as his finished work of art instead of the statue—this, as we know, is the principle of Lautréamont's prose poem: not irony or satire per se, but an exercise in the basic formal self-contradiction of irony.

Irony, or its verbal mechanism, is but one special case of marker permutation. I should describe its function as the generation of idiolectic codes: it has the power to make any given set of representations represent something else than it does in common usage. This transformation does not involve the semantic transfer that occurs in the metaphor or the metonym, and it seems to me it is the basic mechanism, perhaps the only mechanism, of the literary *symbol*.

As will be shown later, conversion ordinarily involves relatively long sequences, such as a descriptive system (or a fragment thereof) or an intertext. For now let us just observe it in a sentence from a Baudelaire prose poem in which the individual meanings of words are subordinated to a single overriding symbolism, and the symbolism is the opposite of the hypogram's connotations:

Satan . . . était un homme vaste . . . dont toute la peau était dorée et illustrée, comme d'un tatouage, d'une foule de petites figures mouvantes représentant les formes nombreuses de la misère universelle. Il y avait de petits hommes efflanqués . . . , de petits gnômes difformes. . . . et puis *de vieilles mères portant des avortons accrochés à leurs mamelles exténuées.* Il y en avait encore bien d'autres.[46]

Satan was a huge man with skin gilt and covered all over with pictures, like tattooing, of lots of little moving figures representing the many forms of universal misery. There were little emaciated men, deformed little gnomes, and then there were old mothers carrying abortions clinging to their exhausted teats. There were many more such.

The sentence I italicize is not derived from semes of the *vieille mère* signifier: whereas in reality it is possible, if rare, for a woman to bear children late in life, and thus for *vieilles mères* to signify in a specific context by referring to such a referent, the stereotyped, compound lexeme *vieille mère,* in the collocations permitted by common usage, excludes any relationship to an infant and precludes the mimesis of breast feeding.[47] Worn-out, dried-up breasts *can* be derived from a mimesis of the old mother, though hardly from that of suckling. Finally, there is no associative string that enables us to derive *accroché* from *avorton.* Thus the sentence does not issue from a sequential generation progressing from word to word. Rather, its continuous pejoration results from the permutation of the plus sign, normal for the mimesis of blooming maternity, into a minus sign—a permutation determined by the allegorical context ("représentant les formes nombreuses de la misère universelle"). In this context the sentence negativizes a stereotyped portrait of the normal mother: "des mères portant des nourrissons suspendus à leurs seins." The negativizing effect is worsened by the polarization that, with each component of the sentence, increases the distance between the hypogram and its transform. Since *mère* in its maximal positive form is *jeune mère,* conversion yields *vieille mère.* As for *nourrisson,* "suckling," often associated with the cliché *plein (éclatant) de santé,* "bursting with health," it generates the word whose semes annul that cliché: *avorton.* The mimesis of the infant's meliorative dependence upon the nipple would call for *suspendus* or a synonym (e.g., Hugo: "O mère universelle! indulgente Nature! . . . Nous sommes là . . . pendus de toutes parts à ta forte mamelle . . . A tes sources sans fin désaltérant nos coeurs"[48] [Oh cosmic Mother, kindly Nature, we are all of us clinging to your strong breast, forever slaking our heart's thirst at that fountain]). The conversion generates *accrochés,* which means the same thing but suggests a frustrated obstinacy, with the emphasis upon the frustration. So the sentence is not a string of realistic details: it means by turning a mimesis of maternity, normally positive, into a code of the universal condemnation to sorrow.

Conversion of Descriptive Systems

Descriptive systems are transformed into codes by permutation of their markers: this is how conversion is able to affect much longer sequences than phrases or sentences and to make one sign out of a whole text. Because a descriptive system is a grid of metonyms built around a kernel word, its components have the same markers as that word throughout; a permutation of the kernel's markers will instantly

reverse the orientation of the entire system from positive to negative
or negative to positive, changing into their opposites the connotations
of every constituent lexeme.

The system centered around *maison,* for instance, has a positive
orientation whenever the context indicates that *maison* is synonymous
with *foyer* and must be understood as a shelter and the architectural
or man-made variant of the *locus amoenus.*[49] Baudelaire's first "Spleen"
demonstrates how the inversion of that orientation turns the *maison*
system into a code of the moral and physical discomfort a home is
supposed to protect us against:

> Pluviôse, irrité contre la ville entière,
> De son urne à grands flots verse un froid ténébreux
> Aux pâles habitants du voisin cimetière
> Et la mortalité sur les faubourgs brumeux.
>
> Mon chat sur le carreau cherchant une litière
> Agite sans repos son corps maigre et galeux;
> L'âme d'un vieux poëte erre dans la gouttière
> Avec la triste voix d'un fantôme frileux.
>
> Le bourdon se lamente, et la bûche enfumée
> Accompagne en fausset la pendule enrhumée,
> Cependant qu'en un jeu plein de sales parfums,
>
> Héritage fatal d'une vieille hydropique,
> Le beau valet de cœur et la dame de pique
> Causent sinistrement de leurs amours défunts.

Pluvius, annoyed at the whole city, pours torrents of dark cold out of his
urn down onto the pale tenants of the cemetery next door, torrents of
mortality over the foggy suburbs. On the tiling, my cat is looking for
a litter to bed down on; he shifts his thin mangy body about restlessly.
The soul of an old poet wanders through the rainspout with the sad
voice of a chilly ghost. The great bell is lamenting, and the smoke-
blackened log, in falsetto, accompanies the wheezy clock, the while, in
a deck of cards filled with foul perfumes—fatal bequest of a dropsical
old hag—the handsome knave of hearts and the queen of spades talk
of their dead loves sinisterly.

World-weariness, the dreary emptiness of life suggested by the title,
seem at first to be expressed straightforwardly enough through the
commonplace symbolism of dismal rain and dank discomfort. The
statement is made twice, once in the conventional language of tradi-
tional allegory, in the first stanza; then in the plain language of descrip-
tive realism, in the second stanza and the sestet. All of which can be

found in any number of run-of-the-mill descriptions of bleak, wet afternoons. What makes Baudelaire's treatment of a hoary theme different and effective is the structural permutation, which converts a mimesis of intimacy into a code negating intimacy and its attendant happiness.

Except for the first stanza's setting the mood and pitch, no detail denoting discomfort or inclement weather is directly stated; each one comes through the negative permutation triggered by the matrix. The sonnet is deduced *a contrario* from the positive system, just as the Black Mass of Satan's votaries was deduced from the Roman Catholic Mass. The sonnet's significance is relative to what it annuls, just as the Black Mass can celebrate Satan only if the true Mass has meaning.

The matrix I hypothesize would be something like *no refuge from misery,* but the cliché *all-pervading gloom* would do as well. In that matrix, *pervading* is precisely the agent that triggers the conversion, for it cancels the "separateness" seme, the "shelteringness," that makes the *maison*-centered system positive.

Every device in the first stanza is calculated to make rain the hyperbole of Nature's hostility to Man.[50] But a radical departure from the normal thematic use of the *maison* system transforms this rough-weather mimesis into a "slough-of-despond" symbol. Normally any description of a hostile exterior heightens by contrast the positive interior; conversely, the *maison* system's positive marking is emphasized by rain drumming on the windowpanes, wind howling in the chimney—these are necessary counterparts to warmth and coziness motifs. The conversion dictated by *pervasive gloom* transforms this opposition *inside* vs. *outside* into an equivalence.

The conversion becomes obvious as soon as the poem reaches what should have been the second pole of the original opposition: the mimesis of the cat (lines 5–6). The cat sleeping in front of the fire is an essential constituent of our descriptive system, since it is metonymic of the hearth (with another analogue of home, the crackling log fire), and of the master of the house—thus a metonym once removed of the *maison* itself.[51] The cat's description should echo the semantic components of the Baudelairean happy household—*luxe, calme et volupté* —we should find the flowing, harmonious feline contours, the glossy fur. In a poem that simply actualizes the system, without conversion, Baudelaire celebrates the *plaisir de palper (s)on corps électrique* and *(s)on dos élastique* ("Le Chat"). Here, however, the markers' permutation derives *maigre,* "skinny," from the ideal cat body, *galeux,* "mangy," from the ideal coat. The soft rug becomes *carreau,* and *carreau* never generates any adjective but *dur* or *froid,* which negate coziness. The meliorative *coussin,* on which the cat normally sleeps, becomes the pejorative *litière.* The animal's reposeful slumber becomes *agite sans repos.* And just as the positive markers of the cat are negativized, other metonyms of *foyer* are inverted in the first tercet: familiar sounds like the fire crackling, the grandfather clock ticking, signify the secret life of the home. They too become dissonant: *fausset, pendule enrhumée.* Again, *bûche enfumée,* "smoking log," nullifies the flames of the fire, its most positive descriptive component. This permutation, incidentally, is reinforced by intertextual opposition: lines 9–10 are the more negative because they counterbalance the almost humanized description of *le feu qui palpite* in the preceding poem ("La Cloche fêlée"). The words *le bourdon se lamente* negate the joyous chimes of that other text: *le bruit des carillons qui chantent.* Not that there is no sadness in "La Cloche fêlée," but at least the standard image of the safe home,[52] the opposition *outside* vs. *inside,* is preserved.

The second tercet strikingly illustrates how a text becomes a formal unit by conversion and enters, as a constituent, a larger, more complex system. Knickknacks, familiar little objects like packs of cards left lying on a table, are common motifs in scenes of intimacy—they presuppose members of the household somewhere about; when no one is there, these objects symbolize the essential continuity of living, they are silent witnesses, the *âme des choses.* An emphatic variant of this motif translates "intimacy" into its hyperbole: the secret life of familiar things. Examples abound: the night-dance of household furnishings, which stops short when an intruder appears or when day breaks; the jig the puppets do while the puppet-master is asleep, a motif exploited by ballet and cinema alike; a quadrille of lilliputian goblins inside a highboy, dreamed up in an 1873 prose poem by Charles Cros;[53] and so on. The rule of polarization applies: the moment it is stylistically emphasized, any statement of motionlessness will generate a statement of motion. The more natural and permanent the movelessness, the more striking the mobilization, and the more suggestive of fantasy. Consequently, the very immobility of furniture or of the knickknacks sitting on this furniture, or of the deck of cards, can be the proof of their unseen mobility, and unseen mobility equals secret life. This derivation is overdetermined for playing cards by the easy animization of their figures, as in *Alice in Wonderland;* love between the characters comes as a logical result (or a thematic one, queens dallying with lackeys).[54]

The whole motif, a complicated story, is verily a subsystem of the *maison* system. It has now been integrated into the overall conversion of "Spleen" and functions as a word—no matter how broad all its connotations—would function, as one constituent in a sentence, on a par with the other words. The conversion within the subsystem (adjectives and adverbs: *sales parfums, héritage fatal, causent sinistrement, amours défunts*) has no independent meaning; no symbolism of their own attaches to the details of this parenthetic story.[55] Their complex negativizations are just a marker like the others, an embedding within the syntagmatic continuum of the sonnet's conversion. The realistic mimesis of the whole tercet has been semioticized into being one word of *maison*'s transformation into *non-maison*, that is, of the transformation of *maison*'s systematic significance into a code of that significance's contrary.

Conversion as Textual Sign

Nowhere is the mechanical nature of conversion more apparent than in surrealist texts produced by automatic writing. This is natural enough, since automatic writing was intended and practiced as a method of putting an end to the literary tradition that prized conscious, calculated writing, which is to say, denied the generative power of the text itself, of the language's own dynamics.[56] Nowhere is it more clearly demonstrated that the transform obtained by conversion is not just a string of words, but a textual unit whose characteristic lexical and semantic features, as well as its beginning and its end, all result from the conversion process. The ungrammaticalities, the model, and the clausula all have the earmarks of a reversal, which means that they cannot be fully understood without the hypogram they transform. Indeed, even if the ungrammaticalities are perceived by themselves as a disorder of grammar, their significance, which is their restoration to a new order, their integration into the norm of another text, does not come about until the reader has traced backwards the path of the transformation.

One of the prose poems that make up André Breton's *Poisson soluble* recounts a long automobile odyssey. The incidents are so far removed from all verisimilitude (driver and passengers in medieval armor, river-leaping instead of bridge-crossing) that the reader naturally looks for some esoteric symbolism: strange happenings remind him of familiar mythological patterns. For instance, the car rides on and on without reaching the end of a shadow cast by a statue, reminiscent of the knights of old who rode all day and still could not get out of the shade of the tree Yggdrasil. The contrast between today's metal charger and the tales of bygone days is too strong—this cannot be the "normal" literary fantastic. The text is now correctly interpreted as a verbal game, a mythic structure realized with the help of that ultramodern code, the language of the automobile enthusiast (1924, the date of the book, is still the Heroic Age of the motorcar). It is rather like when Jarry rewrote the Crucifixion in the style of a sportscaster describing a bicycle race.[57] The myth is more a mimesis of the myth, and the weirdness of the episodes, yielding a semiosis of the supernatural or the esoteric, is created entirely with words. Conversion is one device of this grammatical fantastic.

> C'est dans les faubourgs de la ville 26 que se produisit le miracle: une voiture qui venait en sens inverse de la nôtre et commença par écrire mon nom à l'envers dans un merveilleux paraphe de flamme vint nous heurter légèrement; le diable sait si elle allait moins vite que nous.[58]

> The miracle occurred near the city limits of Town 26: a car was coming in the opposite direction and began by writing my name backwards with a wonderful flaming flourish; it struck us lightly, the devil knows it was going slower than we were.

The narrative abnormalities permit us to reconstruct a hypogram that is the "true" story of an accident—that is, it would look true because it would follow commonplaces, and its veracity would be guaranteed by linguistic usage. "Struck us violently," "God knows it was going faster than we were," where "God knows" is a cliché asseverating the truth of an understandably emotional statement by a witness; where the adverb "violently" is but a variant of stereotypes like "the impact was so violent that" used in similar circumstances; a variant too of that inevitable declaration by accident victims: "The *other* driver was speeding." In fact, the story here would seem to be at the same time a borrowing from a newspaper traffic-accident report, and a parody of it; that is, if it made sense as a parody. It does not, of course, and we catch on when we realize that the text is composed of contraries, that what brings about the "miracle" in *que se produisit le miracle* is a conversion from the expected sentence about a speeding car: *que se produisit l'accident,* and that this is the miracle of mirror-writing, so to speak, the mechanical converse of newspaper discourse; and that the rule regulating the conversion, its model, is a dual sign.[59] For in the dictionary *en sens inverse* has two mutually exclusive meanings, and it is the mark of poetic discourse that whenever usage posits incompatibilities, they are reconciled. The dual sign, *en sens inverse,* at first looks like nothing more than a report of circumstances leading to a head-on collision ("coming from the opposite direction"); but in fact it refers at the same time to a metalanguage ("in reverse order") whose application to the surface text inverts its details. The metalinguistic genotext is made explicit by *commença par écrire mon nom à l'envers* [began by writing my name backwards], a revealing statement that places responsibility for the miracle squarely on the words themselves, as the author's persona is replaced by its mirror image. And, by the way, this will appear retroactively as a variant on the title of the whole *Poisson soluble* collection, since as a title, that is, as the sign of the author's intention, it has been cancelled, its meaning has vanished as would "soluble fish" in water; the title does represent Breton, because it is a fish and Breton is a Pisces, and it does represent automatic writing, because Pisces dissolves.

The conversion, it will be noted, makes the car-crash episode a separate text within the poem, since from the *miracle* of the curious accident to the last detail,[60] the entire sequence is the syntagmatic equivalent of the one lexeme offering the temptation of a double reference.

For the dual sign to generate the automatic brand of conversion, there need not be an opposition of two common-usage meanings, one acceptable in context (here the *sens inverse* of traffic, generating the syntax and lexicon) and one unacceptable (here the logical *sens inverse,* generating the conversive constants). The two may be equally acceptable, if one is the metaphorical and the other the literal meaning of the same word. In this case the text will first develop the implications of the metaphor and then oppose them to the literal denotation. The following "automatic" pseudostory of an ill-fated polar expedition, from Robert Desnos's *La liberté ou l'amour,* is derived entirely from such an actualization, within the same context, first of the conversive transform and then of its hypogram. The cliché description of an iceberg as a *pyramid of ice*[61] generates the description of an Egypt of the North, as if *pyramid* were being taken literally. The passage begins with the explorers' party trapped in the icefields, slowly sinking into ice as insects into amber—a literary theme, but one that owes its hold on the imagination less to the picturesque mimesis of travel literature than to the semiotic structure: the familiar *buried alive* polarization.

La mission Albert avec ses mâts surmontés d'un oriflamme est maintenant au centre d'une pyramide de glace. Un sphinx de glace surgit et complète le paysage. De la brûlante Egypte au pôle irrésistible un courant miraculeux s'établit. Le sphinx des glaces parle au sphinx des sables.

The Albert expedition, a navy flag atop its masts, is now at the center of an ice pyramid. A sphinx of ice looms up and completes the landscape. From burning Egypt to the irresistible pole there now begins the flow of a miraculous current. The sphinx of the icefields speaks to the sphinx of the sands.

Further derivation soon abandons all reference to an imaginable reality. Thus the boats on the polar seas are called *jolis chameaux.* So far so good, since there is a cliché that makes a camel *le vaisseau du désert.* But there is no hope that the reader will be able to invent a metaphoric rationalization for a sentence like "Egypte polaire avec ses pharaons portant au cimier de leur casque non pas le scarabée des sables, mais l'esturgeon" [Polar Egypt with her pharaohs wearing upon their helmet crests not the scarab of the sands, but the sturgeon]; or like "les crocodiles se transforment en phoques" [the crocodiles turn into seals]. The text makes a pretense of translating, as did André Breton, into a miracle narrative what is just a conversion miracle: "un courant miraculeux s'établit . . . Et voici que les temps approchent! On soupçonne déjà l'existence d'une Egypte polaire" [a miraculous current starts to flow . . . A new era is at hand! Some already suspect there is a polar Egypt somewhere]. The conversion itself is double, since it lists successively or alternately the transforms from a "real Egypt" hypogram, and then gives the straight version, in turn derived from its own transform. Ice derived from sand, sand derived from ice.

Pyramide, as a dual sign, is the model for the conversion. Not as a metaphor: its being a metaphor is a phenomenon of the text's semantic level and lies within the domain of surface analysis, that is, stylistics. The opposition between the metaphoric and literal uses of *pyramide* is the model for the successive actualization of the two Egypts, which is in itself a powerful structure of poetic discourse, because it is an exemplary polarization. A variant of the *cold climates* vs. *hot countries* opposition, this theme is common in modern French literature (*zone glaciale, zone torride,* as nineteenth-century geographers put it): quite a few poems are built on it, especially where the contemplator embraces at a glance the whole expanse of the universe, or where the dreamer envisions an impossible reconciliation of extremes.[62] But here the metaphor is the first result, not the cause of a phenomenon appearing at the semiotic level: at that level *pyramide* functions as interpretant between the two Egypt texts, because this language-pretested periphrasis for "iceberg" happens to refer also to a literary intertext.

Pyramid and sphinx are metonyms of each other. There is Jules Verne's well-known *Le Sphinx des Glaces;* and as if to establish the pattern of metonymic description, yet another of his titles: *Le Désert de glace.* In Desnos the intertextual connection surfaces, as it were, one page later, when a character walks incongruously across the narrative carrying a Jules Verne novel under his arm. Jules Verne himself was building on an intertext: Edgar Allen Poe is the first to transport to polar climes the sphinx as a symbol of mystery—another function of the Egypt system, the land being one of esoteric tradition. At the conclusion of the *Narrative of A. Gordon Pym,* the image of a white sphinx concretizes the mysterious world that swallows up sailors wrecked beyond the Antarctic Circle. Jules Verne then wrote a sequel to the adventures of Pym, purporting to "disclose" what his predecessor had not spoken of and to pick up the thread of his narrator's unfinished story. Out of Poe's purely metaphorical sphinx (or perhaps the sphinx dreamed up by his sailor), Verne extracted a reality that "literally" resembles the monster—a mountain with a sphinx profile. Thus *sphinx* in Desnos's text is overdetermined, as is the adjectival *des glaces.* The word "ice" is less descriptive of a reality than it is (as in Jules Verne) the means to a binary opposition, *sphinx* vs. *ice sphinx.* Thanks to this opposition, the descriptive system of the Egyptian sphinx is converted into that of the polar sphinx by modification of each component of the former with an adjective or complement synonymous with *glace.* There is no dubiously valid comparison on the mimesis plane, as in the true travel tale; there is simply a reversal through alteration of "geographical" markers. To be valid the transformation need only be constant; but then, as a constant it formally isolates the episode and makes it a poem qua verbal artifact, for the polar reality it purports to describe is a reality springing not from observation of the outside world but from the negativization of a metaphor. Its literalness is not a mimesis but the reversal of a sign of literariness.

None of this would work if the reader's decoding were left to his uneven attention: what insures the text's control is the same element that authenticates its status as the textual equivalent of *pyramide*'s dual reference. A final metonym of the pyramid (and another stereotype of the Egyptian decor), the Memnon colossus, is the test of correct deciphment, according to the inversion rule. As soon as referentiality disappears, a word's very form is imposed as such: in *Memnon* it is now possible to isolate another word, *non,* and as a consequence to invert it, since every negation bears a bipolar relation to an affirmation. By virtue of this relation, patterned upon the substitution of *ice* for *sand,* the clausula reads, "les colosses de Memnon appellent les colosses de Memoui" [the colossi of Memno are calling to the colossi of Memyes].

Conversion Combined with Expansion

There is one type of conversion unrelated to an external hypogram: this type modifies the generation of a text by expansion. Instead of indiscriminately producing forms more complex than their homologues in the matrix, the expansion here is limited to those more complex forms that also repeat features characteristic of the matrix. The reader's perception entails no reference to a hypogram, but he recognizes that the conversive constants do not result from the expansion, that they are distinctive features of the matrix, and that they reflect the matrix's unchanging identity within the grammatically and lexically multiform, ever-changing otherness of the textual detour. These constants repeatedly actualize one or more semes of the word capable of summarizing or symbolizing the matrix:[63] this the reader grasps empirically.

Conversion of this kind is exemplified in Gautier's metaphorical portrait of the poet as a swallow:[64] we recall that every verb of motion describing the bird's zigzag flight repeated the semic selection of the initial metaphor equating the poet's spirituality, his flights of inspiration and fancy-freedom, with the bird's exemplary escape from the pull of gravity. In that instance the development of the text involved no obscurity or major departure from cognitive language: first because the matrix had already been made explicit at the beginning by the metaphoric model, second because the lexicons of the *esprit* and *oiseau* descriptive systems are to a large extent interchangeable, the same words being used figuratively for *esprit* and literally for *oiseau.* Thus Gautier's expansion could be deciphered, with the appearance of logical sequence, as an extended metaphor. And it is the same with the *aurora borealis* text and "Les Bijoux."

But such clear cases by no means predominate. For one thing, the initial actualization of the matrix may not be plainly decipherable, or it may be recognizable as the model for the expansion only later on, through retroactive reading, when the awareness of textual constants begins to operate. The reader does not immediately realize what it is the successive images of the poem have in common, since he may not at first see them as variants of the same structure. Things are the more difficult because the conflict is at the semic level and is therefore bound to entail a drastic deterioration of the mimesis from variant to successive variant.

My example is a Rimbaud poem in which such deterioration has been made all the more conspicuous by the intellectually foolhardy and sometimes foolish interpretations it has inspired:

> FÊTES DE LA FAIM
>
> Ma faim, Anne, Anne
> Fuis sur ton âne.
>
> Si j'ai du *goût,* ce n'est guères
> Que pour la terre et les pierres.
> 5　Dinn! dinn! dinn! dinn! Je pais l'air,
> Le roc, les Terres, le fer.
>
> Tournez, les faims, paissez, faims,
> 　　　　Le pré des sons!
> Puis l'aimable et vibrant venin
> 10　　　　Des liserons;
>
> Les cailloux qu'un pauvre brise,
> Les vieilles pierres d'église,
> Les galets, fils des déluges,
> Pains couchés aux vallées grises!
>
> 15　Mes faims, c'est les bouts d'air noir;
> 　　　　L'azur sonneur;
> 　— C'est l'estomac qui me tire.
> 　　　　C'est le malheur.
>
> Sur terre ont paru les feuilles!
> 20　Je vais aux chairs de fruit blettes
> Au sein du sillon je cueille
> La doucette et la violette.
>
> 　　Ma faim, Anne, Anne!
> 　　Fuis sur ton âne.[65]

Feasts of Hunger. My hunger, Anne, Anne, run away on your donkey. If I have any taste, it is for hardly anything but earth's soil and stones. Dinn! dinn! dinn! dinn! I feed on air, rock, soil, iron. Turn round and round, hungers, graze the meadows of sound! Then the nice vibrant venom of the morning glories; the stones a poor man breaks, the old slabs of churches, the beach pebbles, children of deluge, bread loaves lying in the grey valleys! My hungers, they are crumbs of black air; the azure bellringer; it's my stomach that aches. It's unhappiness. Leaves have come out on earth! I am going to the flesh of overripe fruit, from the heart of the furrow I pick lamb's lettuce and the violet. My hunger, Anne, Anne! run away on your donkey.

At first blush there seems to be little connection between the successive images. The one riddle that does not require solution is that of the refrain, since a refrain need not have any connection with the song it gives a beat to or divides into stanzas, and it can even be made of nonsense words. This one, at least, repeats the title's basic word—"sings" it, so to speak—and thus functions as a sign for both the poem's subject, hunger, and its form or genre, the celebration of hunger, hence the *anti-blason,* like our poet's *Comédie de la soif.* But the refrain is our only respite. We assume from the title that the text must concern hunger. Yet aside from one familiar turn of phrase (line 17), the bizarreness of the images leaves us in doubt as to why or how these particular forms symbolize hunger. Why should hungers, in the plural, be turning around (line 7), why should they suggest cattle grazing, let alone cattle feeding on sounds (line 8)? This is all so puzzling that one critic simply gives up. Says he: "Rimbaud lets himself go here in free childish association. The effect is fresh, innovative, and naturally uneven."[66] Others, like Suzanne Bernard, author of the most popular and authoritative school edition of Rimbaud, feel compelled to explain away the strangeness of the discourse by referring to the private nature and, out of context, the oddness of the poet's experience. Their reductionism mistakes formal uniqueness for historical accident, biographical happenstance. Bernard explains line 6 by assuming that Rimbaud happened to be hungry in London; that this country boy was "fascinated by the mineral landscape of a city where iron and coal are everywhere"; that he dreamt of springtime and fresh vegetables; that the last stanza (lines 19–22) must be about the fulfillment of the hungry boy's longings: "vegetable fecundity has replaced mineral hardness."[67] This would all be very well for *doucette,* a kind of salad, but in fact spring is not the best season for fruit, certainly not for the more luscious, over-succulent kind. One of Rimbaud's friends, Delahaye, comes to the rescue. He testifies that in Rimbaud's native region you can get frozen fruit at the end of winter—frozen and therefore soft. But this still does not explain *violette,* not a food but a flower.

These lame explanations are quite unnecessary. The mimetic deficiencies that have been piling up from the first stanza on have the appearance—to our hindsight—of accumulating metonyms of hunger. Starting with the self-mocking italics (line 3), "if I have a taste for anything (what a taste!), it is for earth and stones," the poem simply catalogs inedibles. More precisely, since the last stanza shifts to edibles, the entire poem is an expansion on two polar opposites, the narrative potentialities derivable from the sememe "hunger": a tale of unsatisfied hunger, and a tale of its satisfaction. *Avoir faim* has two lexical facets, a negative and a positive: you starve, or you have a good appetite. In either case the craving for food can be expressed in terms of eating, hence a matrix: *eating the inedible, eating the edible,* which covers the whole story of the poem's given, that is, of the title. The two complementary facets are both able to generate "exemplary" literary discourse, since the first is a polarization and the second a tautology.

A denser derivation from this matrix is Eluard's line *Le rêve manger l'immangeable*[68] [the dream of eating the uneatable]. Here the second stage and the first are conflated, in the form of fantasy, instead of the second's actually solving the difficulty of the first.

Consequently, the expansion consists of two paradigms of foodstuff, both on verbs of eating or craving. The first series is modified by the negative converter, the second by the positive one; the first lists uneatables—minerals, air, even sounds, and poisonous vegetables; the second lists eatable substances, vegetables.

This periphrastic recitation or litany of kernel-word metonyms is quite literally a verbal celebration—a feast of hunger—to the same extent that cataloging a woman's physical charms constitutes the conventional *blason* of Woman in Renaissance literature. What is more, both enumerations are fully motivated and seasoned by usage at the very points where they seem nonsensical. At first the reader does not catch on, because each disconcerting (and linguistically established) *exemplum* of the uneatable is out of context; because the whole paradigm is present, when in normal utterance each case would exclude the other; and because the "enthusiastic" grammar (verbs offering or urging this paradoxical consumption) applied to an unappetizing lexicon (the inedible) would, in cognitive language, be a contradiction in terms.

Each variant of this non-food is in fact guaranteed by, and ritualistically refers to, clichés. The air (line 5): *vivre de l'air du temps,* a proverbial phrase applied to impecunious individuals or dieting ladies. The puzzling *bouts d'air noir* uses *air* as a hyperbolic substitute for the famine cliché *des bouts de pain noir.* Whereas *air noir* is sheer nonsense referentially, it carries on the conversion by replacing stale and scanty crusts with the illusion of food, and, as a variant on the model of the stereotype, it makes sense. Again, the deadly convolvulus brings us to familiar warnings to children about poisonous plants. And the revolving hungers refer to the revolving wooden horses of the carousel ("Tournez, tournez, bons chevaux de bois," Verlaine is writing at about the same time) by way of the colloquial *manger avec les chevaux de bois* [eat when the wooden horses eat]—that is, starve. Hence too *paissez,* the verb for cattle or horses browsing on grass. Hence *sons,* a pun on the two meanings, "bran," horse fodder, and in the plural, "sounds." Sounds, of course, because of the bell in line 5, the refectory bell that summons to the table. We need not be wildly imaginative to find this a nice instance of tautology, since "dinn! dinn! dinn! dinn! mangeons" sounds like "dîne! dîne! mangeons!" (as we would say, "Dinner! Dinner! Let's eat!"). A hollow invitation, this being a mineral dinner—wherefore the bitterness concerning *l'azur sonneur,* which unites *l'air du temps* of our aforementioned proverb with the delusive call to dinner. Whence also the bitterness of the allusion to the Mallarmé intertext—the only possible explanation for this strange phrase—a poem in which the blue sky serves as image for a "sterile desert," a haunting emptiness, where "l'Azur triomphe [. . .] qui chante dans les cloches [. . .] il se fait voix pour plus nous faire peur avec sa victoire méchante"[69] [Azure triumphant sings in the bells; it turns itself into a voice the better to frighten us with its victorious wickedness].

But the core of the uneatable sequence is its mineral menu. Rocks, stones, metal have always symbolized the inedible, or food only gluttony can stomach: think of the stuff supposedly found in the gizzards of ostriches; think of Saturn gobbling up a swaddled stone. But we should not see in the mineral conversion anything more than a semic expansion, the poem's playing upon variants of the seme "hardness." *Roc* and *fer* (*charbon* in the second version) are hyperboles of nutritional hardness. An instance is Chateaubriand's humorous account of a besieged and starving garrison: "Cannonballs fell like iron bread loaves rolling amidst famished guests."[70] Literary texts often play, back and forth, on this evidently tempting polarization—Corbière: "Si quelqu'un leur jette la pierre / Que la pierre se change en pain" [the stone cast at the poor, may it turn into bread], and conversely, Tzara's title "La pétrification du pain."[71] So powerful is this polarization that Magritte is inspired to paint loaves of bread made out of grey stone.[72] So the expansion moves forward to its climax, where the *cailloux* in the context *casseur de cailloux* (periphrastically represented by the day-laborer working on a road gang, line 11) presupposes hardness twice: as stones and as stones to be crushed; the *pierres d'église* exemplify stoniness; and the *galets,* always hard in French stereotypes, bring back explicit food, only to cancel it again deviously, since the pseudo–bread loaves of the valley are hard-tack petrified into *galets:* from *galettes* to *galets.*[73]

Once this hyperbolic climax has been reached, the reverse conversion begins and expansion sets to work developing the other facet of "hunger." Since "uneatable" was represented by variations upon "hardness," "eatable" is now represented by the converse, "softness." Hence the fruit of line 20: referentially unacceptable in a nonverbal context of real yearly seasons, it nonetheless ripens and mellows at the level of signifiers. It is generated by the structural change of hardness into nonhardness. Using a strikingly similar conversion, André Breton made a poem out of *adynata.*[74] There the group *flammes froides,* "cold flames," annuls an essential semantic component of *fire.* Significantly, *flammes froides* is followed by *pierres blettes,* "overripe stones," where the adjective is to *pierre* what *froide* is to *flamme:* it nullifies the essential stoniness of *stone.* In Rimbaud's poem this stoniness is doubly nullified by the compound softness of *chair* and *blette.* Thrice nullified indeed, thanks to *doucette.* Without a dictionary I should not have known that this is a kind of lettuce. But I do not have to know. All that counts here is the double softness of the word, with *doux* for its root and a diminutive suffix *-ette,* which in French compounds combines softness with mincing prettiness. Add to this the effect of *violette,* here no more than a synonym of *nonhardness:* first because the flower that "blushes unseen" symbolizes retiring delicacy; second, and most important, because in the context the violet appears as a variation, a sort of reverse declension of the radical on the unchanging *-ette.* Promoted by its reduplication from an appendage to a fullfledged sign, *-ette* is now semanticized as the polar opposite of *uneatable.*[75]

Thus, while every single representation in the poem is well-nigh incomprehensible to start with, it becomes capable of metaphorization or symbolization as soon as it is perceived as functionally identical with the others, as soon as we perceive the sequence that develops one word of the title, or rather one seme of that word, into a text. And once again, maximal catachresis[76] at the lexematic level of individual words or phrases coincides with significance at the textual level.

⋙⋙⋙ FOUR ⋘⋘⋘

INTERPRETANTS

The shift from meaning to significance necessitates the concept of interpretant, that is, a sign that translates the text's surface signs and explains what else the text suggests. Peirce, propounder of the concept, puts it this way: "A sign stands *for* something *to* the idea which it produces, or modifies. . . . That for which it stands is called its *object;* that which it conveys, its *meaning;* and the idea to which it gives rise, its *interpretant.*"[1] Any equivalence established by the poem and perceived by retroactive reading may be regarded as an interpretant: for instance, a paradigm of synonyms, or in Mallarmé's -*yx* sonnet the variations on *rien*.[2]

In this chapter, however, I shall use the term only of signs I believe peculiar to poetry and whose function is to guide the reader in his "comparative" or structural reading. These signs mediate, since by their very form they represent the equivalence of two signifying systems: by this I mean they much resemble *puns* or *syllepses,* being equally pertinent to two codes or texts, the meaning-conveying one and the significance-carrying one.

I shall distinguish between *lexematic* and *textual* interpretants. The latter are mediating texts, either quoted in the poem or alluded to: they themselves contain a model of the equivalences and transferrals from one code to the other, and they lay down the rule of the poem's idiolect, guaranteeing, with the authority a normative grammar, a tradition, or a convention would have, the semiotic practice peculiar to the poem. The lexematic ones are mediating words, which I shall call *dual signs,* because either they generate two texts simultaneously within the poem (or one text that must be understood in two different ways), or else they presuppose two hypograms simultaneously.

Intertextual Punning

As suggested above, the dual sign works like a pun. We will see that
the pun in poetic discourse grows out of textual "roots." It is first ap-
prehended as a mere ungrammaticality, until the discovery is made
that there is another text in which the word is grammatical; the mo-
ment the other text is identified, the dual sign becomes significant
purely because of its shape, which alone alludes to that other code.

The following three passages—the first two by Ronsard, the last by
Olivier de Magny, a lesser contemporary of his—are three variants of
the conventional encomium on the female body. The basic rule of
the genre (the *blason*) is that every part of the feminine form must be
celebrated. One required motif, and the most frequent, is praise for
the lady's snowy breasts. The context of this convention is so well
established, the details are so unmodifiable, so predictable down to
the color of the bosom and the similes of laudation, the expectedness
at all stages of the description is so strong, that what hits us in all
three of these poems is truly startling: the image actualizing so fa-
miliar a motif contains in all three a contradictory representation of
the much-extolled whiteness as green grass. The text makes this contra-
diction absolutely inescapable; there is no glossing over it, because it
holds the conventional milk-whiteness and the greening of the breast
firmly face to face, lexematic incompatibles in a state of syntactic
unity and mutual interdependence:

> Ha, seigneur dieu, que de grâces écloses
> Dans le jardin de ce sein verdelet,
> Enflent le rond de deux gazons de lait,
> Où des Amours les flèches sont encloses!
>
> Belle gorge d'albastre, et vous chaste poictrine,
> Qui les Muses cachez en un rond verdelet:
> Tertres d'Agathe blanc, petits gazons de laict,
> Des Grâces le séjour, d'Amour et de Cyprine:
> Sein de couleur de liz et de couleur rosine,
> De veines marqueté, je vous vy par souhait
> Lever l'autre matin, comme l'Aurore fait
> Quand vermeille elle sort de sa chambre marine.
>
> Et qui void ses petits tetons
> Void de lait deux petits gazons
> Ou bien deux boulettes d'ivoire.[3]

(Ronsard 1) Ah Lord God, how many graces blossom in the garden of
this pretty green bosom and swell the round of two milky lawns . . .

(Ronsard 2) Beautiful alabaster breasts, and you chaste bosom, who keep
the Muses hidden in a pretty green circle; mounds of white agathis, little
lawns of milk, sojourn of the Graces, of Cupid and Cyprine Venus;
breasts the color of lilies and the color of rose, inlaid with veins, it was
my pleasure to see you rise from bed the other morning, like Dawn
herself when she comes forth rosy from her sea chamber. (Magny) Who-
ever sees her little breasts sees two little lawns of milk, or else two
little ivory balls.

Such blatant oddness triggers the usual reaction: flight from the
textual conundrum to asylum in periphrastic rationalizations, in ex-
ternal, nonverbal explanations, or in some compensatory authority
able to extenuate the offending turn of phrase. Readers groping for
textual reference will find it in this case. At least they did during the
sixteenth century, in a famous female-breast *blason*, Alcina's portrait
in Ariosto. Ronsard's and Magny's verses are among many imitations:

> Bianca nieve e il bel collo, e'l petto latte;
> . . .
> Due pome acerbe, e pur d'ivorio fatte,
> Vengon e van come onda al primo margo
> . . .
> Non potria l'altre parti veder Argo:
> Ben si può giudicar che corrisponde
> A quel ch'appar di fuor quel che s'asconde[4]

White snow is the lovely neck, and milk the breast; two unripened ap-
ples, green yet ivory, move to and fro like a wave . . . Argus himself
could not see the rest, but you can judge that what is hidden is a match
for what is seen

The unconscionable images of Ronsard and Magny, far from being
unjustified, derive quite logically from Ariosto's. We have here an ex-
tended metaphor straddling two texts, two languages, two civilizations:
the secondary, or derivative metaphors (green breasts, two round milk-
lawns) are found in Ronsard; the primary metaphor is situated in
the intertext.[5] This primary metaphor ("two unripe apples," *due pome
acerbe*) generates derivative ones that are in fact overdetermined,
since they are also linked by a "garden" sememe, the semic complex of
jardin's descriptive system (an overdetermination likewise at work in
Ariosto and in the French poems). Nor was the selection of the *garden*
system as a code a random selection. It was dictated by the genre (as
a subgenre of love poetry). For ever since medieval poetry woman's
more secret charms have been traditionally represented as a secret
garden or a walled orchard.

But why should Ronsard and Magny have chosen *lawn* rather than *apples?* Why did they aggravate their assault on language by giving the lawn the impossible color of milk? This unlikely shift from the fruit, which at least shares "roundness" with the breast, is the result of the intertextual conflict—a conflict not softened by the reader's recollection of the Italian hypogram or his realization that the key to the unsettling French images lies elsewhere. Even as he gets the point, the reader is seeing through the screen of the initial difficulty. He still sees the image (and will continue to see it, as often as he rereads) in the isolation of the single text; the gap must still be bridged through his own efforts, in his own mind. <u>Difficulty, however surely and however often overcome, remains a component of literariness</u>. Here the conflict is created by a translation problem, an incompatibility of language and of generic or thematic idiolect. The Italian *pome acerbe,* "unripe fruit," praises the young breast, a beauty hardly nubile. But *acerbe* in apple context yields *pommes vertes,* "green apples," where "green" means both the color and "unripe"—either way, scarcely positive. Words more conformant to the matrix (the genre's fundamental rule of praise) must be found, that is, words with positive markers. Hence the change from *vert* to *verdelet, vert* with a diminutive suffix. That the marker is the important consideration here, and that the conversion is the pertinent factor, is proven by *verdelet,* "tart, slightly acid": as a metonym for "unripe" it is not much less negative, while it loses its power to represent a color, since it does *not* mean "a little bit green" or "greenish." And yet we know that the poems stick to the color mimesis: the texts still use the *vert* radical of the diminutive lexeme to generate a mimesis of greenness. The *-let* suffix, indeed, functions only as a marker denoting a positive valorization of the word it modifies. As a class sign, it is overdetermined, first by the topos opposing smallness to bigness—smallness in this binary opposition has the kind of connotation we find in adjectives like *nice* and *cute;* second, by baby talk, again a positive connotation. The *-let* suffix is prevalent in the Pléiade school of lyrical and *blason* poetry, where it also becomes a marker of encomiastic style. Despite the suffix's values, however, suffixation alone cannot positivize sufficiently, because *fruits verdelets* are just as unripe as *fruits verts.* The descriptive system of *sein,* however, does offer a way out, through its network of metonymic links: the simplest solution (one also tried by Ronsard) is *boutons verdelets,* "little green buds."[6] Paradoxically, green reenters the sememe *verdelet* through the adjective's association with *bouton,* for in that sense the noun is often the kernel of a tautological cliché: *vert bouton.* This time the image is quite acceptable, because the same word *bouton* means, according to the text, either "nipples" or "flower buds"—a happy coincidence for one striving to suggest nubility as a promise of beauty to come. In our poem *sein verdelet* must therefore be understood as metonymic: the word for the whole breast stands for the nipple. But the metonymy keeps *verdelet* looking as wrong as ever, because *"sein,"* breast, cannot be any such color. And this wrong look in turn determines the generation of *gazons de lait.* The production of the text compensates for the problem at the semantic level by a pseudo-explanation at the lexical level.

What happens is this: on the one hand *gazon* is an apt metaphor for the breasts in the love-garden complex, and yet we still need *de lait,* incompatible with green grass, for without this modifier the reader may not recognize that the lawns stand for breasts. Yet the incompatibility is there only if the text is used as a reference to reality. The incompatibility vanishes once the text is read the way texts are built to be read, as a reference to its own models, to words further back down the line. In such a reading *verdelet,* "unripe," is singled out, made a special, conspicuous sign, because it is all that is left of a whole text (Ariosto's), because it is equivalent to a famous quotation. Now *verdelet,* singled out as a form, lends itself to punning: it sounds exactly like a fantasy *vert de lait,* "milk green," which thus forms a hypogram for *gazon de lait,* since *gazon* (like *grass green* in English) is *the* word for "viridity" in a garden description. The group thus produced may look no less disconcerting[7] from the viewpoint of a feminine-beauty mimesis (all languages, in fact, seem to make green in human context a consistent sign of pathology or monstrousness: sickliness, morbid decay, envy, outerspace complexion, etc.). But the excuse is that at least *gazon de lait* has the shape of a metaphor, that *de* permits formal statement of an equation and at the same time the statement that this is not in earnest, it is just a conceit. In fact labels like mannerism, or later, baroque imagery, or later still, *préciosité,* or negative value judgments like affectation or *mignardise* (mincing, simpering prettiness of style)—all these are modalities of a perception of literariness, and all are rationalizations of what boils down to an awareness of ungrammaticality. Yet the retroactive association with the equivocal generator, with the pun, since the pun is also a sign of intertextual reference, lets the reader experience one more form of literariness: perception of a tradition in the text, of an allusion to another author—*author* in its etymological meaning, *auctor,* not writer but guarantor, witness to a verbal contract. Intertextuality is to the hypogram and its palimpsest what escrow is to the lender and the borrower.

Nor does the intertextual pun lose its power when cultural changes cause the *auctor* to be forgotten and the link with *pome acerbe* to be lost. For *verdelet/vert de lait* remains a pun: it fits prenubile womanhood and, just as well, the erotic *locus amoenus,* this time because readers have to explain or "excuse" it by direct reference to the courtly theme of Woman as the love orchard.

Such is the nature of this type of double, or equivocal, sign, that when its intertext disappears it reconstitutes another,[8] generating an imaginary referent (here the Garden of Love, that is, the Woman descriptive system rewritten in garden code), and this seems to entail the text that was once presupposed.[9]

Dual Signs

The dual sign is an equivocal word situated at the point where two sequences of semantic or formal associations intersect. Nodal point might be a better image, since the word links together chains of association drawn along parallel paths by the sentence. These parallels meet, in defiance of geometric law, only because the dual sign properly placed in one of the two sequences would have been just as much at home in the other. This potential appropriateness somewhere else, in another text, is a familiar concept at this point in our exploration of the semiotic grid; the difference here is that the other "text" is very close at hand, the sequence is mixed with the one in which the equivocal word rightly belongs. The potential appropriateness is its total or partial homophony with another word (or with itself, in the case of a word endowed with very different meanings) that might be in the other sequence: to put it otherwise, the dual sign functions like a pun.

Such words may carry meaning in ways that cannot be explained as metaphorical or metonymic, and they point to textual significance because they stand for a whole "text," the other text, while at the same time functioning like any other word, in accordance with grammar and lexical collocation, within their more "natural" sequence. For instance, Chateaubriand's description of General La Fayette's funeral, which he attended. If for once I resort to nonfiction prose I may be pardoned, since the only possible interest of the story, or at least of the details I am concerned with, lies in their symbolism. They are removed from the two genres to which *Mémoires d'Outre-Tombe* may belong, for they are of no historical moment and have no autobiographical pertinence. Furthermore, the passage is a separate vignette and should be read as a prose poem:

> . . . au haut de la montée du boulevard, le corbillard s'arrêta; je le vis tout doré d'un rayon fugitif du soleil, briller au-dessus des casques et des armes: puis l'ombre revint et il disparut. La multitude s'écoula; des vendeuses de *plaisirs* crièrent leurs oublies, des vendeurs d'amusettes portèrent çà et là des moulins de papier qui tournaient au même vent dont le souffle avait agité les plumes du char funèbre.[10]

> at the top of the boulevard-incline the hearse stopped; I saw it, gilded all over by a fleeting ray of sunlight, shining above the helmets and the weapons: then shadow returned and the hearse disappeared. The crowd dispersed. Women selling refreshments cried their wafers, men selling toys carried about their paper windmills, which whirled in the same wind that had ruffled the plumes of the hearse.

As reality, the details are indeed minor. As words, however, minor details are worth noticing merely because they have been recorded: their insignificance is but the other face of their importance as signs. And as signs it is clear what they mean: the hearse first shining in the sunlight, then lost in shadows, evidently symbolizes the transience and vanity of all things human. This semantic given is the model for all the other details, which function not just as picturesque notations or constituents of reality, but as embodiments of the semiotic constant. The last sentence, for instance, "vent dont le souffle avait agité les plumes du char funèbre," is built on the model of *des moulins de papier tournaient au vent:* the equivalence of the two sentences entails the equivalence of the funeral decorations, symbols of human pride, and the *moulins de papier* (a variant of *amusettes,* hence trifles doubly childish)—the same wind sweeps over both. This context explains why *oublies* has become the dual sign I am after. *Oublies,* "wafers," "waffles," used to be sold by street vendors the way ice cream is sold today; thus they belong to the mimesis of the street scene, especially on public occasions. They are not to be confused with *oubli,* "vanished memory," "oblivion."[11] Yet the two are quasi-homonyms and full homophones. The reader cannot help feeling that the poem is pretending to talk about waffles but is really talking about oblivion; and conversely, he feels that when the poem speaks of public sorrow, it is really speaking about the empty show of such a ceremonial: official mourning is hardly more than an excuse for public amusement. Now we cannot in conscience maintain that there is much similarity between wafers and oblivion, or that waffles symbolize oblivion. Nor do waffles mean oblivion metaphorically or by analogy. What is happening here is the over-determination of the word *oubli(e)*, doubly appropriate: it is generated by an associative chain of street-scene words, but also by a chain of mourning and death words. Or else, in street-scene code, *oublies* is the word that looks borrowed from the oblivion code, from the "other text." This is not really a pun, for the context does not point to the similarity between *oublies* and *oubli,* and the spelling should efface the impression. But the potential coincidence creates a dual appropriateness: Chateaubriand is speaking of waffles, but in a language that has the sound of death; he is speaking of grandeur, but in a language that has the sound of trifles.

The *vendeuses de plaisirs* offers a slightly different example. The italics make it clear that the word cannot mean "pleasure" but is the colloquial term for "refreshments"; again, this is part of the realism system of the whole passage. But were there no italics, the phrase would be a euphemistic periphrasis for "street prostitutes": they too sell oblivion. I cannot help thinking it was no chance distribution of sex among the street vendors that landed the women in this spot. At the graphemic level, the italics themselves are also a dual sign, because as a linguistic sign they indicate a special meaning, here a technical, limited acceptation of *plaisirs*.[12] But as an idiolectic sign they underscore the equivocation, the way an apologetic intonation at the same time tries to excuse a "bad" pun and calls attention to it.

The above examples demonstrate that the wordplay functions despite the syntactical or lexical restrictions that should ban equivocation. It still occurs; we must therefore treat the phenomenon as a case of ungrammaticality, with its attendant semiotic function.

It remains to be explained why an ungrammatical interpretation is not only possible but in fact so tempting as to be unavoidable, and why it is complementary to, rather than exclusive of, the grammatical interpretation. The reason is that the verbal sequence progresses simultaneously as mimesis and as semiosis. At the mimesis level, meanings of words depend entirely upon syntax and position; they add bits of information to bits of information, and their sole common reference is at most a descriptive system that serves to distribute compatible representations along the sentence. At the semiotic level, contrariwise, the words repeat the same information, usually a seme, or the invariant of a thematic structure (such as *oblivion* in any theme of glory, pomp, grandeur, etc.): all harp upon the same information. The mimetic "text" is syntagmatic, the semiotic one is paradigmatic.

Such is the cumulative power of the paradigm that a word representing it in exemplary fashion, that is, with especial aptness, will carry the significance forward, and if its context-bound, syntagmatic meaning is incompatible with the context-free, paradigmatic significance, the latter will nonetheless shine through the screen. All that is needed for the word's dual allegiance to compel the reader's attention is ungrammaticality.

In the case of homophony, the word is ungrammatical in that it derives two mutually exclusive meanings from, one, its grammatical function, and, two, its shape.[13] The meaning of *oublies* at the mimetic level is irrelevant to its morphophonemic features: its sound and shape do not link it to the other words of the depiction or to their meaning as pieces of a descriptive puzzle that makes sense only because they are grouped together here and now. On the contrary, the meaning of *oublies* at the semiotic level is wholly dependent upon its morphophonemic features, since they happen to coincide with those of the thematic matrix's kernel word.

Since it involves mere homophony, the dual sign in the above example is only an approximation. Perfect coincidings require homonymy. Then the resulting syntagmatic ungrammaticality is correspondingly more serious, the interference more visible, the coincidence of catachresis and appropriateness more effective. Take the following passage from Hugo, where the poet presents his views on metempsychosis. In his universe human sinners and culprits pass on after death to a new life of retribution, in the form of animals or even seemingly inanimate objects. The guiltier they were as human beings, the more grossly material, the less spiritual their new incarnation. Accordingly, every object is the prison of a sinner's soul, and he is tortured there:

> Quel frisson dans l'herbe! Oh! quels yeux fixes ouverts
> Dans les cailloux profonds, oubliettes des âmes!
> C'est une âme que l'eau scie en ses froides lames.[14]

What a shudder in the grass! What fixed staring eyes in the deep stones, oubliettes of souls! And it is a soul too the water is sawing to pieces in its cold waves.

In the conversive sequence that makes Nature a jail, every natural object functions as both a metonym of *Nature* and a metaphor of *punishment*. Water as element metonymically generates *lames*, "waves."

But *lames* in a context of hardware, tools, weapons, also means "blades" and could in this relation be derived from *scier*, "saw." Thus we have the kind of amphibology that in nonliterary discourse prompts the prudent writer to get rid of *lames* to avoid awkwardness and confusion. The adjective reinforces the duality, since *froid* goes just as well with the icy waters of unfriendly seas as with the slashing blade (*froid de la lame*, "cold steel"—a cliché in oldtime murder stories, in Gothic novels, in the duelling episodes of cloak-and-dagger romances à la Dumas père).

Yet we cannot speak of ambiguity in the ordinary sense, inasmuch as the syntax at least (*en ses froides lames*, "in its cold waves") is perfectly clear: the incongruity is with the "blade" meaning (which would demand *avec* or *de ses froides lames*). Nor is it polysemy we have here, since the two meanings are not perceived at exactly the same time, within the same eye-sweep of the text. Because the *punishment* induced by the thematic structure interferes with the description of the sea, syntax forces the reader to choose the descriptive meaning alone (the only one acceptable after *en* [amidst the waves]). But the paradigm has valorized words like *scier* too thoroughly for their associations not to be instantly perceived, and the reader cannot fail to make the connection from *lames* back to *scier*.[15] Here is an instance of split-second, semiconscious retroactive reading: a link that might have been is glimpsed and promptly dismissed, because of the syntactic block. Yet the competing postulations of paradigm and syntax never stop working, and each new reading proposes them again, for the simple reason that they are inescapable because plainly encoded, and unresolvable because the text cannot be corrected or explained away. The sign's dual reference, rather like a system of checks and balances, or a semantic pendulum, sees to it that reading can never yield a stable, secure grasp of the whole meaning, can never, above all, yield visualization: at best we can say that *lames* is the right word for "waves," but that it is appropriate partly because it gives the sea some of the verb's sadistic implications. The verb itself, however, is unacceptable with "water" as its subject, unless we try to imagine some sort of medieval Turkish executioner as a farfetched personification of the sea.[16] But *lames* backs up *scier*, the two words presupposing each other: the reinforcement does not make the scene any more visualizable or the images any more logical, but it does present the fleeting apparition of an idiolectic norm, quoted, as it were, even though it cannot really apply—a seeming guarantee of grammaticality by reference to lexical collocations that in language, at any rate, would be acceptable, if in context they are not.

Retroactive reading thus appears to be the method for decoding dual signs: first, because the sign refers to a paradigm, and a paradigm can be recognized only after it has been sufficiently developed in space so that certain constants can be perceived; second, because any stumbling-block sends the reader scurrying back for a clue, back being the only place to go; third, because the correction made backwards via the proximate homologue creates the ghost or parallel text wherein the dual sign's second (or syntactically unacceptable) semantic allegiance can be vindicated.

The ghost text need not be a ghost temporarily conjured up by a reader struggling to fit together the pieces of a puzzle. It can be fleshed out with actual derivations, created ad hoc: these are manifest at the surface of the text for the most dim-sighted of readers to see. Or the ghost text may embody itself in potential but ready-made stereotypes within the range of any reader's linguistic competence: these need not be fully actualized in the poem, as they are familiar enough for the reader to reconstitute them easily and fill in the gaps from the most fragmentary clues. In the first instance, we have text-generating signs; in the second, hypogram-generating signs.

Text-Generating Dual Signs

In order that the dual sign may be perceived as an equivocal complex, a derivation must take place that actualizes as description or narration the two competing meanings, one after the other, or alternately. Without such expansion and explication the sign's duality could not be a compelling force in reading. Therefore, in order to exist, the sign produces a text. This production may take place before or after the dual sign.

It precedes and motivates the sign in the following Michel Leiris piece. The sentence begins with a metaphorical representation of a rainy day, superimposing a literal statement of rain upon a jail or prison code serving as the metaphor's vehicle:

> J'aimerais dire que la pluie
> nous ligotait de ses cordes,
> qu'elle dressait autour de nous
> les murs de son château d'eau.[17]

I wish I could say the rain is tying us up with its ropes, raising around us the walls of its water-tower.

Château d'eau is the technical term for a water tank at the top of a building, and the *d'eau* modifier effectively blocks out any castle connotations that *château* alone would have, and any prison associations: the Gothic fortress, dungeons, enemy walls, etc.

Clearly it is the context that reactivates these connotations, and a dungeon or prison of water might strike us as a capital image for the low oppressive sky and the damp closeness of a rainy day. The relative boldness of the image, the difficulty we have reconciling a solid, massive piece of architecture and the airy liquidity of the rain it stands for, need not be compensated for by its truth, because what determines it is Baudelaire's fourth "Spleen," the intertext. This is a variant of the world-as-prison theme, illustrating and developing the despair or melancholy of the title. The first stanza compares the sky with a heavy lid, the second compares the earth with a Gothic dungeon; then come the lines, "Quand la pluie étalant ses immenses traînées/D'une vaste prison imite les barreaux" [when the rain, laying its boundless trails, mimics the bars of a vast prison]. These lines constitute the hypogram for Leiris's first image and the model for his second. But the fact remains that he did not write *prison (cellule, cachot) d'eau:* he took advantage of a "happy coincidence," a word that as a pun fits the metaphor of rain as a jailer—as a pun because this particular *château* is not a castle and its *eau* is not rainwater (but rather its opposite, or substitute, the reservoir against dry spells).

In a case like this the equivocal word carries meaning in context only if its meaning in language is destroyed. Only then can it mean in accordance with the other, special language it refers to—the language of the other text, the text this word represents and in a way summarizes. The pun may be seen as a metaphor (or rationalized as such, since puns are not respectable), but this metaphor does not rest upon seme-sharing: it rests upon the deceptive transfer from homophony to synonymy.

In so doing, however, it still receives from language, which it has not violated morphologically and to which it still seems to belong, the guarantee, the stamp of authenticity as an existing word, backed by the highest authority, common usage. It represents and refers to two texts, the intertext and the pseudodescriptive system it would be the kernel of if its intertextual sense were generalized and became the common, cognitive meaning.

So that the peculiar significance of the equivocal word is that at the height of verbal outrageousness it remains true to classical poetic principle, it remains *le mot juste mis en sa place*. It is capable of being at once a catachresis and the right word.

To say that *château d'eau* has received a new meaning would be a tautology. Let us say rather that a new meaning, the image of a castle of rain, is the necessary outcome of the derivation—especially since it was predetermined by Baudelaire—and that this meaning finds its niche in a sign already established and meaningful, thus creating an identical twin, an idiolectic homonym of that word.[18]

The derivation triggered by the need to make the sign's duality perceptible may follow the sign, in which case perception is pronouncedly retroactive:

> Mais enfin où sommes-nous
> Je lustre de deux doigts le poil de la vitre
> Un griffon de transparence passe la tête
> Au travers je ne reconnais pas le quartier[19]

But listen, where are we anyway? With two fingers I polish the fur of the windowpane. A griffin of transparence shows his head. Through that I cannot recognize the neighborhood

This quatrain of André Breton's sets the speaker in a taxicab with a driver who has lost his way—a commonplace little contretemps of everyday life. Which only serves to make greater, by contrast, the shock of the nonsense *poil de la vitre* and *griffon de transparence*. These images radically contradict our concept of things. It would be difficult to think of anything more foreign to the softness of normal hair or fur than the hardness, the cold transparency of glass. As for the *griffon de transparence*, the polarization between the two nouns is further increased by their resemblance to a parody of a familiar stereotyped hyperbole on the model of *monstre d'ingratitude* and *dragon de vertu*.[20] Yet these disconcerting groups derive, of absolute necessity, from two normal but mutually exclusive meanings of *lustrer*: it is just as natural and literal to say *lustrer une fourrure*, "make an animal's fur shine," "stroke his fur till it shines," as it is to say *lustrer une glace*, "polish a mirror." Out of the second meaning a sequence unrolls from *vitre* to *transparence* to *voir au travers;* out of the first meaning comes the griffin.[21] The first sequence is pure logic and fits our experience of reality: wipe the steam off and you can see through the window. As for the second derivation, *poil* might have generated countless real animals sooner than one supernatural; the choice of griffin heightens the strangeness, hence the conspicuousness of the two derivations, the more so because the griffin obviously serves as a verbal detour through phantasm just to reach "see through the pane." Explaining the bizarreness of the detour, its artifice, is irrelevant here, inasmuch as factors foreign to the text itself are involved—Breton's private fantasies.[22] What is relevant is the bizarreness itself, the exaggerated lengths a text will go to under favorable circumstances (where, for instance, in accordance with surrealist tenets, the need for verisimilitude or, more generally, preoccupation with mimesis, becomes secondary) to bring to light the image-creating potential of a word, that is, its latent equivocacy. And again, this latency is uncovered retroactively: the wild ungrammaticality of the windowpane's hair triggers a new consideration of the innocuous, utilitarian verb. Discovering the source of the image in no way diminishes or extenuates the boldness of the derivation, but it removes all stigma of gratuitousness, replacing it with a consciousness of verbal "logic" and demonstrating the creative power of words when left to themselves—another surrealist tenet.

Hypogram-Generating Dual Signs

Here the "ghost text," the word's other reference, is not present in the poem but must be deduced by the reader. Finding himself unable to understand the word as given in the text, and as determined by grammatical function, the reader is forced to look elsewhere for a second, albeit simultaneous interpretation, and to read a pun into the word—even though in common usage the word will not permit equivocation. The second interpretation is supplied by an intertext or by clichés and stereotypes.

The intertext is what puts the pun into a word otherwise quite innocent of double entendre:

> Quel artificier
> Tu meurs! Fauve César[23]

What a pyrotechnist dies with you, wild-beast Caesar

This is the first distich of Francis Ponge's eight-line verse on Nero. Two factors govern the reader's decoding: the anomaly of an exclamation in the second person with a verb like *mourir* instead of *être* (as in "What an artist you are!"); and the phrase in which *fauve*, a familiar ambiguity, may mean either "reddish-haired" or "wild beast," either one applicable to the Roman Emperor. These two factors together make it impossible for the reader not to recognize the text as a distortion of or take-off on a famous quotation (used in French schools to exemplify the pithy Latin style): *Qualis artifex pereo* [What an artist dies with me]—the last words of Nero, who fancied himself a great actor. A pun is thus created, since the context prevents us from understanding *artificier* in its normal and narrow sense of "military explosives expert" or, by extension, "pyrotechnist." The unlikelihood of such a word in Ponge's context thus signals still another incompatibility, this one intertextual: the designation of an antique tyrant as a menial attendant at public celebrations. When we call to mind the Latin word *artifex, artificier* becomes even funnier, for in the context of two languages straddled, it seems to be aping the "accidental" type of pun, which has its place in the traditional joke hierarchy: the schoolboy's mistake when he translates a word with one resembling it instead of one with the same meaning. Ungrammaticality is therefore maximal, since the text has to extrapolate beyond a single language in order to find a homonym. Aptness too is maximal, however, for when we bounce back to the Roman intertext we find that *artificier* in its ordinary French sense is freshly adequate for a Caesar who made his capital into a bonfire.

The preceding example might almost be classed as a new coinage: once the reader notices that the text it stands for is somewhere else, that he has on his hands a borrowing from another language, the impact of the word he thought familiar and now recognizes as a label on quite different merchandise is much like the effect of a neologism.[24] The border is crossed and the intensity of the ungrammaticality-signal increased when the word's double textual reference affects morphology, when the dual sign integrates its duality into one lexical unit, that is, blends into one portmanteau word two lexemes, each of which is the apex of an associative paradigm.[25]

Such a blend is *grouillis,* which no reader can fail to perceive as a new coinage, so clearly is it defined by opposition to *grouillement,* a term for crawling over a surface, for clothes or a body alive with vermin, for crowds swarming through the streets, with other unpleasing or degrading associations. The change of suffix from *-ment* to *-is* may superficially appear merely to rejuvenate the common word and make it more graphically repulsive.[26] These morphological features, though meaningful in isolation, signal a dual sign function in a prose poem of Paul Claudel's. They make the lexical blend a sort of concentrate of the affective connotations and emotional overload that are the significance of that text. The poem plays variations on one of the art-imitating-Nature themes: the romantic theme of the Gothic church born of the forest, or metaphorically a stone forest—trees are now pillars, secret recesses in the underbrush are inner sancta, leaves rustling in the wind are aeolian harps, etc. Most poets have discerned an edifying parallel between the increasing complexity of church architecture and esthetic sophistication. Claudel, for whom the Renaissance and Reformation are the ultimate evil, prefers to convert complexity into miscegenation, and, by selecting only the negative semes of that sememe, to make it an image of deepening corruption and impurity.[27] It all starts with plants and demons sculptured on the capitals of Romanesque pillars:

> . . . souches trapues de l'obscure forêt romane . . . se couvrant . . . de la pâle flore des caves, une moisissure de monstres et d'embryons

> squat stumps of the dark Roman forest gradually overgrown with the pallid flora of basements, a dank rot of monsters and embryos

The evil evolution culminates in the exuberant foliage and grotesque carved animals of flamboyant Gothicism:

> contrainte à contenir le Dieu saint, la pierre païenne dégage extérieurement une vermine grimaçante et démoniaque, et les gargouilles vomissantes, et la grande herbe des fleurs vaines. A mesure que l'heure du Scandale approche, le *grouillis* mécréant se fait plus vivace et plus dense et l'on dirait que la sève de l'église s'épuise dans ce gui parasite.

> constrained to encompass the holy God, the pagan stone breaks out in grimacing, demoniac vermin, and vomiting gargoyles, and the big weeds of vainglorious flowers. The closer the time of Scandal comes, the hardier and thicker grows the miscreant *grouillis*. It is as if the sap of the church were being leeched away by this parasitic mistletoe.

All through the poem two paradigms are being developed; in the above passage their paths cross, and *grouillis* is the nodal point where they join forces. One is a negative animal sequence: the vermin that are monsters, demons, and gargoyles. The other is a negative vegetable sequence, a paradigm of parasitic vegetal growth. The two have the same symbolism. Now whereas the apex of a vermin paradigm is *grouillement,* the height of disorderly parasitic proliferation is *fouillis,* which may be used for any jumble or farrago, but primarily and literally means the tangled vegetal mass of forest undergrowth. In short, *grouillis* is actually a blend of *grouillement* and *fouillis.* The word functions like *oublies,* except that instead of two homophones coinciding in one lexeme, we have a more visible merging, and the reader can react to the signal without a syntactic ungrammaticality, which was needed in the case of *lames*. The telling ungrammaticality is built into the dual sign. Therefore the blend not only unites two sets of connotations; it is the icon of their interchangeability, the interpretant of a new semiotic convention in which vegetable and animal representations are synonymous instead of being fundamentally separate, as they are in language. Thus combined, and both at the extremes of their sequences (an extremity expressed by the portmanteau word's being beyond the pale of the sociolect), they make the dual sign a hyperbole and the lexical equivalent of the two simultaneous or synchronized expansion processes that generated that sign. In a way, the word, whose very morphology is a statement of impurity, and whose components are negative, seems to be a return to the poem's matrix ("mixing is evil"); the vast, convoluted descriptions derived from that matrix have run their course.

The extreme ungrammaticality signalling the dual sign need not be morphological. Instead of altering the lexeme, ungrammaticality may affect the phrases or sentences derived from the equivocal word, in a fashion halfway between the *artificier* and *grouillis* examples. In the former case the context warns the reader that the word is double and has to be broken down into a text-bound *artificier* and an intertext-bound *artificier*. In the *grouillis* case, the word itself warns of its own duplicity. With the "intermediate" type of ungrammaticality, the dual sign is repeated, but each time with different modifiers, which make it clear that the sign initially referred to a different hypogram. Meanwhile the function of the dual sign in context remains the same: repetition does not modify the word itself, but the various modifiers enable it to point alternately to successive referents.

So with *roseau*, "reed," in this verse of Apollinaire's:

> Et vous cils roseaux qui vous mirez dans l'eau profonde et claire
>   de ses regards
> Roseaux discrets plus éloquents que les penseurs humains ô
>   cils penseurs penchés au-dessus des abîmes[28]

and you eyelashes reeds looking at yourselves in the deep clear water of her gaze Reeds discreet more eloquent than human thinkers Oh eyelashes thinkers leaning over chasms

Roseau appears twice, each time in a context that makes it conspicuous: first a metaphor, then an implication of humanization or personification. The metaphor is a traditional image for feminine eyelashes, themselves metonymic of woman as love-object. The second *roseau* is modified by two adjectives (*discrets, penseurs*) that make the word stand for two different hypograms, one mythological, the other a literary allusion with the reed playing the central role. Whereas the adjectives seem farfetched at the text's surface, they are actually translating the image from love poetry into two specialized codes; these in turn reinforce the image with two *roseau* traditions, and most important, confer upon that image a new and more solid propriety.

The first determinant of this passage is the genre selected, the *blason,* for the ethos of the genre dictates the matrix. The matrix is a statement as plain as the beginning of the *Song of Solomon,* something like *Thou art beautiful;* the model actualizes it metonymically as *Thy body is beautiful.* The model then expands in a descriptive sequence where the eyelashes in turn exemplify that beauty. The indirectness of literary discourse eliminates explicit mention of beauty, which is replaced by a comparison to reeds—the word is a positive marker[29]—and by a syntagm denoting superiority (*more . . . than*). The meaning of this syntagm survives the collapse of any attempt to interpret the words *penseurs humains* "normally," that is, referentially, and it survives any doubt the reader may harbor as to the nature of "eyelash eloquence."

I insist upon speaking of the *word* for "reed" rather than of the thing itself, and upon representing a semantic relationship by a syntagm rather than by a full-fledged word. For the choice of "reeds" has been determined not by actual, if distant, similarity to eyelashes (distant because the only natural property they share is *flexibility*), but by two facts that concern lexical distribution only. One is that the word *roseau,* "reed," is metonymically linked with a metaphor (a commonplace in love poetry) that makes the beloved eye a lake or the mirror of a tranquil water surface.[30] This last, central metaphor provides the familiar framework for an analogy (eyelashes are to the eye what reeds are to a lake), which is the stronger because *cils* and *roseaux* can be described in similar terms as to their eye-lake relationship: they both encircle the water, the water reflects them both. Thus we can say that the descriptive system of the word *eye* is one of the hypograms involved in this particular conversion.[31]

The difficult second verse is not so obscure that we cannot read something like *eyelashes silent yet more eloquent than words.* As I said before, the bare grammar of superiority suffices to make this statement work as one more positive marker, as a sustained, increasingly hyperbolic or disproportionate extolment of this minor ocular adornment. Its lexical content, on the other hand, accords nicely with love poetry themes. A silent signal, especially in tense confrontation, is commonly called a gesture, a glance, a wink more expressive than many words. This holds for amorous encounters, when the most discreet flutter of an eyelid can send a momentous message, promise erotic complicity, consent, surrender.

The transformation of "silent" into *discrets* derives from a new model, *roseaux indiscrets,* or as Apollinaire himself puts it in "Mai" (*Alcools*), *roseaux jaseurs,* "tattletale reeds"—a stereotype dating back to the ancient story of King Midas, who had a donkey's ears and kept them hidden under his crown. A confidant of his could not refrain from telling his secret to the reeds. Swaying in the wind, rustling noisily, the reeds betrayed the secret. Thanks to the positive matrix, *roseau indiscret* is converted into its reverse.

As for the disconcerting *penseurs humains,*[32] it has been generated by an oft-quoted sentence of Pascal's.[33] This hypogram reads: "l'homme n'est qu'un roseau, mais c'est un roseau pensant" [man is a reed, but a reed that thinks]. Reeds endowed with thought are a fitting image for eyelashes communicating thoughts. The stereotype says that a subtle, unobtrusive movement of one tiny body part better expresses thought than the grosser activity of human speech. This stereotype can now be actualized as *thinking reed more eloquent than thinking man.*

Obviously, *penseurs humains* remains a troubling phrase. At first we do not understand it. When we do, it may still seem gratuitous. But although they seem gratuitous, the two verses in fact rejuvenate the reed/eyelash erotic symbolism, inasmuch as *roseau,* besides being a metaphor, serves as interpretant translating the *cil* mimesis into two codes equally appropriate to the discourse of love.

Titles as Dual Signs

Titles too can function as dual signs. They then introduce the poem they crown, and at the same time refer to a text outside of it. Since the interpretant stands for a text, it confirms that the unit of significance in poetry is always textual. By referring to another text the dual title points to where the significance of its own poem is explained. The other text enlightens the reader through comparison: a structural similarity is perceived between the poem and its textual referent despite their possible differences at the descriptive and narrative levels.

It may be, for instance, that the textual referent has the same matrix as the poem at hand. Only structures are involved, and contact between the two is made through one sign alone. The two texts are related to that sign in the same way, the relationship being based upon analogy rather than upon similarity. The relationship between poem and textual referent is not one of intertextuality, for there is no conflict between the two.

Apart from this general function with respect to the poem as a whole, the dual title may have its own particular function in the poem's semiotic grid. The title of the first sonnet in Nerval's *Les Chimères,* "El Desdichado," is such a sign. As a Spanish word it cancels (or makes more difficult) the title's natural role, since a title is supposed to inform the reader and facilitate access to the text by stating its subject, its genre, or its code.[34] Thus the title here functions as a sign hinting at a hidden meaning, or a meaning reserved for initiates, or a second meaning in addition to the surface one—to accord with the mystic symbolism that dominates *Les Chimères.* "El Desdichado" alludes to an episode in Walter Scott's *Ivanhoe* involving an unknown knight's shield that bears the motto translated by Scott as "The Disinherited."[35] The knight later turns out to be Richard the Lionhearted; for Nerval's readers, all familiar with Scott, the sonnet's second line is alluding to and expanding on this story: "Le prince d'Aquitaine à la tour abolie" now becomes a periphrasis designating the unhappy prince by naming his Plantagenet domain and by alluding to its spoliation. But the "El Desdichado" title's chief function is as the interpretant that creates the sonnet's significance. We know that the poem is being spoken by a new Orpheus. Orpheus, hence a poet, and a poet who lost his Eurydice and found her again, only to lose her again. But a *new* Orpheus, therefore one who succeeds in his quest ("J'ai deux fois vainqueur traversé l'Achéron" [Twice victorious I crossed the Acheron]), one whose love is born again. It is the title's role to explain this transformation; the first two lines

> Je suis le ténébreux, le veuf, l'inconsolé,
> Le prince d'Aquitaine à la tour abolie

I am the gloomy one, the widower, the unconsoled, the Prince of Aquitaine, he of the tower destroyed

are derived by expansion from the title's *meaning* and are accordingly a statement of sorrow and an introduction to the next two lines, which identify the speaker as *another* Orpheus. But the title refers to Scott, it stands for the story of the knight at the Ashby tournament: this is our cue that the speaker is not just another Orpheus but one who will succeed where the other failed, for the disinherited knight is destined to recover his inheritance and regain his kingdom. The speaker in the sonnet is only a temporary widower, he is an *Orpheus redux* because his Eurydice is to him what his dominion is to Scott's knight— a loss to be recouped.

The interpretant, however, may well be limited to its function as such, with no power to trigger a derivation of its own within the poem. It may serve solely as a converter of the poem as a whole. The prose poem below, from Rimbaud's *Illuminations,* is generated by expansion from its title, but the conversion attendant upon the expansion process is regulated by the Shakespeare text *Bottom* stands for:

BOTTOM

La réalité étant trop épineuse pour mon grand caractère,—je me trouvai néanmoins chez Madame, en gros oiseau gris-bleu s'essorant vers les moulures du plafond et traînant l'aile dans les ombres de la soirée.

Je fus, au pied du baldaquin supportant ses bijoux adorés et ses chefs-d'œuvre physiques, un gros ours aux gencives violettes et au poil chenu de chagrin, les yeux aux cristaux et aux argents des consoles.

Tout se fit ombre et aquarium ardent. Au matin,—aube de juin batailleuse,—je courus aux champs, âne, claironnant et brandissant mon grief, jusqu'à ce que les Sabines de la banlieue vinrent se jeter à mon poitrail.

Reality being too thorny for my exalted personality—I nevertheless found myself at my lady's house, in the form of a grey-blue bird soaring toward the moulding of the ceiling and dragging my wing in the shadows of the evening. At the foot of the fourposter that supported her beloved jewels and her physical masterpieces, I turned into a big bear with purplish gums and fur grizzled with sorrow, my eyes on the crystal and silverware upon the console tables. Everything turned into shadow and flaming aquarium. In the morning—bellicose June dawn—I ran toward the fields, an ass, trumpeting and brandishing by grievance, until the Sabine women came and threw themselves upon my breast.

It is only the *Midsummer Night's Dream* frame of reference that enables us to make some sense of the narrator's metamorphoses. We might make a guess, but we could never link them up to the title. I say nothing of the fact that the last metamorphosis enjoys a privileged relationship to the title, for this jackass and Shakespeare's are not the same. But the title, or rather what it resumes of Shakespeare and his play, for the French reader's imagination, is what confers their significance upon the three animals, including the two non-Shakespearean ones. This significance does not indeed lie in a fabulous tale of man transformed into beast, but in the way the story serves, on the Shakespeare model, as a conventional code in whose ad hoc dictionary any word describing animality substituted for humanness will mean the folly of love. This significance, again, cannot be reduced to an imitation of the comedy plot: Bottom's asininity in the play is born of Oberon's malice, and Titania's infatuation—Beauty enamored of the Beast—symbolizes passion's blindness; the object is unworthy, but the sentiment is noble. Whereas in the poem love makes a man a jackass. I use the term as a general metaphor, not just a reference to the character's third avatar, for no matter what the animal, animality connotes the ridiculous throughout. As we said before, the poem is produced by expansion, since the hypogram—a story of metamorphosis—is repeated in three variants. As for the conversion, it is negative. *Midsummer Night's Dream* is not the hypogram but a different conversion from the same hypogram. The English text is present only as a blurry backdrop for what the name *Bottom* tells French readers: this name filters out for them the components of the play not pertinent to the Rimbaud poem. It tells them that the metamorphosed character is a character in a love story and that he plays a ludicrous part. Not just because he has been given long ears, which would affect only a third of the poem (and besides, one can be turned into a jackass without losing dignity—witness Apuleius's golden ass), but because negativity here is not a matter of situation but of langage, because in the French sociolect *Bottom* is a notorious word.

During the nineteenth century the French neglected foreign languages, but *Bottom* was one English word they knew well. Probably because a commonplace French idea about Shakespeare—regarded as the typical nonclassical writer—was that his comedies consist of light, enchanting fancy, sometimes almost spiritual, mixed with gross earthy farce. The contrast between the brute and the lady captivated by him made Bottom, in the eyes of French critics, *the* archetype of this intermixture. So exemplary was the tale that everyone had come to know the meaning of the name as a common noun. The unmentionable posterior was under such a powerful taboo that in the translation of Shakespeare published in France, while the names of the other characters are all translated—*Quince* becomes *Lecoing, Snout* becomes *Muffle,* etc.—*Bottom* is censored and remains *Bottom.* The one exception is quite as revealing as the rule: a certain Benjamin Laroche does propose a French equivalent for *Bottom,* but this French Victorian too avoids the derrière and lights upon *Lanavette,* "Shuttle"—appropriate, no doubt, for Shakespeare's weaver. Hugo is not so easily abashed, but he still has to find excuses for Shakespeare in classical tradition:

> Quand Horace étale Priape
> Shakespeare peut risquer Bottom[36]

if Horace can expose Priapus, Shakespeare can take a chance on Bottom

The excuse tends to increase guilt by association. All of which testifies to the power the name acquired through its repression. The only possible release is laughter and ridicule, so that the conversion consistently selects the traits, in the three animal pictures, that make the bird, the bear, and the jackass three caricatures of Man rather than mere metamorphoses. The matrix is not *l'amour animalisé* but *l'amour abêtit.*

In consequence, the three representations—the soaring bird, depicting either the naïvely idealistic lover, or love as sublimation; the groveling bear, love's enslavement; the galumphing jackass, sex rampant—these commonplaces of amorous pursuit are travestied by a conversion, of the marker-permutation type, down to the smallest descriptive detail.[37]

The soaring bird—the winged creature whose heavenward flight is cut short by a plebeian ceiling, who negates symbols of spirituality and elevation like the eagle or the phoenix sunward bound, or the Christian dove—this bird is a familiar negativization:[38] compare defeated Hope in Baudelaire's fourth "Spleen," dove into bat, sky into dungeon vault; in Nerval's *La Pandora,* the temptress in a dream, who mockingly disappears not into the *ciel* but into the *ciel-de-lit,* the bed canopy, with a pun on *ciel* and *ciel-de-lit* to aggravate the debunking.[39] As for the fowl itself, in the paradigm of literary birds, sleekness, lightness, and slightness are meliorative features. *This* bird is therefore fat (fatness usually being associated with poultry). *Gris-bleu* negativizes *bleu,* a direct symbol of purity and a metonym of the heaven to which pure birds belong. *Gris-bleu,* however, in its specific emphasis upon a color nuance, should not be misunderstood as mimetic, as a realistic detail. Its semiotic function relies on intertextuality: *gris-bleu* can only be the reverse of *l'oiseau bleu,* the title and principal character of Madame d'Aulnoy's tale wherein a faithful lover is changed into a blue bird so that he can visit his mistress. And why *gris* and not *noir?* Would not a raven have done a better job of annulling the bluebird? Perhaps in isolation, but under intertextual restrictions Madame d'Aulnoy's bird is *bleu couleur de temps* [blue as fair weather], and in French overcast skies cannot be *temps noir:* the only grammatical group is *temps gris.*

The groveling bear: he is a literal variation in alcove code on the proverbial lover-doormat at his lady's feet—the bearskin as bedside rug. This is how it all ends for Heinrich Heine's bear, Atta Troll, on the floor in his beloved's boudoir, poor beast.[40] I could go on with the furniture that metonymically and comically replaces the lady as an object of the bear's adoring contemplation. As for the animal himself, his representation as a positive sign, as the ideal bear, would presuppose white fur. This whiteness is replaced by its negative equivalent: *chenu,* "grizzled," "hoary." He has *gencives violettes,* "purplish gums," not, as one critic maintains, because "the most lyric of all colors is violet . . . and also the color of mourning,"[41] but because *violet* is a negative counterpart of *red* when you describe flesh, while *gum* and its implied toothlessness is the counterpart of *fangs.*

The galumphing jackass: he comes last because the derivation from the title swings back full circle when the final variation rewrites the title *da capo* periphrastically. As with his predecessors, the title's almost farcical connotations color the picture: *brandissant mon grief* is a euphemism but a ludicrous one, as ludicrous as the parodic *Sabines* for the heroines who block his rampaging with their bodies.[42] The special negativizing slant here, affecting euphemism instead of speaking candidly, is further evidence of the interpretant's influence on the poem: the derivation from the title now takes the form of a sexual innuendo, one more constant among the connotations that the name *Bottom* receives from the text it stands for. Witness this remark of Hugo's apropos of the paradox of the lily's maidenly connotations and her erect pistil: "*virgam asini. Une vague esquisse de Titania et de Bottom semble apparaître ici*" [the ass's prick: like a vague sketch of Titania with Bottom].[43]

Thus the words of the text derivable from the title are dual signs: immediate signs pointing to their own meaning, mediate signs pointing to a meaning observable only in Shakespeare, or rather in the set of stereotypes in the French sociolect that embody the presuppositions and connotations of the word *Bottom.* If the facts were otherwise, a title like *Métamorphoses* would have done quite nicely. It so happens that Rimbaud *did* choose that name, then gave it up and replaced it with a word assuredly much less descriptive and in itself foreign to the subject. But it is a word that points to the one text where it has to be interpreted as metamorphosis, and mischievous metamorphosis springing from love.

Dual Title Referring to a Code

Now I should like to examine the case—which may perhaps look like extreme verbalism—where the dual title, instead of referring to another text as text, refers to it only as an example, or as a repository of lexicon and grammar characteristic of a *code*, of a conventional discourse. A poem of Raymond Queneau's has been chosen as illustration precisely because its verbal ways are so obvious, because the poem is so evidently a game. But it will become clear that the game is nowise gratuitous, that the verbal construct it generates differs only superficially from those of more traditional poems.

This is a piece of mock metaphysical poetry. It harps upon the tired commonplace that nothing lasts, everything in Creation is doomed to die. It harps, however, under a formal restriction: the philosophizing must be couched in the language of heraldry. The title has nothing to do with the topic; it merely states the lexical rule. This in itself makes clear that the text is an exercise in form rather than a form with a message. Such preliminary conditions or constraints are of course normal in literature; a meditation upon destiny written in heraldic language differs only in degree from such a meditation in sonnet form. On the other hand, the poem is strewn with verbal jokes: again, the familiar stuff of parody. (Especially familiar to Queneau connoisseurs: an entire volume of his consists of slang, scientific jargon, classical rhetoric and Alexandrine verse, comically interacting with one another—his *Petite Cosmogonie portative* [Pocket Cosmogony], in a genre as old as Hesiod.) But what is peculiar to our poem, what makes it a proper subject for our study, is that the three constants, metaphysical, heraldic, and jocular, are inseparable, and that their intertextual conflict gives rise to a pun, makes repetition of the equivocal word necessary, and makes this repetition the locus of the poem's significance.

HÉRALDIQUE

Le chien courant et l'hippogriffe
sont passés au noir de brou
courant le chien et l'hippogriffe
sont passés—là devant nous

ils passeront là—mèzou?
ils courent chien comme hippogriffe
vers l'abîme qu'engloutit tout
car le tout avale l'abîme
et l'hippogriffe et le toutou[44]

In the Heraldic Manner. The hound and the hippogriff are wall stained
with blacknut. Running, the hound and the hippogriff have passed by—
there, in front of us, they will pass there—but where to? They are run-
ning, hound and hippogriff alike, toward the abyss that swallows every-
thing, for the All gulps down the abyss, and the hippogriff and doggie

Of course my translation cannot equal the text: the transposition
of words in the second line simply indicates, without being able to
render the connotations of *passer au noir,* the presence of a spoonerism
in the French version. Nor can I reproduce the mispronunciation in
the original of "but where to?"; or the heraldic meanings of words
that are both normal and technical in a French blazonry context. The
whole text runs to wordplay, and its focus is a pun: the triple play
on *passer.*

Two heraldic animals have been painted over; you cannot see them
any more. They ran by here; they are here no longer. They will pass
by and be gone, like everything else in this world—it is the way of all
flesh. In each case, we have the verb *passer: passer au brou de noix,*
"stain" or "paint"; *passer,* "pass by"; and *passer,* "pass away" (espe-
cially in an ominous future, as here). So that there are, in effect, three
verbs, but in context they all have the same connotations, since a
picture painted over is a picture blotted out; two running creatures
that have passed are not here, are gone. The third *passer,* picked up
by an image of the race toward the abyss, makes it clear that what we
have here is a jesting Song of Mutability.

Three codes conflict within the text. First, the *jocular markers:* the
triple pun I have just mentioned; the metathesis of *brou de noix* into
the nonsensical *noir de brou;* the inversion of *le chien courant,*
"hound," into *courant le chien,* "running, the dog . . . ," which seems
to imitate the metathesis; the farcical transcription of a phonetic slip
(*mèzou* for *mais où*), a hypercorrect word linkage that betrays semi-
literate pretentiousness;[45] and then the opposite, the vulgar *avale,*[46]
normally reserved for a none-too-dainty food intake; and the silly
baby talk, *toutou,* gratuitously substituted for *chien,* a substitution
made the funnier by the pairing of the lowly *toutou* with the lofty
hippogriffe, and by the apparent stuttering of the cosmic *tout.*

The second code is the *discourse of heraldry;* first of all, *passer*—a common-parlance verb, but in heraldry a highly technical one: heraldic animals shown walking on an escutcheon are said to be *passant.* In the context of the title, this specialized sense is inevitably activated and must seem particularly appropriate. *Chien courant* and *hippogriffe* are naturally understood as armorial bearings, not because they really are, but because they both look to be derived from the title, having features commonly found in armorial language: *chien courant* is a technical hunting term and hence has an archaic and aristocratic flavor, quite fitting here; the mythological hippogriff seems to be one of the fantastic emblematic beasts, all the more so because morphologically it looks like a hyperbole of "griffin," which *is* heraldic; modern readers are sensitive above all to the strangeness of the emblem—to them "hippogriff" looks even more like the real thing than does the simpler word. Finally, *abîme,* the word for the symbolic void toward which all living things are destined to rush headlong and unswerving, is also the technical term for the center of a coat-of-arms.

The *significance-bearing signs* constitute the third code. These are the ones that refer explicitly to the matrix, which should be *tout passe,* or "Nought may endure but Mutability." They are again *passer,* again *tout* and *abîme:* all Creation, the Law of Life, the Fate common to all. It is through these words too that the expansion process manifests itself, through them that the generating power of the theme is felt. Each is repeated: *abîme* twice, *passer* three times, *tout* twice (and twice more in the distorting mirror of *toutou*), and there is not a sentence that is not a transform of one of them.

The distribution of these signs is nowhere random, and even phrases that look like the free play of fancy are in fact overdetermined. The first *passés* is determined by the combination of matrix, heraldic lexicon, and a stereotype borrowed from cabinetmaking—"to give a walnut stain." This means more than just covering up and ruining a coat-of-arms: in blazon code it really means "the way to go out of existence," for *passer au brou de noix* is a specific synonym of *badigeonner,* "color-wash a surface," and during the French Revolution this was the standard method of defacing or destroying the detested symbols of the fallen aristocracy.[47] The inversion of the group, which has the effect of making the expunction yet more radical (black being worse than walnut), is facilitated by the instability peculiar to any compound or phrase whose constituents either have meaning when taken separately, or are at least symmetrical and comparable (both being nouns, or adjectives, or syllables). This instability is the generative model of countless spoonerisms:[48] when Rabelais satirizes Sorbonne doctors whose main activity is tautological—they are *sorbonisant*—he stands them on their heads, hinting, perhaps, at a circularity in their logic: *niborcisant;* Breton transforms the logical *hache dans la forêt* into a surreal *forêt dans la hache;* Lautréamont turns traditional anecdotes inside out: *l'âne mange la figue* becomes *la figue mange l'âne;*[49] and Leiris rewrites the Biblical "dust to dust" by deriving *mon lit,* "my bed," from *limon,* used in the French Bible for the clay from which the Creator made Adam.[50] This formal instability, it would seem, sometimes triggers reversion as a game played merely for the sake of verbal gymnastics,[51] but in our case the inversion, duplicated as it is by that of *le chien courant/courant le chien,* is literally an icon of the basic rule of blazon code: when an escutcheon is read and the position of each figure noted, the positions must be deciphered not from the reader's standpoint but from that of the shield-bearer facing him, so that *senestre,* "left," in normal (if archaic) usage means "right" in heraldry, and *dextre,* "right," means, conversely, "left."

Even the grotesque swallowing of the abyss that gulps down everything (line 8) is overdetermined, since it is superimposed upon a Latin quotation: *abyssus abyssum invocat*[52] [abyss calls unto abyss], and is therefore just as much a verification of language by language as *courir vers l'abîme* (6–7), a cliché of doomsday talk.

It must be stressed that overdetermination continually crosses over from one code to the other. It is not just that the joke signs and the heraldic signs are interdependent—that is the minimum condition of any take-off: you need two texts to make a parody. The point is that the "metaphysical" message itself is generated by this intertextual conflict and by this conflict alone: without the literal, factual interpretation of *abîme,* there would be no play on the heraldic, symbolic meaning of the word; but without the joke there would be nowhere for the animals to hurl themselves, and they could not function like another answer to Lamartine's question:

> . . . où donc allons-nous tous?
> A toi, grand Tout! . . .
> Vaste océan de l'Etre où tout va s'engloutir![53]

Where are we all going? To Thee, immeasurable All, vast ocean of Being where all things rush to be engulfed!

The nodal point of the poem is the comic play on *passer,* but this equivocation would not be perceived without the repetition, which allows the reader to compare retroactively three successive meanings, and to discover that they add up to a statement of mutability or a meditation upon the truth that all who live are ephemeral, creatures of a day. Thus repetition cracks the joke, which is an intertextual conflict twice over, between a heraldic hypogram and its mock actualization, but also between a "serious" or sobering reflection on Man's fate and a bit of banter.[54]

This intertextuality, however, is the very agent of *textuality:* first because the repetition it evokes gives the text a chance to enumerate the components of the escutcheon (the figures, the field, the quarters they charge, the *abîme*), thereby fulfilling the promise of the title. Second, because the repetition of *passer* is the index pointing to the "philosophical" significance of the verb, for repetition of a word with pathetic or sententious potentialities activates those potentialities. This is a common and conventional device for suggesting the emotional or momentous, as in Apollinaire's nostalgic line, "Passons passons puisque tout passe."

The poem's significance lies not in its philosophy, of course, but in its formal conformity to the title. The title functions as an interpretant that, through an otherwise pointless parody, makes the armorial code an apt metaphysical expression. The poem's significance is that it discovers an appropriateness to what it says in the very words that would seem most inappropriate.

Textual Interpretant

Finally, the interpretant may be a *textual sign*. Instead of being symbolized by a word referring to the text in which the reader is to find his hermeneutic clues (for Rimbaud's prose poem, the text of Shakespeare's play, or its sociolectic "ghost"), the *interpretant is a fragment of that text actually quoted in the poem it serves to interpret.* There may be no typographic symbols to differentiate it from its context; the quotation may be incomplete and may demand that the reader make an attempt to complete it by remembering or guessing.[55] As usual, the poetic discourse coyly resists decipherment and discourages speed reading; here again we are forced to recognize that in the reading of poetry there is an initiatory period and a delay in realizing what a given text is actually about.

This *textual interpretant* guides the reader in two ways. First, it helps him focus on intertextuality, especially on how the poem exemplifies the type of intertextual conflict where two conflicting codes are present within its boundaries. Indeed, the hypogram from which the poem is derived is also quoted in the poem,[56] as is the interpretant, in fragmentary form. These fragments, physically present and visible at the surface of the poem (but perceived as foreign bodies with an independent textual preexistence elsewhere), pair up into binary oppositions with the very derivations they have triggered.

Second, the interpretant functions as the model for the hypogrammatic derivation. In Francis Ponge's prose poem "Des Cristaux naturels" (a meditation on the mineral phenomenon),[57] two incompatible sets of images vie with each other in praising natural crystals, and the epigraph is the interpretant. (Because the poem is so long, translations are provided only where needed for discussion of specific passages.)

> Oh! les pierres précieuses qui se cachaient,
> —les fleurs qui regardaient déjà.
> (Rimbaud, *Après le déluge*)

L'on découvre au LITTRÉ, ce coffre merveilleux d'expressions anciennes, que Fontenelle, prononçant l'éloge de Tournefort (le botaniste), en vint à évoquer la nature se cachant en des lieux profonds et inaccessibles (les grottes d'Antiparos) "pour y travailler, dit-il, à la végétation des pierres". Comme René-Just Haüy, le cristallographe vers la même époque, parla de "fleurs", il arrive que nos minéralogistes sans y croire retombent parfois dans ce lieu commun, par penchant sans doute vers un académisme dont notre raison d'être, s'il en existe, est évidemment de les dégoûter, comme avec eux tout le public.

Dominant donc, à la vue des cristaux naturels, ce tout le contraire d'un trouble mais fort violent qui nous saisit, et profitant d'un sang-froid en l'occurrence bien de mise, nous prierons d'abord l'idée de la fleur d'aller honnêtement se rasseoir. [. . . .]

Pourquoi donc, à la vue des cristaux, nous trouvons-nous si brusquement saisis? C'est peut-être parce qu'il s'agit là de quelque chose comme les meilleures approximations concrètes de la réalité pure, c'est-à-dire de l'idée pure: qu'on le mette dans l'ordre qu'on veut! [. . . .]

Ainsi depuis longtemps la matière minérale n'est-elle plus qu'un chaos amorphe, si jamais elle fut ordonnée. On sait d'ailleurs que l'état solide de la matière est celui où l'énergie est la plus basse. Ainsi le règne minéral ne règne-t-il qu'à la façon dont on dit que règnent indifférence ou veulerie. Il y a dans les pierres une non-résistance passive et boudeuse à l'égard du reste du monde, à quoi elles paraissent tourner le dos.

Mais voici qu'au sein du terne chaos—à la faveur de ses failles ou cavités—croissent les rares exceptions à cette règle. D'où, à leur vue, notre saisissement à coup sûr! Au lieu des sempiternels nuages, enfin le ciel pur momentanément avec des étoiles! Enfin des pierres tournées vers nous et qui ont déclos leurs paupières, des pierres qui disent OUI! Et quels signes d'intelligence, quels clins d'œil! . . .

Without the dated aspects, simply in point of structure, the poem belongs to an obsolete subgenre of descriptive poetry, perhaps unjustly out of fashion, the didactic poem. The ethos of the genre, that is, its encoded intent, is encomiastic: it praises things, it proposes that what is natural is also admirable.[58] That is why the matrix of literary mimesis within the genre is an oxymoron: *The Wonders of Nature,* or, to heighten the opposition, *Nature is Preternatural.* This generic matrix entails two complementary derivations, one offering a thing to be wondered at, the other describing the endeavors of the awed and baffled beholder (a persona of the poet)[59] to match with words the miracles wrought by Nature. The first derivation necessarily follows established descriptive patterns; the second follows new patterns, and a parallel path produces new images to rival—or even supplant—conventional praise. The twist in this poem is that the conventional imagery is rejected only to be taken up again, endowed with a different meaning, which is derived from the original one by negativization. Thus the conventional imagery functions as a hypogram of the new.

This conventional imagery, true to the genre's matrix, is based on a model of the hybrid, straddling or overstepping the frontiers of the natural kingdoms—the crystal is described as miraculously mineral and vegetal at once:[60]

L'on découvre au LITTRÉ, ce coffre merveilleux d'expressions anciennes, que Fontenelle, prononçant l'éloge de Tournefort (le botaniste), en vint à évoquer la nature se cachant en des lieux profonds et inaccessibles (les grottes d'Antiparos) "pour y travailler, dit-il, à la végétation des pierres" . . . René-Just Haüy, le cristallographe, vers la même époque, parla de "fleurs"

In Littré, that wonderful jewel chest of ancient locutions, you discover that Fontenelle, delivering the eulogy on Tournefort (the botanist), came to speak of how Nature hides away in places deep and inaccessible (the Antiparos caves) "there to work (says he) on the vegetation of stones" . . . At about the same time Haüy the crystallographer was speaking of crystals as "flowers"[61]

The poet spurns tradition and proposes instead a praise cleansed of cloying lyricism, in images drawn from the appropriate language, the scientific discourse of crystallography. He begins with the scientific differentiation between crystal—of organic, defined, predictable shape

—and the other, inorganic stones—the class of amorphous rock. But hardly has *amorphe* set the tone of technical accuracy when a pun undermines it, twice, as denotation and as connotation, since puns are equally incompatible with didactic poetry and scientific discourse. The sentence generated by *amorphe* is not derived from its mineralogical meaning, "amorphous," but from the adjective's colloquial meaning: the listless, spineless, sullen individual is in everyday French *amorphe*. The amorphous rocks are thus comically humanized, and negatively:

> On sait d'ailleurs que l'état solide de la matière est celui où l'énergie est la plus basse. Ainsi le règne minéral ne règne-t-il qu'à la façon dont on dit que règnent indifférence ou veulerie. Il y a dans les pierres une non-résistance passive et boudeuse à l'égard du reste du monde, à quoi elles paraissent tourner le dos.

> Besides, we know that solid matter is the state in which energy is at its lowest. Thus the mineral kingdom reigns only the way we say indifference or inertia reign. There is in stones a passive, sullen nonresistance to the rest of the world, on which they seem to turn their backs.

Conversely, crystals will make a positive showing, through expansion of *amorphous* vs. *non-amorphous,* carrying on the pun. Since they are the opposite of *amorphe,* they will be cheerful, lively, a mineral of good will:

> Enfin des pierres tournées vers nous et qui ont déclos leurs paupières, des pierres qui disent OUI! Et quels signes d'intelligence, quels clins d'œil!

> At last, stones turned toward us, with their eyelids opened, stones that say YES! And what signs of intelligence, what winks of complicity!

This conforms to another matrix of the miracle-of-Nature mimesis: the structural transformation of the polar opposition *animate* vs. *in-animate* into an equivalence. Thus the lowliest inanimate object conceals a secret life, which gives birth to texts like Nerval's "Vers dorés":[62]

> Chaque fleur est une âme à la Nature éclose;
> Un mystère d'amour dans le métal repose;
> . . .
> Et comme un œil naissant couvert par ses paupières,
> Un pur esprit s'accroît sous l'écorce des pierres!

> Every flower is a soul unclosed to Nature; a mystery of love lies inside of metals; and like a nascent eye still covered by its lids, a pure spirit is growing underneath the peel of the stones!

The bantering tone, however, or the obviousness of the pun, is too foreign to the mystic connotations of this structure; the text would probably jar the reader if the farfetched images did not gather just at the point where the action of the interpretant begins to be felt. The epigraph, "Oh! les pierres précieuses qui se cachaient, les fleurs qui regardaient déjà . . ." [Oh, the precious stones that were hiding, the flowers that were already looking], is culled from the prose poem that opens Rimbaud's *Illuminations;* it will be a rare reader who is hard put to recall the omitted context.[63] The epigraph's first impact on the poem is produced indirectly by that omitted context, which dictates the terms in which conventional imagery is dismissed: "nous prierons d'abord l'idée de la fleur d'aller honnêtement se rasseoir" [we shall first ask the idea of flower to be nice and go sit down]. This uncalled-for vulgarism forces the reader to read the text through Rimbaud, for the first sentence of his "Après le déluge" [After the Flood] reads not "as soon as the flood was over" but "Aussitôt que l'idée du Déluge se fut rassise" [As soon as the idea of the Flood had sat down again]. But the epigraph's function as interpretant is to guarantee the appropriateness of the new imagery, to guarantee that its precedents are authoritative and its grammar tested (here the animization of stones, for which the epigraph refers the text to Rimbaud). More precisely, the interpretant provides the poem with a set of oppositions: *stay hidden* vs. *look around, shutting out others* vs. *opening out to others, negative* vs. *positive.* These oppositions now become the means of reconciling old and new discourse of praise and of demonstrating unexpectedly that the flower is after all an appropriate image for crystal, that it fits the mineralogical definition.

In the Rimbaud epigraph, in fact, the stones are negative and therefore amorphous as in the poem, that is, not only because this is the physical nature of stones, but because they are sulky. Conversely, since Ponge's crystals look, that means they are flowers in the Rimbaud code. It may be objected that Ponge does reject the flower image; but this is a momentary repression, which generates an *implied flower* text, a periphrastic or metonymic compensation for the void opened up by *fleur* used in the wrong (traditional) way.

The repressed flower imagery pops up to the surface of the text; at a turning point in the poem the statement is made, in terms of vegetable growth, that the crystal is an exception among stones: "Mais voici qu'au sein du terne chaos—à la faveur de ses failles ou cavités—croissent les rares exceptions à cette règle." [But here they are, in the bowels of drab chaos, in the shelter of its cracks and hollows, here grow the rare exceptions to the rule]. The sentence makes the "rare exception" grow, and grow where flowers usually do. And then, what is more startling, crystals are called *des pierres qui ont déclos leurs paupières* [stones that opened their eyelids]. The floral code here is the verb alone, but the verb alone suffices, for it is a rare one in French; every French child knows it as the verb for *roses* only, from frequent recitation of Ronsard's most celebrated lines: "Mignonne, allons voir si la rose/Qui ce matin avait déclose/Sa robe de pourpre au soleil" [Dearest, let us go and see the rose that opened her crimson bodice to the sun this morning]. So much so that since the crystal is a stone indeed but a stone that behaves like a flower, the intertextual conflict is resolved or translated into a reciprocal equivalence, the text's esthetic (lexical) unity is demonstrated, and verbal appropriateness is proven again at the point of maximal departure from cognitive language.

FIVE

TEXTUAL SEMIOTICS

The purpose of this my final chapter is to scrutinize the mechanism of various reader-perception modes that seem typical of poetry. All have this in common, that the reader experiences textuality, that is, the something holding his attention, soliciting his ingenuity, exciting in him a pleasure or irritation that he feels to be an esthetic sensation. This something he recognizes as a finite, well-defined text, and the features characterizing this text he rationalizes as typical of poetry. In all cases his perception of the continuous semiosis-producing distortion of mimesis impels the reader to find the significance in the triumph of form over content.

My analysis will bear upon:

1. perception of the text as member of a class, that is, of a *genre*. I have chosen the prose poem as being a genre with no conventionally fixed form to alert the reader, and with only the play of meaning to explain the paradoxical identification of a prose sequence as a poem;

2. *humor* as text-formant and as the sign of language as game, or of poeticity as artifact;

3. *nonsense* perceived as another kind of artifact, or as the ultimate detour or catachresis;

4. *genre-induced obscurity:* obscurity, commonly thought of as one of poetry's most typical and frequent departures from ordinary language, is a text-formant, like humor, when the interpretant is a genre. In such a case words no longer mean by reference to descriptive systems. Instead, their significance is regulated by reference to a literary genre's semiotic system.

In all of these categories we will find that the semiosis-producing ungrammatical constants result from *intertextuality*,[1] the text either being built on conflicting hypograms or containing conflicting expansions.

The Semiotics of a Genre: The Prose Poem

Students of the prose poem usually succeed in analyzing as such any text offered to them, if only because author or critics have labeled it "prose poem." These students are even able to demonstrate that it works. But they find it much harder to show how it works differently from literary discourse in general. Attempting to define the universals of the prose poem, they get stuck. Contrast it with verse and of course you can tell the difference. It is not so easy when you set it up against prose, let alone poetic prose—which latter is hardly a twentieth-century concern anyway. Aragon's dismissive remark that there are no "règles qui permettent de reconnaître un morceau de prose isolé d'un poème en prose"[2] holds true only for a very special case: where the writer arbitrarily isolates such a fragment and gives it a title or calls it a poem. The text becomes a poem only because the margins set it apart and define it as an object of contemplation, regardless of its meaning; because it has been separated from its generator and from the sequences that might be derived from it. It becomes a poem for the same reason that some quotations isolated qua quotations attain independent literary status as maxims, for the same reason that an object put into a frame or set up on a pedestal becomes a ready-made.

But since readers make the literary event, and since they harbor the belief that there is such a thing as a prose poem, we should at least try to identify the poetic components that give us the feeling of "unity —its totality of effect or impression."[3] This formal unity is none other than significance itself, the perception of invariant features as the reader gradually discovers equivalences. Overdetermination at sentence or phrase level could not of itself produce a unified text: it is peculiar to all poetry, prose as well as verse, and also characterizes certain novels, like those of Claude Simon and Ricardou. The overdetermination here must be suprasegmental, since only at that level is it possible to read hermeneutically, to compare variants.

I shall attempt to take a step toward solving this difficulty by finding out what in the prose poem—defined empirically as a short, overdetermined, and clearcut unit of significance—replaces verse, or plays an equivalent role. I am not the first to think of this, but so far all efforts have aimed at discovering in the prose the rhythms and phonetic features of verse, whereas many prose poems display nothing of the kind. Yet irrespective of meter, rhyme, etc., verse offers a basic shape relatively impervious to and partly independent of content, a shape that as such is an index of difference, of artifact, perhaps of artifice. The solution, it seems to me, is to find in the prose poem a similar formal continuity. This constant must be morphological—not just semiotic like ordinary significance—if it is to indicate, as would verse, that the various components of the text are more than merely arranged in sequence, that they are also characterized by a detour, or catachresis, as verse is a detour from its prose version. If there is such a constant, it must be determined like the rest by the matrix that generates significance—a matrix on which all the text's sentences are variations. Such a matrix may be implicit or it may be partly actualized, that is, represented by a word (if fully actualized, the matrix would spell out in sentence form semes or presuppositions of that word).[4]

I propose that what characterizes the prose poem is a matrix with two functions instead of one: it generates significance, as in all poetry, and it generates a particular formal constant, such that the constant is coextensive with the text and inseparable from the significance. There are no margins or neutral areas before or after. Two sequences derive simultaneously from the matrix; their interferences differentiate the poem from the prose, as would verse: not only is the text over-determined, it is conspicuously overdetermined.

I shall distinguish three types of double derivation. With the first type, *only one of the two derivative sequences is present in the text. The other is only implied.* The explicit derivation is a conversion of the implicit one (a conversion by permutation of markers). My example is Eluard's *Toilette* (Lady Dressing, Lady at her Mirror). The matrix is represented by the title. It is a title twice over: the name of the poem and, in French, the name of an iconographic theme.

> Elle entra dans sa chambrette pour se changer, tandis que sa bouilloire chantait. Le courant d'air venant de la fenêtre claqua la porte derrière elle. Un court instant, elle polit sa nudité étrange, blanche et droite. Puis elle se glissa dans une robe de veuve.[5]

She went into her little room to change. The kettle was singing. The draft from the window slammed the door behind her. For a brief moment she stood polishing her nakedness, strange, white, erect. Then she slipped into a widow's dress.

The poem is almost bare of pronounced stylistic devices: there is a kind of alliterative sequence—*chambrette, changer, chantait*—and a metaphor, *elle polit sa nudité*. These features, however, are not related or specific to the poem's prose-poetic quality, for there is no visible link between the devices as form and the whole as meaning.

The link, the significance-bearing feature, is a derivation from the title that is exactly coextensive with the text, not just because it ends with the text, but because it cannot continue beyond it. Its constant feature is the repeated actualization of the seme "simplicity" or "unassuming intimacy": a little bedroom, a singing tea kettle, innocent surroundings, the door slamming shut in a draft, then the *robe de veuve*—in context less a widow's weeds than a black dress unadorned, the plain, almost threadbare, all-purpose attire of a woman with a limited wardrobe—in the world of words, indeed, the only pertinent world, a cliché symbol of the thrifty or impoverished female. All goes to paint a scene of gentle realism, not unlike the poetry of humble life that François Coppée's corniness brought into disrepute at the turn of the century. It is all in the language: the slamming door is a familiar literary cliché for normal living going on unseen but overheard somewhere in the house (the Flood is hardly over in Rimbaud's *Après le déluge* when a slamming door symbolically proclaims the return of the universe to the status quo ante).[6] The *bouilloire* is another such stereotype: it speaks of little household comforts.

Everything I have just listed is clearly derived from *toilette,* inasmuch as it is, among other things, a word for humble, intimate objects like *table de toilette* (a compound without the elegant connotations of *vanity table* or the hasty sprucing-up connotations of *faire sa toilette*). In fact it is more specifically derived from the diminutive implications of *toilette,* since the etymological (little *toile,* little kerchief) and now-forgotten meaning of the suffix is brought back to mind by the derivation *chambrette.* I cannot be suspected of reading too much into this, since Eluard himself changed *petite chambre* into *chambrette,* at the price of a silly pseudorhyme.[7] And finally, the derivation does impose order upon the entire poem, since *robe de veuve* is the last variant of the sequence. Indeed, it is not enough to say that the poem ends because she has finished dressing. Although putting the dress on is the final step in *se changer,* the model or initial variant issuing from the matrix, it is also its equivalent, its homologue in terms of marking, since the shabby clothing is at the same level, in the verbal paradigm, as *se changer,* the lowly or utilitarian synonym of *s'habiller,* which can either be the neutral "get dressed" or suggest sophisticated preening for a formal evening.

Now all this might still be just a bit of nondescript realism, except for the fact that as a title *toilette* generates two parallel texts. For as a title it already has its place in a pretested, preestablished scale of esthetic values. As a title it refers to a genre, or to a set of familiar representations. *Toilette* is the stock label for a subject much exploited by the Dutch school of painting: Van Mieris's *La Toilette,* for instance, at the Louvre, or the numerous "Ladies Before the Looking Glass." These pictures are always full of boudoir luxury if the personage is naked, or full of splendid, colorful, complicated clothing if she is dressed: mirrors play with one another as the maid or lover holds one up to the fair heartbreaker. All of which stereotypes are negated, one by one, in our poem.

So that Eluard's text is not an orderless fragment of realism, based upon the direct mimesis of a scene and setting with circumstantial, real-life variations,[8] but is rather a well-ordered morphological system comprising a limited number of stereotypes. The form of this system is dictated by its first word, and its realism flows from the intertextual conflict between the explicit derivation and its implicit traditional derivation, normally a symbol of fantasies of luxury and pleasure. Its significance lies in the union of meaning and form, and in the fact that its reference is to the discourse of painting rather than to reduced material circumstances.

With the remaining two types of double derivation, the derivative sequences are both actualized in the poem. The second type is characterized by *one derivation representing the subject of the matrix sentence and one representing its predicate*. They are opposed to each other by semantic incompatibility.

Paul Claudel's prose poem "Splendeur de la lune" is about moonlight. The matrix is represented by the title, or rather by its ungrammaticality. It is ungrammatical in its lexical collocations, since *splendeur* normally applies only to the sun. What goes with moon is either the compound *clair de lune,* or the weaker *lumière,* often further weakened by adjectives like *pâle, faible,* or *vaporeuse. Splendeur* transforms the *moon* vs. *sun* opposition into an equivalence. The matrix can be written: *the moon is the (reverse) sun.* It would be better to write *the moon is shining,* if only we had a verb in English reserved exclusively for sunlight.

On the one hand, the matrix generates a variable—the successive details of a moonlight landscape. On the other hand, it generates a formal constant: every detail is modified by a predicate selected from a *daylight* lexicon. The text would be a poem of our first type if the conventional moonlight remained implicit. But nocturnal and diurnal words are subordinated to one another despite their mutual incompatibility. The text owes it distinctive unity to the fact that the moon-light is translated into *sunlight* code:

> . . . je vois toute la capacité de l'espace emplie de ta lumière, Soleil des songes! . . . tel qu'un prêtre éveillé pour les mystères, je suis sorti de ma couche pour envisager ce miroir occulte. La lumière du soleil est un agent de vie et de création, et notre vision participe à son énergie. Mais la splendeur de la lune est pareille à la considération de la pensée[9]

> I see all capacious space filled with your light, Sun of Dreams! Like a priest awakened to celebrate the mysteries, I left my bed to face this occult mirror. Sunlight is an agent of life and creation, and our poetic vision partakes of its energy. But the splendor of the moon is like the contemplation of thought

Every pertinent sentence or phrase, being a variant of the matrix, has for its subject the word *lune* or its metonym, and for its predicate the word *soleil* or its metonym. Hence we have phrases syntactically correct but semantically deviant: *soleil des songes; soleil de l'après-minuit; splendeur* shifted from sun to moon; *lumière* shifted from moon to sun; a sentence like, "Et déjà ce grand arbre a fleuri: droit et seul, pareil à un immense lilas blanc, épouse nocturne, il frissonne, tout dégouttant de lumière" [This big tree has already blossomed: straight and alone, like a great white lilac, bride of the night, all dripping with light], where *épouse nocturne* paradoxically crowns a hyperbolic description of light; or again: "là-haut l'étoile la plus loin-taine et la plus écartée et perdue dans tant de lumière" [up there, the star farthest away, set farthest apart, lost in so much light], where the motif of the remotest star, almost invisible in darkness, is inverted into a star almost invisible in brightness.

Rimbaud was the first, I believe, to set up oppositions of this kind. His also are the most extreme. For instance, *Enfance II,* second of the poems so named in his *Illuminations:*

> C'est elle, la petite morte, derrière les rosiers.—La jeune maman tré-passée descend le perron.—La calèche du cousin crie sur le sable.—Le petit frère (il est aux Indes!) là, devant le couchant, sur le pré d'œillets.—Les vieux qu'on a enterrés tout droits dans le rempart aux giroflées.

> It is she, the little dead girl, behind the rosebushes. The dead young mamma comes down the front steps.—The cousin's carriage squeaks on the sand. The little brother (he is in India!), there, against the sunset, in the field of carnations.—The old folks buried standing up in the city wall overgrown with wallflowers.

The problem we face in deciphering this text is that the members of the family are carrying on normal activities (the mother walking down the steps, the brother out among the flowers), but the nouns designating them are modified by adjectives of death or statements of absence, making any such activity impossible. Mimesis is destroyed, or if you prefer, two mimeses are competing within the same sentences. Indeed, the incompatible representations, despite their polar opposition, are always set forth within one sentence. These oppositions within grammatically compatible sequences create antinomies that cancel visualization and verisimilitude—unless we fall back upon the supernatural or interpret the text as referring to hallucination. Critics have done this, betraying what a quandary they are in. But this quandary is also the key to the significance of the text as a whole. If this significance is to be apprehended, it demands that we accept the premise that representations point to a meaning wherein reality, once cancelled as referential, can be used as a textual sign referring to a concept—the motif, or theme, or subject, or the poetic idea informing the text.

The life Rimbaud depicts is the life of childhood. Every word naming relatives seems to be what a little kid would call them: either the witness is of tender age (*jeune maman, vieux*), or else he speaks child language (*petite morte, petit frère*). The unexplained garden setting, which also consistently contradicts death, is a repetition of child language. The garden of early infancy is a theme of sweet childhood in recollection—either real, as in Hugo's *jardin des Feuillantines,* or metaphorical, as in Baudelaire's *vert paradis des amours enfantines.* There is the town (in the next paragraph) that everyone has left, like the one in Keats's *Grecian Urn.* The town too can be seen as a childhood setting, built like an anticipation of Combray with its curé, and its Swann side (*la maison du général*), and its *côté de Guermantes* (*le château, les loges des gardes*). In short, these settings are perceived as a direct derivation from the title, *Enfance.* But the significance of the grammatical combining of incompatibles is that this past (past because it is dead and gone, a spatial representation of time gone by) is still present—thus the significance is *memory* or *memories,* another version of *enfance* or its pathetic equivalent. The matrix sentence can be written as an expansion of the word *memory* into *childhood living yet dead,* a variant of the theme *Life in Death,* so dear to the hearts of romantic writers.

In the third type of double derivation, *both sequences are present in the text and are opposed to each other at the level of style* by the

presence of tropes in one, their absence in the other. One derivation is
literal and plain, the other *figurative* and periphrastic.

In Francis Ponge's *L'Ardoise*,[10] the prose poem looks like a playful
description of *slate* as a mineral, as a color, as a school supply, and so
on—it is given all the meanings in the dictionary, so accurately, in-
deed, that no mineralogist or lexicographer could demur. Thus a
case similar to *Toilette*, an explicit matrix, the title, and a literal
derivation, which here very nearly exhausts the word's descriptive
system. But at the same time the poem is full of cockeyed images, such
as the slate as a dried-up old maid schoolmarm, or the slate as news-
paper prose. True it is that a pun sets a humorous tone at the begin-
ning: it offers the poem as merely a surface reflection on the subject,
that is, literally on slate: "à y bien réfléchir, c'est-à-dire peu, car
[l'ardoise] a une gamme de reflets très réduite" [if we reflect well upon
this (*slate* as a topic), that is, if we reflect a little, because slate (the
thing) has a very narrow reflecting range] (this mineral being glossy
rather than reflective). But even if this initial given justifies the play-
fulness, and thus a certain unity of tone, it does not make the images
any less gratuitous. And yet they are all rigorously deduced from the
matrix through a metonymic derivation. The constant here is that
each apparently motiveless metaphor for *slate* is begotten by a meto-
nym of *slate*. For instance,

> s'il y a un livre en elle [dans l'ardoise] il n'est que de prose: . . . une
> pile de quotidiens . . . illustrés par endroits des plus anciens fossiles
> connus

> if there really is a book in slate [as who should say of a future writer,
> there is a book in him], it is only in prose: a pile of news dailies illus-
> trated with the oldest known fossils

Here the only referential justification (a very weak one) is that slate
is made of thin laminations vaguely resembling newsprint. Possible
proof of the language's referential function is that others have thought
of this image too: Claudel compares slate to a "liasse de feuilles noires
arrachées aux archives de la nature"[11] [a sheaf of black pages torn
from the archives of Nature]. I rather suspect that Claudel, like Ponge,
was using images already stereotyped. The difference here is in the
derivation, for the true motivation is a formal one, working retro-
actively, since we understand or acknowledge the aptness only as the
next image comes along. From among other possible thin-layered ob-

jects, the newspaper is chosen as a hyperbole of prosey writing, and slate is prose compared to marble. *If* marble is poetry—for two lines later it is stated that slate is dull while marble gleams brilliantly; this in turn is fancifully explained: "les filles de Carrare," the daughters of Carrara, that is, marble, were "touchée(s) à l'épaule par le doigt du feu" [touched on the shoulder by the finger of fire]—a geological truth couched in the language of poetic visitation by the Muse. Now if you are wondering, why explain the volcanic origin of minerals in poetic terms, and why contrast slate with marble, of all stones—the answer is in the intertext, the Du Bellay quotation every French child has learned by heart: "Plus que le marbre dur me plaît l'ardoise fine."[12]

The personification *filles de Carrare,* a classical poetic convention, expresses belonging or nearness—as wine is *fils de la vigne,* etc. And this in turn generates the schoolmistress. "Ces demoiselles sont de la fin du secondaire": marble was formed in the Secondary or Mesozoic Age, so if marble be girls, then they are finishing secondary school. And since slate dates back to the Paleozoic Age, we have primary or elementary school:

> elle appartient aux établissements du primaire, notre institutrice de vieille roche, montrant un visage triste, abattu: un teint évoquant moins la nuit que l'ennuyeuse pénombre des temps

> she belongs to the primary schools, our vintage teacher, with her sad face, depressed: a complexion that conjures up less the night of time past than its tedious penumbra

Farfetched perhaps, yet the verbal derivation is rigorous, for the school-marm is stereotyped as aging, but aging here is expressed through rock imagery (*de vieille roche*), equally stereotyped; in the hierarchy of teachers the *institutrice* is in charge of the first-graders. The slate is therefore her metonym, and she is the metonym of the slate.

So that the further the text departs from direct representation—the sillier or funnier or more artificial it looks—the closer it is to the verbal cognates of *slate.* In fact humor is only a result of ungrammaticality, and as such it points to the intertext. What is more, ungrammaticality consists in the deviant use of metonymy instead of similarity for choosing metaphors: the schoolteacher, as a metaphor, stands for slate, not because she resembles slate but because slate is her mythological attribute. In such a case the poem's formal constant is inappropriateness, verbal detour, carried to an extreme—the *ardoise* as *no-slate,* so to speak, *ardoise* described as what it is not. But this lexical otherness is not random, for every inappropriate representation does indeed employ a wrong word, but one that presupposes the right one. One derivation, the literal, actualizes the *ardoise* system, and another, the figurative, is, as it were, shaped by the repressed presence of that system. Such a prose poem thus displays perfect circularity, since the metaphor's tenor, *slate*, takes as its vehicle the periphrastic equivalent of that tenor. A triumph of verbal self-sufficiency, or the purest form of literariness as artifact.

To conclude, what is special about the prose poem is that its generator contains the seeds of a contradiction in terms. The text develops either by resolving this contradiction, as in Ponge, or by repeating it, as in Claudel, Rimbaud, and Eluard. The prose poem is thus an example of perfect, unmitigated expansion.

Hence the significance of the prose poem lies wholly in intertextuality, that is, it depends entirely upon the reader's ability to perceive (but not necessarily to describe) the interplay, both relatedness and conflict, between the two derivations. The prose poem therefore demands considerable participation on the reader's part. (It fits Barthes's definition of real, live literature: the kind that requires a "scriptor" rather than a passive reader). This is its true difference from verse: for verse does not need a matrix, nor does it depend upon the poem's matrix. It antedates the text, like other conventions, like a genre, for example. In the prose poem the matrix substitutes an ad hoc idiolectic form for the prefabricated one. Born with it and of it, the defining constant of the prose poem is consequently wholly adequate.

Finally, the significance issuing from intertextuality is meaning, but not necessarily content. This meaning tends to be the perception of form: the act of *donner à voir* in Eluard, the conceit in Francis Ponge. Hence the prose poem comes very close to being a mimesis of the literary artifact itself.

Humor as Continuous Catachresis

Humor[13] is frequent in modern poetry, particularly French. It manifests itself either within the limits of the linguistic code, or, especially among surrealists, in ungrammatical forms such as nonsense poetry. Two trends can be distinguished, depending upon whether the reader is able to rationalize the humor as a method of satire, a product of the author's comic bent, or an expression of his attitude toward life—as in Laforgue, for instance, in Corbière, perhaps in Charles Cros; or whether the reader cannot so interpret it, as in the literary forms introduced by

Mallarmé and Lautréamont. In the latter case humor is most gratui-
tous, that is, least motivated by the topic or the rules of a genre. Study-
ing humorous texts of this second kind should thus afford us an oppor-
tunity better to understand the nature of literary language. For if we
recognize that literature can be defined as a linguistic phenomenon in
which form is more important than content, and that this phenomenon
is above all a playing with words, then humor offers the most extreme
and easily observable examples of these two features. Most revealing
of these qualities is humor whose characteristic absurdity stems from
the presence in the text of codes semantically or formally incompatible,
that is, where the mechanism of the humor is but one variety of inter-
textuality. These incompatibilities, rationalized by the reader as jokes,
define a poem as such. For a poem is a verbal complex with its own
rules, and the rules of *this* idiolect are the reciprocal negativization of
codes resulting from these incompatibilities.

I shall examine just how this text-generating conflict comes about and
how its decipherment as humor insures that the text shall be deci-
phered according to the rules, how this limits the reader's freedom of in-
terpretation and regulates his decoding. My example is a descriptive
prose poem from Francis Ponge's *Grand Recueil:*[14]

[1]L'appareil du téléphone

[2]D'un socle portatif à semelle de feutre, selon cinq mètres de fils de
trois sortes qui s'entortillent sans nuire au son, une crustace se décroche,
qui gaîment bourdonne . . . tandis qu'entre les seins de quelque sirène
sous roche, une cerise de métal vibre . . .

[3]Toute grotte subit l'invasion d'un rire, ses accès argentins, impérieux
et mornes, qui comporte cet appareil.

[4](*Autre*)

[5]Lorsqu'un petit rocher, lourd et noir, portant son homard en
anicroche, s'établit dans une maison, celle-ci doit subir l'invasion d'un
rire aux accès argentins, impérieux et mornes. [6]Sans doute est-ce celui de
la mignonne sirène dont les deux seins sont en même temps apparus dans
un coin sombre du corridor, et qui produit son appel par la vibration
entre les deux d'une petite cerise de nickel, y pendante.

[7]Aussitôt, le homard frémit sur son socle. [8]Il faut qu'on le décroche:
[9]il a quelque chose à dire, ou veut être rassuré par votre voix.

[10]D'autres fois, la provocation vient de vous-même. [11]Quand vous y
tente le contraste sensuellement agréable entre la légèreté du combiné
et la lourdeur du socle. [12]Quel charme alors d'entendre, aussitôt la
crustace détachée, le bourdonnement gai qui vous annonce prêtes au
quelconque caprice de votre oreille les innombrables nervures électriques
de toutes les villes du monde!

[13]Il faut agir le cadran mobile, puis attendre, après avoir pris acte de la sonnerie impérieuse qui perfore votre patient, le fameux déclic qui vous délivre sa plainte, transformée aussitôt en cordiales ou cérémonieuses politesses . . . [14]Mais ici finit le prodige et commence une banale comédie.

At the end of five yards of three different kinds of wire twisted together without spoiling the sound, a gaily humming crustacean is unhooked from a portable stand with a felt base . . . the while a metal cherry is vibrating between the breasts of some mermaid underneath a rock. . . . Any sea-cave with built-in set suffers invasion by a laugh, its silvery outbursts, imperious and gloomy. (*Other version*) When a small rock, heavy and black, carrying its snagged lobster, settles down in a house, the house must submit to invasion by bursts of laughter, silvery, imperious and doleful. It is probably the laughter of that cute little mermaid whose two breasts have showed up meanwhile in a dark corner of the hall. She sends her call by vibrating the little nickel cherry hanging there between her two breasts. Forthwith the lobster quivers on its stand. It must be taken off its hook! it has something to say, or else it wants to be reassured by your voice. At other times the provocation comes from you yourself. When you are tempted by the sensually pleasurable contrast between the lightness of the handset and the heaviness of the stand. The moment the crustacean is unhooked, how nice to hear the cheerful humming that declares the innumerable electric nervures of all the cities in the world are ready for any caprice of your ear! You have to work the mobile dial, then, having noted the imperious ringing that perforates your patient, you must await the famous click that delivers you his groan, instantly transformed into cordial or ceremonious civilities. . . . But here the miracle ends and a banal comedy begins.

What lets the reader know this is a poem is the very cancellation of a poem's traditional defining features. For nothing can be cancelled or negated that has not first been asserted. Accordingly, the label, if nothing else, and the basic minimal definition of a poem *are* posited. What does the trick is the general title of the collection: *Pièces*. Though more commonly used for a theatrical play or a musical *morceau,* the word is the minimal designation of a text as an art object.[15] At least the topic of every piece confirms this embryonic classification: each describes an object, outside of any context, isolated in the blank margin of unspoken presuppositions, focussing upon one sensory experience with or without a "meditative" sequel. Each is thus understood as the written equivalent of the painter's still life. That is enough to prevent the prose poem from being read as just plain prose, even though the text looks like just plain prose. This initial assumption being made, a text can realize the poetic model either in conformity with or contrary to the expectations raised. Such expectations are the awareness of an intertext. The reader perceives "L'appareil" as a token of a class, and this class he knows from comparing texts and recognizing what features they have in common. The absence of the traditional verse features cannot be seen as simple nonexistence because the title of the collection belies this; the absence must be negativization, the reverse of the negativization of nonpoetry, which traditionally defines verse through formal features such as meter, rhythm, rhyme, word-order inversions. The poem is thus defined in opposition to conventional poems not because its prose is prose but because it is nonverse, nonrhythm, nonrhyme.

The poem negativizes this intertextual definition of a poem in yet another way: even a prose poem is supposed, like any other art form, to be polished and complete—that is, a masterpiece, a finished product. Whereas this poem is made to look like a preparatory sketch (dots in 2, [4] *autre* making 2–3 look like a first draft of 5–13). But we have here more than a subversion or diversion of the meaning of typographical instructions (i.e., that the sketch is not a real one, but rather a sign that the poem is defining itself *a contrario,* as a nonfinished product). With a wink to the reader, a novel element is added to pinpoint the subversion, a bit of fanciful variation on the conventional language of the memos a craftsman scribbles to himself in the margin: instead of the plain (but indeed bracketed and italicized) indication of a variant by something like *variante* or even *ou bien* or *ou encore,* we come upon the unexpected, manneristic dangling adjective [4] *autre.* The effect is parodic, its almost superfluous function to insist that this sketch is a mimesis of *the* sketch, A Portrait of the Easel, as it were. Nor is this an isolated instance: some of Ponge's texts are built entirely of paragraphs alternately entitled *Variants* and *Autre.*[16] In such a case the humor—still only faintly perceptible in our [4] *autre*—is rendered inescapable by repetition. In fact these make-believe markers of the unfinished text acquire the function performed by subtitles in a finished text. The playful, parodic *variante* and *autre* substitute for formal, "straight" conventions such as the alternation of *strophe* and *antistrophe,* of *ode* and *épode.*

Now this function of humor, substituting for the forms it negates, may still be viewed as merely a stylistic variation pinpointing the intertextual conflict, yet exterior to it. The text as a whole, however, evidences a humorous constant inseparable from intertextuality—the sustained discrepancy between the expectations raised by the title and what we actually find in the text. At first blush the title seems to be announcing a didactic or descriptive poem.[17] But the rather obvious teasing in certain phrases,[18] the excessively extended metaphors, the far-fetched siren personification (2, 6) and the lobster animalization (2, 5, 7), all add up to a jocularity inconsistent with the serious or objective style of a still life, let alone the encomiastic tone of proper didactic poetry. The immediate effect is that of gratuitous fancifulness, but it lasts only long enough to compel the reader's attention. Thus alerted, his sensitivity to form heightened, the reader gropes for some rationale and becomes retroactively aware of a different meaning in the title. The apparent wandering of the description from the plain reality of a telephone is now discovered to be the necessary, justified, cogently logical, though verbal, consequence of the title seen in this new light. Gratuitousness in the mimesis becomes the index of consistency elsewhere, for it derives the poem from the title's aberrant syntax. Indeed, underneath a title that seems to function as a content, that is, to designate the topic, a title functioning as a formal matrix is unmasked. Its very ungrammaticality provides the idiolectic rule or model that generates intertextual incompatibilities. The title is a pun. We speak of *l'appareil téléphonique*, or *l'appareil de téléphone*. Whereas *appareil du téléphone* transforms the matrix *appareil*, "set," into *appareil* as synonym of *apparat*. Consequently, the reader cannot be a telephoner looking for or reading instructions, and the telephone cannot be perceived as the object of a mimesis, but becomes a pretext for a sort of ritual wordplay, a verbal celebration.

Accordingly, the title generates the whole poem in such a way that two texts develop side by side. One is the descriptive discourse derived from *appareil* as a metonym for *téléphone,* with the meaning it has in the phrase *appareil de téléphone*. The other is derived from *appareil du,* that is, here, an Ode to the Telephone, or the Epic of the Telephone.[19] Perhaps it is closer to the baroque genre of *blason,* since the *blason* was written in praise or dispraise of an object that usually had little significance in itself, the point being to lend it significance through a disproportionate verbal construction.

The descriptive text involves both a mimesis and literary themes concerning telephones. It is factual, even technical, describing the instrument's portable base, the dial, the wires (2), the bell (6, 11), the dial tone, as well as how to dial a number (13). It has a moralizing voice and leans toward philosophical attitudes, exploiting the positive and negative motifs of the new-discovery theme. The positive: the power of such inventions to harness the elements and triumph over man's physical limitations (12), electricity, or lightning tamed, distance abolished, the opposition *intimacy* vs. *absence* annulled; in 13, the hold the new contrivance gives you upon others. The negative: invasion of privacy, a motif now forgotten as far as the telephone is concerned, but still alive in connection with television, or at least its commercials (3, 5, 8, 13). The negative motif is the exact reverse variant of the positive: the inventor enslaved by his own invention.

The *blason* is metaphorical. Its ethos as a genre is expressed by maritime imagery (sea-cave, rock, lobster shell, lobster, siren), but the rub is that these images, however ornamental and embellishing, are comical when used for the telephone or its mythology, because the semantic fields and descriptive systems of tenor and vehicle are so extremely remote from one another, and because there is no similarity or analogy to justify bringing them together.

These two derivative sequences keep referring to each other, each text cancelling out the other. The technicality of the descriptive text, like any engineering code, is incompatible with imagery in general. The moral epicality of the themes is threatened by the drollness of the imagery. Conversely, the inner logic or consistency of the *blason* metaphors is destroyed because the syntax organizing these representations is different from the syntax of the telephone descriptive system.

Sentence 3 is an example of technical discourse conflicting with the poetic phraseology that fills its lexical slots. Despite the nonsense of *l'invasion d'un rire,* the sentence manages to sound like a theorem, thanks to the statement of a constant *(tout+Noun+Verb)* observable when and only when a given condition is fulfilled *(qui comporte +* Noun, the clause being postponed in typical textbook fashion): *tout (A) (x, y, z) qui comporte un (B).* But, if *A* be a *grotte,* we hardly expect *appareil* as *B,* and vice versa. They do not fit together, even though their disparity is not so obvious as, or is more acceptable than that of *rire.* The point is, however, that this incompatibility results less from *rire*'s abnormality in this microcontext than from the blatant conventionality of the literary diction used to describe it:[20] the hyperbolic image *(invasion)* and the *accès* periphrasis with more images *(argentins, impérieux).*

Or take the non sequitur twice linking *crustace, bourdonner,* and *gaîment* (2, 12), despite the fact that a noun referring to a crustacean (whatever the exact meaning of this noun may be) cannot possibly have humming or purring as a predicate, and the fact that the adverb

hardly fits such sounds but goes rather with the buzzing they meta-
phorically represent: a metaphor normally proposes a "better," cer-
tainly a more striking representation of its tenor; the twist here is
that the tenor interferes with its metaphorical vehicle, making it
nonsensical.

These intertextual incompatibilities, although they are, or rather
because they seem to be bizarre or absurd, create the humor that gives
the text its shape and the adequate form and content that make for the
organic unity one expects of a poem. To begin with, its oddities never
cause the text to veer away from its announced subject. Instead of
jeopardizing the representation of reality, a seemingly freewheeling
fancy brings the picture of the telephone back into sharper focus,
thanks to the surprising twist. The absurdity of make-believe animation
(the pseudopsychological motivations of telephonic functioning), for ex-
ample, reaches a climax with the representation of the phone bell as a
mythological siren or mermaid (2, 6). And yet the image is fitting after
all, for a ringing telephone has to be answered, just as a siren's song
cannot be resisted. In fact, the telephone is the only appliance whose
call casts upon us the spell of a siren's voice. And the breasts of the
mermaid are just right too, though not quite so obtrusively for the
American reader, whose telephone has its bell inside the box. But this
text is aimed at the French reader, and *his* telephone has its bell sep-
arate from the instrument. The bell hangs on a wall, hidden away
[6]*dans un coin sombre du corridor.* It consists of two nickel cupolas with
a hammer in between, each cupola fastened with a screw at its center:
they much resemble breasts indeed, or rather their familiar crude
stylization—two circles, two dots—in graffiti, cartoons, boys' doodles.
So we have a reference not merely to reality but to an established
semiotic of visual humor.

But there is more to the unity of the poem and the aptness of its
forms than descriptive accuracy or completeness. Humorous effects
stem from a continuous polarization between the words actualizing
both components of the intertext. This very continuity, however, is
entirely determined by the semantic given of the title, and it therefore
forces the reader to sense at all times that the text is neither more nor
less than the zigzagging expansion of that given. These variants, for
instance: [2]*une crustace se décroche* and [7]*le homard frémit sur son socle.*
[8]*Il faut qu'on le décroche,* play upon a verb substitute for the noun
téléphone. The two verbs central to the descriptive system of this noun
are *décrocher* and *raccrocher.* These are verbs never used in everyday

French except for insignificant, practical, down-to-earth actions such as hanging a utensil up on a hook (cf. *accrocher* and the colloquial *décrochez-moi-ça*). Now these negligible lexemes suddenly become the agents of human presence and contact. For in the act of telephoning, and in its mimesis, they are literally the alpha and omega of what two human beings have to say to each other. This humanized transform of a mechanical contraption is what generates the make-believe animation in sentences 8–9, making a metallic vibration masquerade as a silly, trembling emotionality that must be calmed down. The conventional animation cannot be taken seriously, as it would be in an ode: *décrocher* remains too close to its plebeian connotations for that. Even one of the zaniest bits of nonsense—*[5]petit rocher . . . portant son homard en anicroche*—is really a neological hyperbole of *décrocher*,[21] reaffirming the verbal consistency of the text through a most striking ungrammaticality born of the intertext. For *anicroche* is a rather rare, hence highly visible, vaguely comical, clearly colloquial term, meaningless after *portant son homard en.* The distraught reader's reaction is to rationalize it as a pun on *en accroche-cœur* and *en croc.* This does not make any sense either, but it does focus attention on the positional relationship indicated by *en: anicroche* then appears to be a transform of *en écharpe* or *en bandoulière,* or better yet, of *en sautoir*—and that does make sense. But it also makes the transform sound like a translation of "sling" or "strap" into *téléphone* language, because *anicroche* is so closely related to its basic verbs. Only seven words in French begin with *ani-.* Of this small group, *anicroche* is the only one with a last syllable recognizable as a full-fledged word: *croche,* the word for the musical quaver. We sense *croche* as descriptive, iconic, since it alludes to the actual hook of the musical symbol for the quaver; a word doubly graphic, for it also sounds like the feminine of *croc. Anicroche* is perceived as having a root, or a pseudo root, which makes it an extension of the *raccrocher-décrocher* paradigm.

The text is thus self-sufficient even when it departs from the linguistic code, because even departures are transforms of the title: <u>linguistic ungrammaticalities are still grammatical in the idiolect and they produce what would be called harmony in a conventional poem.</u> This self-sufficiency can be verified by the way the derivation governs the shape of the poem and delimits its textual space. The boundaries of this space are not just a beginning in the typographical sense or an end because the verbal output has tapered off. There is a verbal logic to these limits; the beginning and the end are not that just by virtue

of their position, but because of a formal, semantic, and semiotic re-
lationship between the opening and the closing words. Since textual
space is filled by playing a complex game, it is fitting that the text
should start with the rule of the game, that is, the pun in the title. And
that it should close with the statement that words stop when the game
ends and reality begins again: [14]*ici . . . commence une banale comédie.*
The fact that this reality should be given the name of still another game
(*banale comédie* instead of extraordinary, instead of the game of verbal
fireworks) points to another difference between an ending and a textual
clausula: the finis would be a typographical blank space, leaving the
reader free to return to his experience of the real world; the clausula
is a representation of reality as nonliterature. And in a way *comédie*
is the esthetic antithesis of *appareil.*

Nor is this all: [14]*prodige* justifies *in fine* the poem's indulgence in
the verbal pomp of *appareil* at the outset—as if a hymn were to begin
with *praise* and end with *glory.* Lastly, the endocentric nature of the
poem, its self-sufficiency as a closed system of words, is underscored by
a final touch in its use of perfect verbal equations to replace truth as
reference to things. The name of the genre is annexed or contaminated
by the designation of the subject: using *appareil* in the sense of *blason*
or *ode* is like translating these literary terms into a telephone language.

But now the gratuitousness of humor must be reinterpreted. It is two-
fold. The gratuitousness that makes us perceive an intertextual conflict
is in fact part of the overdetermination system. But what about the ini-
tial decision to speak humorously of the telephone? That at least seems
to be quite pointless, or else a genuine creative fancy. Either way, it is
a cut-off point. We might say that this is where creative humor falls be-
low creative imagination, the latter presumably being rooted in reality,
whereas the former is just arbitrary. Or, without taking sides, we might
say that overdetermination vindicates the choice, but only retroactively,
just as the reader must do a double-take before spotting the anomaly
of *du* and noticing the pun. Not so. Overdetermination antedates the
initial selection, for it is latent in the very principle of the poem. We
have here an exact analogy between the semantic structures of *télé-
phone* (as a word and as a theme) and the basic rule of the genre. For
a commonplace view of a given subject as unworthy, the *blason* sub-
stitutes the revelation of its real worth, polarizing an initial flat, ob-
jective statement of the subject and a panegyric thereon. And here the
most obvious and ordinary synonym of telephone, that is, *appareil,*[22]
is at language level, before the text is born, both the word for "me-

chanical device," a clichéd epitome of insignificance, and a synonym of *panegyric*. The pun in the title merely actualizes the two potentialities simultaneously. The [14]*finit* vs. *commence* opposition at the end, as a narrative, i.e., sequential transform of the title, separates them once again, in the reverse order of a *da capo* movement, as if the text, after rising from *appareil* to *apparat,* ends by descending from *apparat* to *appareil.* This entire mechanism—the point must be emphasized—remains within the realm of words: the poem simply rediscovers, through humor exactly as through other forms of verbal creativity, the first, basic meaning[23] of the word *appareil* as *apparat, pompe,* or *fête,* with all the more impact because this meaning is disappearing from common usage altogether.

All that precedes, it will be noted, is based upon facts observable entirely inside the text. The intertextual incompatibilities discussed so far are actualized *in toto* in the letter of the poem. We may speak here of an *explicit* or *idiolectic* intertext, to which the rules of overdetermination apply just as they do to its initial given. But even if the choice of humor were determined, we would be hard put to explain why this particular code—the sea code—was hit upon. The wherewithal of humor, the content of the metaphorical text, seems still to be the most gratuitous factor.

Let us assume that the *sirène* metaphor is fully explained by the imperious ringing of the telephone, and that the whole sea code can be derived from that personification. This derivation would still not confer any aptness upon the extended metaphor that turns the telephone receiver into a lobster, its base into a rock, and the house into a grotto. It is certainly not impossible to find enough semes common to a house and a grotto to justify this last. Mallarmé, for instance, calls a home the *grotte de notre intimité.*[24] The rock can be justified by the weight of the telephone,[25] and its mobility (5) derived therefrom by oxymoron: such would be the mechanism of humor at this point. Whereupon the mermaid will make grotto and rock marine. But why should the handset of the phone be a lobster's carapace, when a minor literary motif makes a very different shell into a transmitter of the sounds of the sea (almost as good as the electrical sound waves this poem is about)? We must conclude that no *intra*textual derivation will explain the extended metaphor as a sequence. Nor will it explain satisfactorily the selection of the primary metaphor that triggers the sequence, if it is indeed the mermaid, or explain what determines the humorous distortions in each of its components. The problem is com-

pounded by the fact that the incongruity of the sea imagery peaks in
three instances of extremest nonsense—which happen, of course, to be
the high points of the poem's humor.

These all occur at the lexical level: they are [6]*mignonne,* [5]*anicroche,*
and [2, 12]*crustace.* All three, above and beyond the stylistic contrasts
they create in context, do violence to the very fabric of language, not
just to the idiolect. They are not all equally upsetting. *Mignonne* is
no worse than foreign to the connotations of *sirène,* and it alters only a
system of word collocations that is loose anyway. As for *anicroche,* I
have shown the morphological kinship between *anicroche* and the
telephone code, but the semantic displacement remains puzzling, all
the more so in the metaphorical context. *Crustace* is the most powerful
of the three because it is a new coinage, and it is puzzling in the con-
text of both the telephone and sea metaphors, in the latter case be-
cause *homard* alone would be sufficiently incompatible with telephone
if only the explicit intertext were involved.

To find out the deeper roots of the gratuitousness in these examples,
we must take into account an *implicit intertext.*[26] Implicit because the
poem actualizes it in the form of allusions. These look like deviant
components of the text's lexicon. Their anomalousness vanishes when
the reader recognizes that they refer to texts outside the poem. Whether
these are identified or not, however, the anomalous words contribute
to the overdetermination of the metaphorical code.

When identification does take place, it is because their deviant char-
acter has a deictic function. It triggers the reader's memory, enabling
him to retrieve another text that contains the same formal component,
or a text whose components may have motivated the deviant form and
may be summarized or symbolized by it.[27]

Mignonne, for instance, cannot be explained by the fact that a tele-
phone is being translated into briny language. And the *femme fatale*
glamor of the mythological siren makes such a namby-pamby adjective
unacceptable. This very unacceptability, however, prompts the reader
to grope instinctively for a reassuring precedent, and eventually he
may connect Ponge's unlikely mermaid with one in Mallarmé. *Un
Coup de Dés* contains not only a siren who is *mignonne,* but also a
darkness that hides her:

> au front invisible
> scintille
> puis ombrage

une stature mignonne ténébreuse debout
en sa torsion de sirène[28]

at the invisible front there scintillates then casts a shadow a dainty
figure dark standing in her siren twist

Mallarmé's text functions as Ponge's hypogram, and *²sirène sous roche* must be regarded as the icon of the hypogram, since its meaning is compounded with an unavoidable allusion to the French cliché *anguille sous roche*—that is, to a secret or a double entendre.

The more unsettling unacceptability of *en anicroche* (its solecistic substitution for *en sautoir*), or, more accurately, the twofold (positional and morphological) unacceptability of *homard en anicroche,* calls to mind Alfred Jarry's fable "Le homard et la boîte de corned-beef."[29] Irresistibly, for Faustroll is shown carrying the lobster's counterpart, a can of corned beef, *en sautoir.* The fable, by the way, is built, like our prose poem, upon an intertextuality that generates a back-and-forth lexical exchange: the can is described as a chained, motionless lobster, the lobster as a living, automotive can (*la petite boîte automobile de conserves vivante*). The animal is translated into a negativized inanimate code, the inanimate into a negativized animal code.

Crustace tops my list, being the ultimate departure from language because it is a neologism and thus sure to attract the reader's attention. All the more so, in fact, because it is at the same time comical per se, as a superfluous coinage, and finally, as a reference to the already gratuitous lobster. Per se because it calls to mind, as no existing word could, the words it rhymes with, i.e., not only those with an *-ace* suffix, but also those ending in *-asse,* a derogatory suffix. It is comical because it is uncalled for: its shape suggests it has been formed on the model of adjective-noun pairs like *glacé* and *glace, menacé* and *menace.*[30] Accordingly, *crustacé* yields *crustace* for the hard outer shell that characterizes this class of invertebrates. But, of course, there is already a word for this, *carapace.* The play on forms cannot fail to emphasize the idea of carapace. It morphologically underlines its metonymic link with the animal that is indeed, in French, the typical crustacean. *Crustace,* as a paronomasia of *crustacé,* resembles this eminent crustacean more closely than does *carapace.* This emphasis heightens the absurdity of the lobster's masquerading as a telephone receiver, because it underscores the reality of the lobster,[31] thus making it more different from the mechanical appliance. This also ensures memorization and textual rapprochement. And once the implicit intertext is linked with our poem, the compounded nonsense becomes precisely the locus of greatest sense.

The intertext here is another piece of Ponge's (found in the next volume of the collection), which reveals *homard* as the true matrix of the metaphoric code in our poem, the element that triggered the linkage with Jarry and Mallarmé and to which these intertexts are functionally subordinated. In that piece Ponge develops his peculiar view of civilization and defines manmade mechanical contraptions in a crustacean code. This key to *crustace* is Ponge's jocular explanation of man's superiority over animals: many animals have built-in tools, weapons, and defenses, and the best examples are shellfish, like lobsters, crabs, etc.; their pincers, mandibles, and shells are susceptible of geometric, machinelike representation. What makes man superior is that he has been able to cast away his tools, cast off his shell. Man can relax, leave his impedimenta stored—in a cave, significantly, and that cave is, of course, his house (a cave well motivated in context, since Ponge, speaking of the early stages of man's evolution, his first steps away from other animals, adopts the conventional representation of the caveman).[32] If our poem is read in the light of this intertext, wherein man is defined in opposition to the crustaceans, and as superior to them, the lobster looks like a lesser man, a man less perfect. Now within the lexicon of crustaceans, *homard* seems to be just that, thanks to a pseudo etymology, for the French derogatory suffix *-ard* pretends that the lobster *is* a lower variety of man, that *homard* is determined by the latent model *homme-ard*.[33]

Implicit intertextuality is highly vulnerable to the erosion of time and cultural change, or to the reader's unfamiliarity with the corpus of the elite that bred a particular poetic generation. But even when the intertext has been obliterated, the text's hold on the reader is not affected.[34] The fact that he is unable to decipher the hypogram of reference immediately does affect the content of his reactions, but not his perception of the grid of ungrammatical or nonsense phrases. They function as buoys marking the positions of a sunken meaning. If retrieval is blocked, this denial of the reader's right to language as communication is not taken lying down. The reader looks elsewhere for a meaning, as well as for the reason why the text is playing tricks with language—that is, he tries to find within the inner system of references of words to words the justification he cannot find in the semantic system of language at large, in meanings based upon referents.

If he does not perceive the connection with Mallarmé, he at least sees *mignonne* as a first step away from the mermaid and toward the household appliance, the personification finding its rationale in a human interpretation of familiar domestic sounds—symbols of home intimacy (thus compounding the humor, since the siren song reverses the symbolism and denotes home privacy intruded upon). This first step is the action of the adjective turning her into a diminutive female, on a par with the average *genius loci,* who is ordinarily small, whether goblin or cricket on the hearth. If the connection with *homard en sautoir* is lost on one who is a stranger to Jarry, the word *anicroche* must still be understood as equivalent to *sautoir* (or to a synonym), and the reader will therefore be aware of at least a variation for the sake of variation. He will see the text as a trope, which is a modality of the literary experience. In point of fact, whether or not the reader is able to solve the riddle of ungrammaticality is so secondary that there was indeed a time when our poem had no semantic core, since its intertext had not yet been written—Ponge's text on the superiority of man over lobster was written fifteen years after *L'appareil du télé- phone.*[35] Even in such an extreme case, the perception of a verbal de- tour around *carapace* suffices to force upon the reader an esthetic per- ception of the text, albeit in a parodic way: *crustace* looks like the perfect *mot juste,* that ideal so often sought in vain. It is somehow too fitting—that a crustacean should wear a *crustace* is like saying *Kleider machen Leute.* It is too good to be true, it smacks of verbal sleight-of-hand, reversing causality, a regressive word formation, as if the slug were to be so named because it is sluggish.

If the discovery of the intertext makes the intertextual relation ex- plicit, the basic semantic relation of signifier to referent is replaced by a relation of text to texts. The deictic function of humor is therefore a cardinal one. But we must realize that it can just as well point to the invisible—elements unrealized in the poem and undiscoverable by this or that reader. It marks where the unidentified intertext should be, al- though the latter remains implicit. Humorous gratuitousness is then an icon of verbalism: as the trace left by an intertext unactualized in the poem, it renders visible the outline, the geometry of a structure, without our having to deduce it from a variant. The deictic function of humor thus has two facets: humor is the nonmotivated at text level, and therefore the motivated at the level of the intertext.

The two possible readings are compatible: in fact the reader usually begins in the dark and discovers the implicit intertext later on. Hence we must include in the definition of the literary phenomenon the concept of time lag: the poem is not only the object of progressive and retroactive readings of its text, it is a system whose complexes are capable of extensible (but always verbal and always controlled) reference. More precisely, the absurdity or inappropriateness of humor is only a deferred appropriateness.

The deictic function of humor in a poem, by pointing to intertextual relationships, gives the poem its form and posits its structural polarities. In some cases humor can consequently replace conventional features of poetry such as meter or even tropes. It destroys the meaning of the text in the usual sense of meaning (our poem cannot be said to be about the real telephone or its mythology). It replaces referential meaning with references of words to texts and of texts to texts, it replaces literalness with literariness. The praxis it demands of the reader is therefore the awareness that the text always refers to something said otherwise and elsewhere, the continuous experience of a verbal detour.

Catachresis may be a general feature of all types of poetic discourse. But most of the time it appears to be motivated by the subject (hyperbole, for instance, or litotes): because humor is perceived as absurd or unmotivated, despite being just as determined as any other poetic form, it must be regarded as an extreme form of catachresis, and therefore as the symbol par excellence of the verbal game, which is precisely what literature is.

Finally, as we saw in the case of the title (resuscitating the *discours d'apparat* under *appareil*), this catachresis is the means of rediscovering the potentialities of language, the means of testing new semantic and semiotic relationships. This suggests that humor is nothing other than a special case of poetic language, and that poetic language is a special case of metalanguage.

Nonsense: Intertextual Scrambling

Some poems are characterized by nonsense. It may or may not be completely opaque, but it is always absurd or unacceptable as language used for communicating. Nonsense varies in range: it may involve the entire text or only crucial parts, but it always bears upon the semiosis-producing paradigm, affecting at least the matrix's successive variants or any derivation from the model.

This nonsense is a phenomenon linked to intertextuality, for as soon as the reader becomes aware of the hypogram, an interpretation becomes possible—perhaps not a complete hermeneutic process, but the reader at least gets the feeling that the wording of the text, however disconcerting, is no longer gratuitous.

What we have here is much more than an extreme case of conversion and resulting ungrammaticality: the difference that justifies our classing it under the head of textuality is that ungrammaticality does much more than point to the latent hypogram. It has a further role in that it is a sign of its own, not just of literariness (we have observed again and again that ungrammaticality is a sign of literariness, because even when it has been solved or understood it remains active as difficult reading, therefore the contrary of nonliterary reading, which tends to facilitate interpretation). Nonsense is its own sign because it adds a dimension to retroactive reading. Not only does the reader become capable of a structural reading, he becomes sensitized to the semiotic constants pointing to connotations rather than to denotations: he realizes that each nonsensicality corresponds to textual signs in the hypogram, which are hyperactivated by the stylistic buildup received in their hypogrammatic context.

This particular type of intertextually determined nonsense, which enables the resulting unit to impose itself upon the reader as a well-formed one despite its unacceptability to linguistic usage, I call *scrambling.* The linear shift or displacement the term implies is what differentiates this type of derivation from that represented by quotation, allusion, or parody. Where the text contains words, phrases, or sentences also found in a hypogram, but with their order changed, and where, further, the links in the sequence they form in the hypogram have been perhaps completely destroyed, or at least bypassed or made implicit—that is scrambling. The functions of words, phrases, or sentences in the syntagm are consequently upset, their original meaning mixed up. A distinction must be drawn between hypograms: some have already been actualized in texts, others are potential descriptive systems. With the latter, obviously, the reader needs only normal linguistic competence to perceive and interpret that scrambling.

For instance, the first line of an automatic-writing surrealist text posits a sentence that may not at first glance appear nonsensical. Vaguely absurd, perhaps, since it has such a low level of expectedness, although it states a possible fact. Only retroactively does its absurdity become blatant, the ensuing story growing less and less acceptable as it unfolds, and this unacceptability looking more and more like an expansion of the initial sentence:

Il y avait une fois un dindon sur une digue.[36]

Once upon a time there was a turkey on a dike.

The text is so constructed as to make it impossible to read it referentially: the turkey's adventures are not compatible with what either language or experience teach us to expect of this bird, and their departures from verisimilitude forbid us to interpret them as a mimesis of the fantastic.[37] Story, plot, and representations can only be called absurd. L. Jenny has shown, however, that the text progresses without violating narrative structures, that in fact it follows rules no different from those of a "normal" realistic narrative. What makes even the absurd thus acceptable is the fact that the text is a series of events unfolding out of a given whose "truth" is tolerable for the simple reason that it is grammatical.

What has not been recognized, however, is that the narrative well-formedness only corresponds to the possibility that a turkey might happen to be on a sea-wall. Whereas the unlikely or uninteresting nature of this circumstance, that is, its descriptive improbability (or near impossibility) corresponds to the text's semantic absurdity (despite its narrative correctness). Now this improbability derives from the first sentence's scrambling of a hypogram that is none other than a familiar refrain of children's rhymes—once even elevated to literary status by the nineteenth-century songwriter Béranger: *diguedondaine diguedindon.*

Like most refrains, this one is nonsensical by definition (although Béranger motivates it in *his* song by making it a sound-symbolization of bells ringing). The scrambling isolates *digue* and *dindon* by reversing the order that made these two-syllable groups a variation on *diguedondaine,* and thus brings to the fore the meaning they happen to have as separate words, "dam" or "dike" and "turkey." But obviously, this scrambling process cannot quite erase the memory of the refrain, which makes it quite plain that the fowl and his locale are figments of nonsense and nothing else, that they are purely verbal creations. The text immediately develops this with *il y avait une fois,* the standard fairy-tale and fable opening; I hardly need emphasize that this "once upon a time" only *seems* to suggest that what is going to be told did actually happen, that in fact the phrase functions as a genre marker of unreality, an assurance that the tale is a mere fiction. The *dindon* itself becomes another marker of fiction, since in the "once upon a time" context it refers less to the winged gobbler than to the proverbial or popular *c'est le dindon de la fable.*[38] It matters not that this refers colloquially to the foolish or gullible; what matters is that *dindon* is associated in a stereotype with *fable,* and thus is metonymically turned into a sign of nonexistence. The nonsense resulting from the hypogram's scrambling is a sign of itself, so to speak, since the poem's significance lies in its very semantic emptiness, in the lesson surrealists meant to teach by their automatic writing—that beneath the words there is nothing but more words.

Scrambling affects clichés and stereotypes as well. In fact, the more firmly rooted the form thus modified, the more effective its nonsensical violation as the agent of semiosis. The following quatrain, again a "collective" poem from the heroic age of surrealism, owes its form and its significance to the scrambling of a well-established cliché (and one charged with emotional overtones), *soif du sang*—almost always encountered in the phrase *avoir soif de sang* [to be bloodthirsty]:

> Le jeûne des vampires aura pour conséquence la soif
>   qu'a le sang d'être bu
> La soif qu'a le sang d'épouser la forme des ruisseaux
> La soif qu'a le sang de jaillir dans les endroits déserts
> La soif qu'a le sang de l'eau fraîche du couteau[39]

a consequence of the vampires' fasting will be the blood's thirst for being swallowed, the blood's thirst for taking on the shape of brooks, the blood's thirst for spurting out in deserted places, the blood's thirst for the fresh water of the knife

The poem is built on an anaphora (*soif* introducing a succession of four relative clauses, with *sang* as grammatical subject of each), which expands on our cliché but also distorts it in such a way that its components, isolated as *dindon* and *digue* before, evoke other stereotyped versions of a most shocking transgression: blood being spilled, a violation of a transcendent sociomythic taboo—for blood is the precious liquid par excellence, no drop may be let without awesome symbolic consequences.

Soif du sang[40] is never used literally, "thirst *for* blood" (which meaning would fit the vampire's peculiar appetite). *Soif du sang* plays punlike with two possible meanings of *du*—as if it meant *the blood's thirst* instead of someone's thirst for blood. In which case "thirst" is a metaphor for "desire."[41] Fasting triggers not the hunger of the faster but his prey's craving to be consumed. The blood's thirsting for someone to drink it complements someone's thirsting for blood in one instance: in the thematic structure of the vampire myth, where the monster's lust is reciprocated by his victim's desire to be possessed by him. This reciprocation is the secret of the hold the myth has kept on man's imagination; it is what makes the myth a variant of man's death wish.

It also means that the text offers a false, discursive reading at first decipherment, when it is read as a chain of separate statements, as a musing upon an individual who longs to be stabbed, who seeks fulfillment from a knife between the ribs in some deserted alley.[42] False, because the series of these separate statements bears no relation to the given.[43] Except for the first one, they are even incompatible with the myth, since their only common factor in a linear, nonliterary reading is that *blood* could be a metonym for *violent death*, and this is excluded by the vampiric seduction.

The true reading is the reading that makes the text a synonymic variation on its model—the reading that from beginning to end keeps matching up blood and thirst in accordance with the presuppositions implicit in *vampire*. The text actualizes several components of the *sang* descriptive system, but only such as can also be read as components of the *soif* descriptive system.

The first line contains *boire le sang*, which is not just any derivation from the model but is a hallowed cliché of frenetic literature (also reinforced by *buveur de sang*, until the turn of the century a commonplace term for political or religious fanatics). In the second line, *forme des ruisseaux* has for its hypogram the stereotypes *ruisselant de sang* and *ruisseau (rivière) de sang* [dripping with blood; stream, river of blood] at home in tales of battle. And finally, *the* verb for the spurting or gushing of blood is *jaillir*, found in the third line, while *couteau* in the fourth is associated with descriptions containing that verb.

Boire, ruisseau, and *eau fraîche* also refer to ways of slaking your thirst (*ruisseau* may not be the most obvious one in everyday life, but in French literature down to romanticism, it regularly relieved the parched throats of such stock characters as travelers and shepherds). *Jaillir* looks like the exception that can refer only to blood; but while the sentence seems to be and actually is about the dangers of deserted streets, we recognize in it the hypogram *jaillir dans le désert* [gush forth in the desert], the standard allusion to the spring that flowed out of the rock smitten by Moses in the Sinai. A hyperbole (a miracle) of thirst-quenching that must be completed by mention of the liquid, *eau fraîche* (not just plain *eau* because of the polarization from *désert*). Since that group is displaced by *sang*, which the matrix dictated, *eau fraîche* surfaces as a meliorative qualifier of *couteau*.

Of course this is nonsensical in a language still conforming to referential function, and so is the impossible circularity of *soif d'être bu*. But these forms are meaningful as transcodings of the metaphorized desire we saw as a corollary (the *conséquence*) of the matrix. Scrambling substitutes for referentiality (the relationship between the words for blood and blood itself) new semantic equivalences (here, between the words for blood and the words for thirst). This is no metaphorical transfer: blood does not "stand for" thirst. These equivalences are due solely to a double entendre carried through the whole text, a single verbal sequence simultaneously actualizing two conflicting texts (two descriptive systems). We read one but have the feeling that it is couched in the language of the other (blood in "thirst code," as it were, and vice versa).

This intertextual referentiality defines as semiotic units groups recognized as clichés, groups made especially effective by their stylistic structure, and at the same time deflected from their ordinary meaning by their membership in two systems. Where grammar precludes this dual allegiance at the lexical level, nonsense embeddings such as *l'eau fraîche du couteau* maintain it at the syntagmatic level. Thus linear, horizontal nonsense becomes significance vertically, along the axis of the text, that is, the vertical axis of adding up: significance is the sum, an image, appropriately enough, of obsession.

Scrambling also affects literary images (perhaps I should say "signed" clichés). For example, it is common (perhaps only in *littérature édifiante*) to describe the body as the prison of the soul; a frequent, extended metaphor exhausts the lexical resources of the *geôle* [jail] descriptive system: the flesh is the chains, death is the key, etc. This transcoding uses the grammar that goes with the lexicon; that is, it respects the natural relationship among these words, thereby making for verisimilitude. Indeed, the aim of the extended metaphor is to prove its aptness by pursuing the analogy, step by step, between a believable body and a believable jail. Whereas Lautréamont, practicing intertextual scrambling for the purpose of destroying traditional literary conventions, writes:

je sens que mon âme est cadenassée dans le verrou de mon corps[44]

I feel my soul is padlocked in my body's bolt

Certainly *cadenas* and *verrou* belong to *geôle*'s descriptive system,[45] but the second cannot contain the first: *dans* is the wrong grammar, and *verrou* replaces the cell it is supposed to lock.

The scrambling of the hypogrammatic descriptive system can be so complete that it entails contradictions, mimetic incompatibilities.

When Lautréamont's narrator squashes a snake, for instance,

> plaquant sur le gazon rougi, d'un coup de mon talon, les courbes fuyantes
> de ta tête triangulaire.[46]

> crushing flat on the reddened grass, with a blow of my heel, the receding
> curves of your triangular head.

The triangular head is a cliché of snake descriptions, and so is *courbes fuyantes* for the rapid creeping, undulating motion of its body; but body and head, coils and triangle are mutually exclusive.

In both our passages, then, the lexical slots of the descriptive syntax are filled with misplaced words. But these words all refer to the matter of the text. The effect is that of a color print where the colors have run over their proper boundaries. The destroyed syntax, the encroaching lexicon annul the mimesis but leave intact the repetitive insistence upon essential characteristics of prison and snake. The words are not permitted their normal hierarchy or mutual collocability, hence are deprived of power to organize a picture, but they retain their power of repetition, that is, they all refer to one kernel word that is un-uttered yet all the more effectively evoked through repeated allusions concentrically pointing to the latent prison and the unmentioned snake. Or better still, by piling up the constituents of the descriptive system *en vrac,* so to speak, they let only the significance show through: in the first case, *the bondage that is life,* in the second, the reptile's very *reptility.* If the descriptive system is thus reduced to a paradigm of metonyms of the same kernel, this amounts to its being a paradigm of synonyms. The text this paradigm generates is attention-getting be-cause as a mimesis it is all wrong. But since the syntactic variations seem unable to distribute the words in a reasonable way, they have to be read not as language but as a kind of musical variation on a single motif.

When the scrambled hypogram is an actual text, part and parcel of the literary corpus, the reader's linguistic competence may not be enough.[47] When he recognizes the intertext and decodes the text as referring to that hypogram, his interpretation comprises not only a decoding but an awareness of a tradition or of a filiation; this aware-ness informs and guides his esthetic evaluation. For in such a case intertextuality parallels the chronology of the text's genesis. A poem of Pierre-Jean Jouve's associates the melancholy of autumn with the boredom of dead desires. The lines

Et la blessure intime et noire qui s'accuse
Du *prince pluvieux* plus mort même que vieux[48]

and the secret black wound—it is getting worse—of the rainy prince
who is indeed more dead than old

do permit a superficial interpretation as one more symbol of *ennui*,
but *prince pluvieux* is absolute nonsense unless taken as shortcircuiting
Baudelaire's third "Spleen": "Je suis comme le *roi* d'un pays *plu-
vieux*."[49] And once this connection is made, the reader must shift from
the temptation to dismiss Jouve's poem as perhaps a trite harping on
a tired theme, to a recognition of the open challenge to Baudelaire:
the text is no longer about *acedia,* it is about the language of ro-
manticism; it is no longer plain lyricism, it is a variation on a phrase
of Baudelaire's.

The personal circumstances of one's cultural acquisition are infinitely
varied. It is thus a frequent accident of the reading process that one
discovers the hypogram long after reading the text whose decoding
problems that hypogram solves. No matter when the discovery is made,
the first reading stage, that is, the perception of ungrammaticality, is
already interpretative, even though it has to fail in part or remain
incomplete. During this phase personal symbolisms come in.[50] Even-
tually there follows a second stage—the hypogram is at last identified,
in part because the cruces left at the first stage loom so large in the
reader's mind that when he finally does encounter the hypogram, the
faintest perception of similarity will trigger contact. So that the more
arrant the nonsense of the derivative text, the more likely its bizarre-
ness is to facilitate the hypogram retrieval process. It is entirely pos-
sible for a reader to miss the hypogram, if only because part of the
intertextual corpus always drops out of memory as time flies and culture
changes. Since there are degrees of scrambling-induced nonsense, the
less blatant may yield to interpretation of the first-stage kind, whereas
the more extreme keep the reader shut out. But in both cases, while
the meaning of the successive sentences may be separately grasped, the
poem's significance (its nonreferential meaning as a whole) remains
stored away in the lost hypogram.

My example here is a Jules Laforgue poem. The subject: a lonely
man's daydream, his longing for sex. The scene: a stifling summer
afternoon; the narrator is panting in the sultry heat.

Le blanc soleil de juin amollit les trottoirs
Sur mon lit, seul, prostré comme en ma sépulture
. . . .

4 Je râle doucement aux extases des soirs

. . . .

Tout est un songe. O! viens, corps soyeux que j'adore,
10 Fondons-nous, et sans but, plus oublieux encore;
Et tiédis longuement ainsi mes yeux fermés.[51]

the white sun of June melts the sidewalks. On my bed, alone, I am
prostrate as in my grave, my death rattle sighs out softly into the ecstasies
of evenings . . . It is all a dream. Oh come, silky body that I adore, let
us dissolve into each other, and without purpose, more oblivious yet. . . .

The narrator's peak of morose frustration is also the climax of the
reader's frustration by obscurity—a significant coincidence, for therein
lies the key to intertextual decoding. This climax involves the two
cruces forming the second stanza. I count two because the first yields
a decipherable symbolism even if the true solution remains unfound,
while the second more effectively blocks understanding—almost com-
pletely, in fact—even at the second reading stage. The first crux:

5 Un relent énervant expire d'un mouchoir
Et promène sur mes lèvres sa chevelure

an enervating scent breathes out of a handkerchief—the scent passes its
hair lightly across my lips

We are in some doubt as to whether this is the hair of a handker-
chief or the hair of an aroma—two proposals equally audacious and
equally ridiculous. Since a hairy handkerchief would be a bit much,
our instinct would rather give the hair to the scent: it is at least com-
mon knowledge, and a literary theme into the bargain, that woman's
hair is fragrant. But the inverted order within the group and the
equivocal role of *mouchoir* are too striking: the text must go on look-
ing like a well-nigh mad animization of the perfume. This interpre-
tation is all the easier because perfume is an obvious metonym for
woman. In other words, the ungrammaticality is compensated for by
the reader's readiness to fantasize. The very anomalousness of the sen-
tence qua grammar delineates a verbal unit qua context, and within
this context the mere collocation of *mouchoir, parfum, lèvres, cheve-
lure,* however impossible grammatically, is in itself enough to license
an imaginary construct (starting with the four close-together words,
fragments, as it were, of a broken sentence) wherein longed-for sex sym-
bolizes a yearning for perfect harmony. The contextual aptness of
this symbolism is confirmed in this case, once the hypogram is iden-

tified, that is, when Laforgue's ungrammaticalities succeed in pushing the reader toward contact with Baudelaire's "La Chevelure":

> O toison, moutonnant jusque sur l'encolure
> O boucles! *O parfum chargé de nonchaloir!*
> Extase! Pour peupler ce soir l'alcôve obscure
> Des souvenirs dormant dans cette *chevelure,*
> Je la veux agiter dans l'air comme un *mouchoir!*

Ecstasy! To fill the dark alcove tonight with the memories sleeping in that hair, I want to shake it out in the air like a handkerchief!

Here, then, is where the rule is laid down that establishes the equivalence of scent and memory. Implicit reference to this poem permits the Laforgue text to omit or bypass the beloved and replace her with the lingering presence of her perfume (substitution is not too strong a word, since her perfume assumes the woman's function and makes love to the fantasizing narrator). Out of a metonymy in the hypogram, intertextuality has made possible an otherwise unacceptable metaphor. The substitution here is comparable to the shortcut in Jouve's poem. Even though it causes, in each text, a kind of semantic "scandal" (the transfer of a symbolic value from kingdom to king in Jouve, from woman to perfume in Laforgue), still this very scandal points to a highly acceptable meaning, a preestablished symbolism valid in any context (bad weather as symbol of melancholy, fragrance as symbol of sexuality). So that this formal and semantic unit, delineated in the text by elements derived from the hypogram, guides the reader with its very gaps, with the omitted constituents of the hypogram. *These implied constituents exercise as much control at the hermeneutic stage as the explicit ones.*

The second crux (lines 7–8) offers much more resistance to any attempt at solving it:

> Et, comme un piano voisin rêve en mesure,
> Je tournoie au concert rythmé des encensoirs

and while a neighbor's piano beats a dreamy tempo, I am waltzing to the rhythmic concert of the censers

A first reading turns up no acceptable meaning. For one thing, the speaker's spinning about is, strictly speaking, incompatible with his prostrate position on the bed. True, the reader takes care of this by hypothesizing a metaphor or a sensory illusion, like the dizzy whirl of a fainting spell. Either one is consistent with the depressiveness or even death-throes of stanza one, although perhaps not consistent with the actual musical accompaniment in line 7, which swings away from giddiness toward waltzing. Any first-level interpretation must be strained here, since the text hardly permits a visualization of what goes on. This alone, by the way, would suffice to establish the literariness of this portion of the text, for cognitive language allows or at least seems to promise visualization (and of course a metaphor like the piano "dreamily" keeping time confirms the literariness).[52] Further, even if this difficulty can be dealt with, nothing at all can be done with the censers. For censers are not musical instruments, and fancy as we will their ritual pendulum-swings beating out a musical rhythm, they remain unmotivated in context. So that the image in line 8 has two functions. First, its ungrammaticality (the *encensoir*'s nonsense) looks like a hyperbole[53] of the connotations of the two words to which incense may be remotely related: *extase* (line 4) and the intoxicating fragrance in line 5. The second function of the image stems from the fact it stands so stubbornly in the way of the reader's interpretation: its formal conspicuousness and its semantic opaqueness suggest an incomplete statement crying out for completion by the rest of the sentence, which lurks somewhere in an intertext.

And completion does indeed take place, since there is only one French text that links incense-burners and twisting movement within the same sentence; where the whirling is at the same time waltzing and dizziness; where perfume and music are equated, and both perfume and music are bound to an evocation of evening; and where the significance is a representation of harmony between man and woman, the spiritual correspondence, either realized now or remembered or longed for, being symbolized by the couple. That text, "Harmonie du soir," happens to be very familiar—one of Baudelaire's most quoted, most imitated poems, and also one most often set to music:

> Voici venir les temps où vibrant sur sa tige
> Chaque fleur s'évapore ainsi qu'un encensoir;
> Les sons et les parfums tournent dans l'air du soir;
> Valse mélancolique et langoureux vertige!

Now come the times when every flower, quivering on its stem, evaporates like a censer; sounds and perfumes swing round in the air of evening; melancholy waltz, languorous vertigo!

Here the scrambling is even more pronounced than in "La Chevelure," since Laforgue's line 8 conflates Baudelaire's lines 2 and 3, and metonymically represents, and implicitly alludes to, Baudelaire's line 4. In fact, the synonymy the line posits between waltz and giddiness is the presupposition now enabling the reader to interpret correctly not only the speaker's whirling sensation but also the connection between piano and dizziness. On the surface it looked like a mere superimposition of sensory impressions: nauseated depression exacerbated by the sounds of normal life going on close by. Now the superimposition appears to be a general law, attested as it is in the intertext: the statement of a law of mystic correspondence between music, perfume, and the sense of loneliness or yearning—that is, a representation of potential harmony.[54] This potential harmony clearly constitutes the significance of Laforgue's poem as a whole, as a single unit of meaning. This much is obvious now that the reader, thanks to the Baudelaire hypogram, can see that line 8 is a cryptic, initial statement of the message set forth a second time, and more plainly, in the third stanza: the dreamed-of union. Without that context the reader would not recognize this synonymy or repetition or formal variation on the same meaning, which is an essential feature of the literary text.

Again, the very obscurity of *encensoir* in Laforgue, if read in isolation, would suffice to give the word its function: it hyperbolizes, as we saw, connotations of fragrance. But it fully performs this function only if backed up by the Baudelaire hypogram, because only then does the hyperbole focus on a word that is already *the* metonym for "fragrance," that is, *fleur; encensoir* as a metaphor for *flower* is thus the more effective because it summons up a vast intertext, the stereotyped simile so many times encountered: flowers as incense-burners.[55]

Last, an indirect reference to Baudelaire's throbbing violin (in his second stanza: "Chaque fleur s'évapore comme un encensoir;/Le violon frémit comme un cœur qu'on afflige") motivates in Laforgue's poem a final image that would otherwise be a gratuitous and ludicrous combination of the devil's-fiddle or pied-piper theme and the hooked atoms of Lucretius:

> Depuis l'éternité, croyez-le bien, Madame,
> L'Archet qui sur nos nerfs pince ces tristes gammes
> Appelait pour ce jour nos atomes charmés

Since all eternity, believe me, Madame, the violin bow that scrapes these dismal scales across our nerve-strings has been summoning together our enraptured atoms, for this happy day

Thus the correct, that is, the complete interpretation of the poem is made possible for the reader only by the intertext. This neatly frees us of any temptation to believe that in such a poem there can be referentiality to a nonverbal universe: *the poem carries meaning only by referring from text to text.*

Two final remarks: first, scrambling and the hypogram it necessarily points to presuppose the presence of an author, an intent on his part to play with another text and stimulate a comparison. In this particular case, it is at least possible to say—without questioning intentional fallacy in general—that the *scrambled text is an icon of intention.* Second, the fact that this comparison is the reader's responsibility does not make reading dependent upon his idiosyncrasies: the system of inescapable ungrammaticalities makes *reading* a *restrictive process.* The only freedom left to the reader is the certainty that his reading is wrong, his task unfinished, so long as the ungrammaticalities are not removed.

Genre-Induced Obscurity

Obscurity results from an interference of the genre's structures and of those of descriptive systems. Obscurity bespeaks literariness not just the way nonsense does, symbolizing artifice, or cancelling utilitarian communication. Obscurity betokens literariness by symbolizing the reader's participation in an activity reserved to an elite: the perception of the generic interpretant presupposes that enough texts have been read to enable the reader to recognize them as class tokens, belonging to a genre.

An example from Mallarmé is in order: the Goncourt brothers were not distorting his intent when they quoted him as saying that "a poem is a mystery and it is up to the reader to look for the key."[56] I have chosen *Don du Poème*—one of his simpler poems. Simpler in that they are easy to paraphrase or translate. Here is the story: At dawn, after a long day's night of work on a poem called *Hérodiade* (concerning a native of Edom, or Idumaea), Mallarmé finds himself hating the poem. Nevertheless he decides to offer it as homage to his wife, who is now nursing their child of the flesh. To quote one of Mallarmé's commentators, Mauron, "the symmetry of situation awakens in him emotion tempered with humor," and he playfully suggests to her that she suckle his infant poem:

> Je t'apporte l'enfant d'une nuit d'Idumée!
> Noire, à l'aile saignante et pâle, déplumée,
> Par le verre brûlé d'aromates et d'or,
> Par les carreaux glacés, hélas! mornes encor,

L'aurore se jeta sur la lampe angélique.
Palmes! et quand elle a montré cette relique
A ce père essayant un sourire ennemi,
La solitude bleue et stérile a frémi.
O la berceuse, avec ta fille et l'innocence
De vos pieds froids, accueille une horrible naissance:
Et ta voix rappelant viole et clavecin,
Avec le doigt fané presseras-tu le sein
Par qui coule en blancheur sibylline la femme
Pour les lèvres que l'air du vierge azur affame?

Gift of the Poem. I bring you the child of a night in Idumaea! Black, with bleeding wing and pale, plucked, Through the glass burnt with aromatics and with gold, Through the frozen panes, alas, still dreary, Dawn threw herself on the angelic lamp. Palms! And when Dawn showed this relic To this father attempting a hostile smile, The blue and sterile solitude shivered. O lullabying woman, with your daughter and the innocence Of your cold feet, welcome a horrid birth: Your voice is reminiscent of viol and harpsichord, With a withered finger will you press the breast From which Woman flows in whiteness sibylline For the lips starved by the air of the virgin azure?

One thing is certain: any reader familiar with Mallarmé will recognize images that are true verbal obsessions, occurring in a number of his poems. If we make a comparison, for instance, between our poem, one entitled *Sainte,* and the prose poem called *Le Démon de l'Analogie,* we shall find windowpanes, archaic musical instruments, a finger pressing on something like an instrument, a wing in all three poems (with the feathers plucked out in two), and an angel, in person or deducible from the wing and the palm. Moving from poem to poem, we can plot lexical coincidences that shape the image of a musician-angel always associated with a window or a windowpane. These coincidences, the fact that they are always elliptical—the unchanging components, the *Knotenpunkte* of analysis—enable us to reconstitute a consistently repressed or displaced narrative whose fragments remain obscure only so long as they are out of context. Once set back into context, they become meaningful and, of course, symbolic in Mallarmé's subconscious. For example, Jeffrey Mehlman,[57] who pointed out the shortcomings of the first French attempts at literary psychoanalysis, nonetheless believes that the narrative thus strung together is the only possible explanation for words like *Palmes,* which cannot be explained solely inside the poem. *Palmes* would thus be the surfacing of the latent angel linked in other texts with the palm and the wing. French psychocritics (*their* term) insist upon recognizing in the angel Mallarmé's elder sister and his mother; both died when he was still a child, both were the objects of his incestuous fixation (their angelization is based upon a Roman Catholic euphemism used around French children: a deceased female relative is alluded to as an angel who goes on living in Heaven). A nonsensical remark overheard by the narrator in *Le Démon de l'Analogie,* "La pénultième est morte," is supposed to be about the mother, dead ten years before the sister—penultimate indeed. The sound of old or broken musical instruments must certainly represent the voices of the lost loved ones. And the window must be a transform of the tombstone. Like the tombstone, the window separates creatures who love each other. (In literature the window shuts you out; you see through it without being able to touch what you see, or else you wait in vain as you gaze through the glass.)

Charles Mauron tries to demonstrate that the *doigt fané* belongs to the dead female who haunts Mallarmé. He also points out that this finger is significantly weak ("withered" being a variant of this debility). Way back in an early story, *Three Storks,* which supposedly contains the key to the latent network of the poet's imaginary universe, the dead is sewn into his shroud, unable to lift it with his finger (*sans le pouvoir soulever du doigt*). The stained-glass saint of the poem *Sainte* places this same finger on an otherworldly harp made of an angel's wing. Finally, in *Le Démon de l'Analogie,* the narrator with his finger awakens in an instrument played by Memory the sound of no sound (*son nul*). This finger is laid upon lips that open less on a mouth than on a netherworld (*orifice du mystère*).

Our text's latent significance is that the poet's wife and his newborn daughter (*avec ta fille*) now hide his dead mother and sister. This breaks through in details like the coldness of the feet, and the voice reminiscent of viol and harpsichord, therefore the voice of the past, the voice of death.[58]

This explanation is no doubt tempting, since it accounts for many different things at the same time, and it may be valid for some hidden meaning of the poem. But it is a meaning that remains hidden. In any event, we do not have to discover the meaning concealed by the text in order to interpret the traces left by that meaning on the surface, for these can be read as plain realistic detail, as components of the system of verisimilitude. *Fané* evokes a woman weary after giving birth. Cold feet are a familiar inconvenience of nocturnal congress in the marriage bed. Remember, for instance, Charles Bovary's dissatisfaction with his first wife: "he had lived for fourteen months with a widow whose feet in bed were as cold as icicles."[59]

No matter what their secret motivation, such details never lack surface motivation, and at no point is the secret one relevant to a reading of the poem. Nowhere in *Don du Poème* do we have elements that if recognized as components of the latent network would signify differently from the words surrounding them. All we can say about the lexical traces left in the poem by the network is that they provide a kind of fingerprint evidence that the text belongs to the Mallarmé corpus.

Even if the latent network generates unusual word clusters, any reading problem they may create is palliated by the context. "Withered" (*fané*) is certainly a strange adjective for "finger" (*doigt*), but much less strange for occurring only half a line away from "breast." For we have the cliché *sein flétri*, "withered breast," commonly applied to the flaccid breast of an aging female worn out by many nursings. *Fané* particularizes for flowers (and, by extension, for feminine beauty) the general *flétri*. It is thus Mallarmé's scrambling of the cliché: *sein fané* is found in another poem, *Le Guignon*. The finger pressing milk from the nipple is as withered as the nipple itself—verbal contamination of a whole scene permeated in every detail with *post partum* fatigue. Words, apparently explicable only if we assume a system of repressed representation, are remotivated and overdetermined at the surface level of the text. This is the case even with *Palmes*. Critics have done plenty of squabbling over this: it is a symbol of triumph, a symbol of martyrdom, a resplendent image (its veins are to the palm what the sun's rays are to the dawn—I do not exaggerate), etc. Whatever it may mean, it has been stuck there at the back of our minds ever since *Idumée* appeared at the head of the text. Not because of Vergil's "Primus Idumaeas referam tibi, o Mantua, palmas"[60] [I shall be the first, O Mantua, to bring thee back Idumaean palms]—a line to which every exegete makes sure to refer his hapless reader. But because *palmes d'Idumée* entrenched itself as a cliché, from Ronsard (who uses it eighteen times) to Chateaubriand. *Palmes* is thus always attracted by *Idumée*, and its occurrence here is triggered at the point of interference by another sequence of words in which *palme* figures, that is, the *ange* descriptive system—palm being the allegorical attribute of the angel. Once *angélique* has interfered with the Idumaean derivation, *palmes* surges forth twice motivated. The startling suddenness of dawn calls for an exclamation. Alexandre Dumas is said to have

carelessly written of one of his heroines: "Ah! Ah! she cried in Portu-
guese." This is probably apocryphal. But *palme* need be nothing more
than an exultant *Ah!* in the angel language of Edom: the transfer of
the exclamatory intonation from a mere interjection to a meaningful
word is all the easier because the palm, as a symbol of victory, happens
to be the visual equivalent of a triumphant cry.[61]

The real difficulty of the poem stems from the fact that a set of
generic rules supersedes the mimetic rules. The entire piece is derived
from its title, which constitutes the semantic given; this is both neces-
sary and sufficient for complete decoding. The title tells us about the
content of the poem, but it so happens that this content has a form.
Perhaps I should say it *is* a form: it is a genre, an entity that is per-
ceived through comparative readings in an intertext. The genre sets
limits to a text's potential verbal associations and allows the reader to
harbor certain expectations once he has identified the text as belong-
ing to the maxim, for instance, or to the Gothic novel. The difference
between a fixed form (like the sonnet) and a genre is that the genre
has a grammar and this grammar merely develops a very limited
number of matrix sentences. The Gothic novel, for example, is built
upon the expansion of sentences linking innocence and a threat to that
innocence, and linking the threat and the past, with the corollary that
the past is secret.

Now there are titles that simply indicate that the poem belongs to a
certain genre; they are pointers letting the reader know what rules the
text will follow. I am thinking of such titles as Bucolic or Elegy. Mal-
larmé's title differs from these only by conversion. Here the conver-
sion transfers the name of the genre from one stylistic level to another.
For the words *don du poème* are a periphrasis of the word *dédicace*,
[dedication]. They are a variant in lyric poetry style of that matrix
whose variants in the genre's normal style would be *A Madame X,* or
Au lecteur, or *Le poète au lecteur.* This conversion cannot be read
without calling the reader's attention to the very fact of the verbal
detour, since nothing seems to justify this detour (and yet it is not
so farfetched as to prevent him from identifying the matrix and there-
fore the genre this given points to). This genre, limited enough histor-
ically and dying today, is the dedicatory epistle. The word *don* here
actualizes (as a Mallarmean variant) an essential semantic component
of "dedicatory."

Even though it generally has little to do with the content of the
work of art it is dedicating, the dedication must mention the title of

that text. In Mallarmé's poem, this rule generates the first line; but instead of simply the title, *Hérodiade,* we get the periphrasis *l'enfant d'une nuit d'Idumée.* Here *l'enfant* refers to both a character born in the country of Edom and to a poem about this character composed during the night.

The dedicatory epistle solicits both the reader's indulgence and the godparent's protection. It is thus the variant of a structural invariant whose three functions—giver, gift, and recipient—are embodied in three concrete forms: the author, the work, and the reader. The work is at the semantic crossroads of a creator-to-creation relationship and a story of difficult beginnings, of risks taken. The threatened and vulnerable work will inevitably be metaphorized as a child, hyperbole of vulnerability and object of protection. For example, from the pen of Rousseau—the poet, not the philosopher—Jean-Baptiste, not Jean-Jacques:

> Vous me dites qu'il faut brûler mon livre
> Hélas! Le pauvre enfant ne demandait qu'à vivre[62]

You say I must burn my book: Alas! the poor child asked only to live

It is clear that the transformation of the title's *poème* into the *enfant* of the first line derives its significance from the genre's semantic structure. The aim of the dedicatory epistle (a genre permits the encoding of intention within a text) is to insure the success of the work. The relationship between giver and receiver of the gift will therefore be that the giver asks the receiver to protect the child. Since a request usually presupposes compensation, some return to the person of whom the request is made, this request will take the form of a transfer of ownership. Here the giver asks the recipient to assume the responsibilities of an adoptive parent.

In many cases, especially in the seventeenth century, when writer and patron were socially far apart, the request for child adoption was not direct; it was expressed as a mere hope that the work might be found worthy to bear the receiver's name, worthy of a nobler family. But when there is no longer any need for discretion, texts become more explicit. If the receiver is male, the boon sought is adoption, guardianship, or at least avuncular benevolence. An example is Robert Herrick's epistle "To His Verses":

> What will ye (my poor Orphans) do
> When I must leave the World (and you)
> Who'l give ye then a sheltring shed,

Or credit ye, when I am dead?
Who'l let ye by their fire sit? . . .

I cannot tell! unlesse there be
Some Race of old humanitie
Left of the large heart, and long hand
Alive, as Noble *Westmorland;*
Or gallant *Newark;* which brave two
May fost'ring fathers be to you.
If not; expect to be no less
Ill us'd, than Babes left fatherless.[63]

If a woman is being approached, the appeal for protection is inextricably bound up with a suggestion of amorous complicity between her and the author. The following stanzas, translated from a Théophile Gautier "Sonnet of Dedication," seem to be saying "I offer you my child," and at the same time saying "I should like to have a child who looks like you":

Venus wants a hundred doves. . . . For my goddess I have nothing but a pen! I dare raise myself up to you. And trembling I lay upon the white altar of your knees divine, my offering, my book.

Your guardian name shines on the frontispiece. . . . And in your portrait, set in cameo, the beauty beams that beams not in my verse.

Since Homer, certainly, touching the knees has been a gesture of the suppliant. But in the foregoing text, contemporary with Mallarmé's (1869), the knees and the glimpsed whiteness of those knees, the touching of the flesh, can only be erotic. It is but a step from taking care of a child together to going to bed together, and we have quite a few texts that rewrite the generic invariant in genetic terms. Listen to Molière's Trissotin giving *his* sonnet to his bluestocking paramour:

Alas, it is a newborn child, Madame. Its fate must surely move you. And it was in your Courtyard that I just gave it birth. . . . Your approval can be a mother to it.

An error made by the scholar Denis Saurat, from whom I borrow this quotation, is rather revealing. Instead of *Cour,* "courtyard," he writes —and thus brings to light what the text has been suppressing—"Et c'est dans votre Cœur que j'en viens d'accoucher" (And I just gave birth to it in your bosom).[64]

Acceptance of the role of mother by the woman to whom the epistle

is addressed generates descriptions of either maternal protectiveness
(here, *O la berceuse*) or even of a functional substitute (again in our
sonnet, the suckling in the second tercet).

Such is the system of restrictions established by the semantic given
of the genre, restrictions governing the narrative and descriptive gen-
eration of the poem. Now, as we have seen, the basic semiotic mecha-
nism is that any sign system can structure another of a higher level of
complexity and become a mere code serving to signify something else.
Thus with a poem of Hugo's entitled "Envoi des *Feuilles d'automne*,"
subtitled *A Madame * * **. The lady in question is Marie Menessier-
Nodier, and French students are still taught, for what it is worth, that
Hugo was pursuing her. But even without such instruction, they could
make a shrewd guess, for the poem was removed from the *Feuilles
d'automne,* the collection it was supposed to preface and dedicate, and
was included in another collection (*Chants du Crépuscule,* XVIII),
where it is irrelevant. The metaphor of the dedication therefore re-
sumes its literal meaning, and the appeal for protection of the de-
fenseless opus serves only to encode an appeal for sympathy with the
author:

> Ce livre errant qui va l'aile brisée,
> Et que le vent jette à votre croisée
> Comme un grêlon à tous les murs cogné,
>
> Hélas! . . .
> Le froid, la pluie, et mille éclairs obliques
> L'ont assailli, le pauvre nouveau-né. . . .
>
> Voici qu'il boite après avoir plané! . . .
>
> Ouvrez, Marie, ouvrez-lui votre porte,
> Raccommodez ses vers estropiés!
>
> Dans votre alcôve à tous les vents bien close,
> Pour un instant souffrez qu'il se repose,
> Qu'il se réchauffe au feu de vos trépieds,
>
> Qu'à vos côtés, à votre ombre, il se couche,
> Oiseau plumé, qui, frileux et farouche,
> Tremble et palpite, abrité sous vos pieds!

This wandering book with its broken wing, that the wind hurls against
your window like hail driven against walls, alas! . . . cold, rain and
lightning bolts pursue it, poor newborn child. . . . Here he is, limping

by, when not long since he flew. . . . Open, Marie, open your door to him. Mend his broken feet. Let him, for a moment, rest in your sleeping alcove. . . . Let him take comfort at the fire of your foot warmer. Let him lie down beside you, in your shadow, a plucked bird, chilled and wild, trembling, all aflutter, sheltering beneath your feet.

Obviously this somewhat risqué entreaty seeks benefits for the writer rather than for his writings. "Let him lie down beside you" is really a bit much for Diogenes' feathered biped. The other one is what the text is really talking about. We have here another genre—erotic lyricism—or rather a subgenre, the propitiatory offering. The change in the semantic given of the genre does not modify the invariant, though, since the functions remain the same. Only the beneficiary changes, since he is no longer the transferred but rather the transferer. As for the object to be protected, the metaphor replaces the child at the breast, present or future orphan, with a wounded bird. But the substitution, however complete, does not destroy the function of the orphan's transference: significantly, Hugo calls the bird *le pauvre nouveau-né*.

The new image is generated by a triple hypogrammatic derivation—the bird linked with the book, with the woman as Good Samaritan, and with the woman as sexual target. The resulting semantic overdetermination makes the bird[65] the interpretant for the poem's imagery and gives it its aptness. The bird readily becomes the metaphor for the book as such, or a metonym for verse, or for the writer, because the soaring of the bird has already been linked to images of poetic inspiration. The bird walks as well as it flies, or somewhat less well: this opposition comes in handy for representing the duality of man and *vates* in the poet's persona. An opposition easily polarized—"lofty flight" versus "lamed wing." In Hugo's poem, after having soared, the bird limps.[66] The opposition is further determined here by a pun: you can say that an unmetrical line is crippled (*estropié*) or limps, a wordplay on "feet," anatomical and prosodic. Second, the wounded-bird theme coincides at one point with the literary representations of woman: the motif of the maiden who nurses the little bird's broken wing back to health—a cliché dramatizing female tenderness (or tender femininity). Third, the theme of woman as an object of desire is conveyed by a narrative stereotype as old as the Latin elegy and Lesbia's sparrow. The beloved carries her feathered pet in her bosom, thereby turning it into a metaphor for the lover who would like nothing better than to be metamorphosed instead of being metaphorized. The French, sly by nature, have occasionally exchanged the bird for a character even tinier and more intimate, such as the flea on a fair lady's breast (celebrated in a garland of love poems, *La Puce de Mademoiselle Desroches,* 1583). In Hugo's *Envoi,* however, structural interference scrambles the stereotype and chooses as shelter for the shivering bird the lady's feet instead of her bosom. For the dedicator is still only a suppliant and must restrict himself to kissing feet.

I have not dwelt upon this text just to demonstrate once more the mechanics of derivation, or its readiness to yield to any modification of the matrix. I have dwelt upon it because Mallarmé used Hugo's poem as a prefabricated code. Instead of activating the dedicatory-letter genre directly from its invariant, Mallarmé used the ready-made variant he found in Hugo. Awareness of the latter and the double reading that follows on this awareness are in no way essential to de-cipherment of the form. Comparing the two is simply one possible reading for one or two generations of readers. Traditional philologists can also have fun discovering that the cold feet of Mallarmé's women are only a step away from Marie's and from her *trépied.* All this is of course irrelevant to our experience of the text. Taken by themselves, the structures of Mallarmé's sonnet are adequately encoded for a complete reading.

What *is* relevant in Mallarmé's variations on Hugo is that the functions, the setting, and the scene enacted in it are left intact. Mallarmé's text seems much looser or less coherent than Hugo's. And yet overdetermination by the genre's matrix must be the same. We still have a symbolic visitation, a wounded bird, a call for help. The obscurities stem from the fact that, within a syntactic frame left untouched, new words have been inserted. "Dawn" is substituted for "bird," that is, the moment of inspiration is substituted for inspiration itself or the poem it gives birth to. The broken wing is rewritten in the words most natural to Mallarmé on such a topic, that is, his obsessive angel lexicon. The adoptive mother is the writer's wife, a conquest already made, so to speak, but she must still be seduced into suckling her husband's bastard. Some scholars assume that allusions of this kind to the poet's intimate personal life must be obscure, but here at least the poem tells us all we need to know. The real difficulty lies in a conflict of verbal sequences. The grammar derived from the matrix (the grammar of the bird scene) does not quite fit the lexicon of dawn, the stereotypes of that lexicon and *their* grammar, and it fits even less where the possibilities of association are further restricted by the lexicon of the Mallarmean bird—the angel.

This is all a matter of description, for the *fact,* the mechanics of the

substitution itself, are no problem. The bird has been totally human-
ized elsewhere: Musset's Muse in *Nuit de Mai* or Banville's in *Roses
de Noël* comes tapping at the window with her wing. Or the bird
loses its feathers and becomes the mere geometry of a bird: André
Breton's inspiration comes to him in the shape of a *sentence* knocking
against the pane (first *Manifeste du Surréalisme*, 1924). Of the tenuous
bird only its flight may be left and still the symbolism remains unim-
paired. In our poem, however, the difficulty is that the bird is meatier,
the scene is sketched more precisely. In short, we have the elements
of realism, the more opaque appearance of real objects, and this stands
between us and their symbolic role. But the trouble is only a retarda-
tion; this is only pseudorealism, the objects are still just words, not
things. Commentators compound the difficulty by filling out a com-
plete angel with the aid of other Mallarmé texts, because then the
scene is too small for all three birds—the real one, the mythic, and
the metaphorical. The contradictions become manageable the instant
we recognize that they are all a matter of lexicon. The adjectives de-
picting the wing's shattered condition apply comfortably to a mere
real bird except for the humanization of "pale"—but humanization
itself is very acceptable in an allegory. Of the exploded angel, only the
fragments remain that fit the matrix: the adjective *angélique* alone
is left. Freed of its burden of representation, the adjective simply means
what it always means in a context of portent and miracle. The lamp is
not angelic because its light is so lovely, as some critics actually believe,
but because it illuminates a remarkable birth, because it is an agent
of Annunciation. The dawn and the bird lexicon filter each other
out, as it were, in similar fashion. Dawn is topical, since its light re-
veals the product of a night's work. *Relique* has to be added to make
clear that night has left something behind. And the window glass is
multiplied by two: the panes are retained in the poem, since they are
the obstacle against which the bird hurls himself. But the glass of
the lamp is also needed, because this bird is dawn; the theme of
struggle between lamplight and daylight is well established: the lamp
casts its rays upon an orgy of the flesh (as in Baudelaire's *L'aube
spirituelle* [Spiritual Dawn]) or upon an orgy of the spirit. In quite
a few poems and novels written since the French romantic era, the
unequal combat signals the end of nocturnal tribulations and a new
beginning.

Thus it is that the genre, because it is a grammar, reorders the
words and destroys or threatens their connotations in the language.

Hence the obscurity. Dawn, for example, is a positive representation in the language. Describing it as a wounded bird subverts established relationships so that the reader is confused. Starting with *noire* in the second line, the accumulation of pejorative statements insists that dawn be seen as negative, as if the following four-line sentence were a blow-up of a dark dawn oxymoron. As always, this ungrammaticality is at one and the same time the locus of obscurity and the index to the solution. It signals that the words cannot be taken at face value, that they are forced to conform to a structure other than that of their referents—here, the transference structure defined by the genre.

The poem ends on another such incongruity, which again functions as a signal that the genre structure is transforming the mimetic into the symbolic. This incongruity is the description of the breast feeding. Everyone sees the scene, of course, as an affectionate, smiling allusion to Mallarmé's personal circumstances. But that does not account for the double anomaly: a strange adjective, *sibylline*, and the slight but unmistakable vulgarity of a phrase that implies the nurse has sprung a leak (*le sein par qui coule*).

Critics, to be sure, do their best to explain *sibylline*, but their explanations are mere paraphrases. Says Walzer, "the milk is a philter"—I suppose he means it is both nourishment and mystery. Here is Chisholm: "A young mother suckling her baby is performing more than a physiological act. She is participating in a mystery as old as mankind and the animal world, penetrating into the arcana of disinterested maternal tenderness." Jean-Pierre Richard: "Where does this milk come from? and how does it reach us? Where has it found its nutritional power?" Questions which of course remain unanswered. But *sibylline* puzzles critics only because the text has grown older. The system of the poem fails because language has changed. In the French of today *sibylline* is the hyperbolic equivalent of "incomprehensible," since tradition has it that the Sibyl's oracular message was always so ambiguous and arcane that it only hid more darkly the future it was supposed to be revealing. In the nineteenth century, however, and for our poet's contemporaries—as one glance at the Littré dictionary (Mallarmé's favorite tool) will show—*sibylline* meant only prophetic, or laden with portentous meaning.[67] For instance, Mallarmé recognizes genius in a child by the sign on his forehead—a sibylline star. In his sonnet on Wagner (*Hommage*), the ink of the musical score, the music's poetic message, is described as *sanglot sibyllin* [sibylline sobbing]. As for *couler*, it upsets the critics, but they dismiss it—revealingly, perhaps

—as an instance of Précieux or baroque explicitness in imagery. In fact, the anomaly of the reified mother points to another statement of paternity transference. In our own time, Cocteau spoke of the writer's ink as his inner night pouring out, and of his inspiration as a hemorrhage (*le Sang d'un Poète*). Most Western literatures compare inspiration to an outflow, sometimes seminal, and if painful, of sweat and tears and blood. In Mallarmé this commonplace monopolizes a verb always embarrassing when it refers to a person—it must be as direct a representation as our repressions can tolerate of man's most intimate fountain of fertility. Mallarmé speaks of Loie Fuller as a fountain, and a fountain gushing herself out—something akin to the overflowing woman of *Don du Poème*—and significantly this overflowing, her dance, is a text, since the ballet, says Mallarmé, is a hieroglyph.[68] Elsewhere he describes writing itself as a flowing (*coulée*), and the page as its outfall (*déversoir*).[69] He allegorizes musical inspiration into a Chimaera (the then commonplace image for fantasy) bleeding out a line of melody.[70] It seems to me these examples prove that *couler* is referring not just to milk but to literary output, especially here within the frame of an analogy positing that woman is to child what poet is to poem. Nor is this all. Whiteness, by the same analogy, calls forth a parallelism that fits the genre-defined relationship between dedicator and recipient. Mallarmé says that writing can flow white as well as black: "one does not write white on a dark background, except the stellar alphabet . . . ; man on the contrary keeps writing black on white"[71]—you could not find a more symmetrical pair of variants of the same structure, except where a parallelism like the recurrence of the same epithet makes that symmetry even more obvious: for example, the sibylline weeping of ink in *Hommage à Wagner*,[72] and the sibylline flow of milk in *Don du Poème* clearly mirror each other. Inasmuch as under the rules of the genre motherhood is parallel to authorship and, in the "story" or "plot," the pathetic substitute for the writer when he fails as a parent, the white flowing from the mother is the exact counterpart of the black flowing from a pen.[73] Or else: she is depicted in an *ink* code (the more easily because ink as blackness is the antithesis of milk as whiteness in French as well as English), and this, as it were, fulfills the speaker's wish that she feed the infant. The text does not actually say she will, but at the semiotic level breast feeding has already been translated into writing.

Everything I have said suggests that Mallarmé sticks to the tenet he once set forth in a letter to Stuart Merrill, that poetry must indeed baffle comprehension, but only for an instant. His critics have taken heart from his qualification and have tried to reduce his poetry to music. His poems are in fact built to be intellectually understood. But this understanding is not to be achieved by translating, which leaves the poem behind and yields nothing but a content either trite or trifling. It is to be achieved by the backward and forward comparison, renewed with each rereading, between the poem and its genre's intertextual blueprint. It is only in isolation that the poem is difficult and, when made easy, trite. It makes sense only when read as a metonym of the whole genre—like the antique tessera that was just a shard by itself, but a message when fitted to its matching piece. And its significance lies not in hidden depths, but in the fact of its being a variation on a motif. Not so much a musical variation, since the motif is semantic, as a logogriph.

CONCLUSION

I should like to conclude by returning to the reader, the only one who makes the connections between text, interpretant, and intertext, the one in whose mind the semiotic transfer from sign to sign takes place. Indeed, if the poem—as I have tried to show it does—results from the transformation of a word or sentence into a text, or the transformation of texts into a larger whole, then its form is felt to be a detour or circuitous path around what it means, and this feeling must have two consequences. First, the form or shape of the detour is interpreted as an artifact, with visible joints and props. Hence a constant component of poetic significance is that the poem's language looks as much like a ritual or a game (in many cases the poem is akin to a generalized pun), or pure artifice, as it does like a means of conveying sense. Second, the poem's content, that is, what the detour turns about, is perceived or rather rationalized as an equivalent form at its before-detour, pretransformation stage. The reader more or less explicitly subsumes this content as a colloquial or ordinary-language version of what he is reading. The paradox is that while the poetic text is interpreted as a departure from a norm, that imaginary nonliterary norm is in effect deduced, or even retroactively fantasized, from the text perceived as departure. But no matter what the reader may think, there is no norm that is language as grammars and dictionaries may represent it: the poem is made up of texts, of fragments of texts, integrated with or without conversion into a new system. This material (rather than norm) is not the raw stuff of language; it is already a stylistic structure, hot with intensified connotations, overloaded discourse.

Something else I have had to underscore repeatedly is that any ungrammaticality within the poem is a sign of grammaticality elsewhere, that is, of belonging in another system. The systemic relationship confers significance. The poetic sign has two faces: textually ungrammatical, intertextually grammatical; displaced and distorted in the mimesis system, but in the semiotic grid appropriate and rightly placed. This coincidence of catachresis and propriety influences the hermeneutic process by making reading at once restrictive and unstable.

Far from freeing the imagination, far from giving the reader greater leeway as it invites him to greater participation, reading is actually restrictive: retroactive reading is comparative and sets up equivalences despite the reader's instinctive feeling that the elements equated should not be. In particular, the embedding in the poem of textual borrowings from the hypogram (or the inclusion of textual signs) creates a new hierarchy of words, a new grammar whose very novelty or strangeness makes it harder to ignore or bypass. All the harder because such factors usually occur repeatedly in the poem. The reader's freedom of interpretation is further limited because of the poem's saturation by the semantic and formal features of its matrix: in other words, continuity and unity, that is, the fact that the semiotic unit is the text itself, forbid the attention to wander, deny the opportunities for hermeneutic deviance that the multiple facets of mimesis offer. Finally, the hypograms, whether in intertextual conflict or not, are always incomplete in the poem: they are either pointed to by textual signs or are fragmentarily actualized. Even the dual signs, however equivocal or ambiguous they may appear, do not refer to *n* texts, but to two specific texts. The original architecture of these "other texts," their grammar, the distribution of their lexicon, the sequence of their components, are nonetheless obvious to the reader, since they are part of his linguistic competence; he is therefore under strict guidance and control as he fills the gaps and solves the puzzle. Since reading is restricted, the reader's interpretation is a scanning of the sociolect's commonplaces, the practice of a lore of well-tested *exempla,* the recognition of forms and hallowed symbols through a scrambled transmission.

But reading is also unstable, and interpretation is never final, because the text cannot be corrected or amended, and the ungrammaticalities, however revealing they may be, however hermeneutically indicative, are still an obstacle (whether the obstacle blocks understanding or just looks like an abnormality, an error, a violation of the code rules). Because these ungrammaticalities threaten language as representation, the reader continually seeks relief by getting away from the dubious words, back to safe reality (or to a social consensus as to reality). Which

is possible, however illusorily, only when the reader works from dis-
crete components of the poem considered separately, only when the
retroactive reading process is ignored. But the reader is reconverted to
proper reading when the structural equivalences become apparent all
at once, in a blaze of revelation. This revelation is always chancy, must
always begin anew, since each rereading, or even the instinctive re-
checking of a difficult passage, forces the reader to undergo again the
experience or temptation of a decoding obedient to mimesis, hence
to relive the block of the distortion. The reader's manufacture of mean-
ing is thus not so much a progress through the poem and a half-random
accretion of verbal associations, as it is a seesaw scanning of the text,
compelled by the very duality of the signs—ungrammatical as mimesis,
grammatical within the significance network. This seesawing from one
sign value to the other, this alternating appearance and disappearance
of significance, both in spite and because of unacceptable features on
the plane of mimetic meaning, is a kind of semiotic circularity[1] char-
acterizing the practice of signification known as poetry. In the reader's
mind it means a continual recommencing, an indecisiveness resolved
one moment and lost the next with each reliving of revealed signifi-
cance, and this it is that makes the poem endlessly rereadable and
fascinating.

Notes

1. On the role of text-reader dialectics, see Fish 1970; Riffaterre 1971a, 1971c.

2. Or at least challenge its premises, such as the establishment of a verisimilitude level (like the *effet de réel* of French critical terminology, see Barthes 1970), which becomes the norm for a given text and by opposition to which we can perceive departures—e.g., the fantastic or the supernatural.

3. Significance, to put it simply, is what the poem is really about: it arises through retroactive reading when the discovery is made that representation (or mimesis) actually points to a content that would demand a different representation in nonliterary language. Yet my use of *significance*, however specialized, does not contradict Webster: "the subtle, hidden implications of something, as distinguished from its openly expressed meaning."

4. For an exact definition of sign, especially the differences between index, icon, and symbol, see C. S. Peirce 3.361–62; also Greenlee 1973, and Sebeok 1975. Strictly speaking, Eco 1976, p.16 ("everything that, on the grounds of a previously established social convention, can be taken as something standing for something else") would exclude poetic signs valid only within the idiolect of a text: they are then only context-established (of course Eco deepens his definition considerably, and his whole book, especially the "Theory of Codes" chapter, is essential in this connection). I rather like Peirce's pithy definition in his letter to Lady Welby of 12 October 1904: *a sign is something knowing which we know something more.*

5. The last class, idiolectic signs and space-oriented signs, may provide an answer. But that would still leave unexplained the relationship between the other two categories (by far the more numerous signs) and the poem as a whole. Also, the very definition of the third-class signs seems to demand preliminary knowledge of what makes a text a closed, structured unit—hence the serious risk of circularity.

6. Paul Eluard, "Comme deux gouttes d'eau" (1933), in *Œuvres complètes,* ed. Marcelle Dumas and Lucien Scheler (Paris: Bibl. de la Pléiade, 1968), vol. I, p.412.

7. Lightning is a Second Empire euphemism for orgasm: Michelet, for example, in his treatise on love published seven years after the sonnet, alludes to the sexual act as a *ténébreux éclair* [dark lightning] (*L'Amour,* p.201); and later on, prompted by the Baudelaire intertext, Charles Cros will write:

"La mort perpétuera l'éclair d'amour vainqueur" [Death will make eternal the lightning flash of love triumphant].

8. Cf. Eco 1976, p.126: "every item in the code maintains a double set of relations, a systematic one with all the items of its own plane (content or expression) and a signifying one with one or more items of the correlated plane."

9. See Eco 1976, pp.314 ff. Also pp.48 ff. (especially p.57).

10. As defined by Peirce 5.484. Cf. Eco 1976, pp.71–72, 121–29.

11. On literary competence, see also Ihwe 1970.

12. See my definition in chapter 2, pp.39 ff. and note 24.

13. Since the text is a multilevelled discourse, the perception of *sign-functions* (in Hjelmslev's sense, 1943, p.58) necessarily changes, the correlation of functives being transitory: it depends upon the reader's gradual discovery of new coding rules, that is, upon his working his way back to the structures that generate the text (the reader is performing an *abduction,* in Peirce's sense: Peirce 2.623).

14. Which should not be confused with adherence to the referential fallacy. This is a matter of effect. Whether the reader believes the mimesis is grounded in a genuine reference of words to things, or realizes the mimesis is illusory and is in truth built upon an entirely verbal, self-sufficient system, the impact of the representation of reality upon his imagination is the same. It has to be a norm before the well-formedness of any of its components can appear questionable.

15. Maurice Jasinski, ed., Gautier, *España* (Paris: Vuibert, 1929), pp.142–45.

16. I prefer *hypogram* to *paragram,* since the latter is identified with Saussure's forgotten concept, brought back to life in Starobinski 1971. In Saussure, the matrix of the paragram (his *locus princeps*) is lexical or graphemic, and the paragram is made out of fragments of the key words scattered along the sentence, each embedded in the body of a word. (My hypogram, on the contrary, appears quite visibly in the shape of words embedded in sentences whose organization reflects the presuppositions of the matrix's nuclear word.) Saussure was never able to prove that the key word's role implies "une plus grande somme de coïncidences que celles du premier mot venu" (Starobinski 1971, p.132). Such proof must be looked for, and the question asked is hard to reconcile with the reader's natural experience of a literary text, namely, his greater awareness of the *way* things are said than of exactly what is meant. The fact that the saturation of the text by a phonic paraphrase of a key word is more assumed than perceived is hard to reconcile with the poetic function as defined by Mukařovsky, and followed by Jakobson, as a focussing of the language system on the form of the message. These problems, it seems to me, can be avoided if the analyst starts from what the surface features of the text, that is, its style, force him to perceive. These features can be defined as variants of a semantic structure that need not be realized in a key word present intact or as *membra disiecta* in the text, so long as decoding emphases and other formal distortions sensitize the reader to their recurrences and hence to their equivalences, and thus make him perceive them not just as forms but as variants of an invariant. This natural decoding procedure

should obviate the difficulty of proving the existence of a key word, because the structure's complex network of relations is self-defining outside of and above any word that may implement it.

17. Cf. the American joke—a polar bear in a snow storm. Alphonse Allais, *Album Primo-Avrilesque* (1897), in *Œuvres posthumes,* vol. 2 (Paris: La Table ronde, 1966), pp.371–79; Benjamin Péret, "Allô," in *Je sublime* (Paris: Editions surréalistes, 1936). Allais's piece is in the parodic catalog of an imaginary *Salon* of paintings, in which every exhibit is monochromatic. He offers his own version of the first of our three jokes. The plaques on five other "paintings" function similarly to the one I commented on here, but raise problems irrelevant to my point.

18. Robert Desnos, "Apparition," in *Fortunes* (Poésie) (Paris: NRF, 1942), p.62. Thus a Desnos exegete: "strange, violent, fascinating poem, modulating one long shout," etc., etc. (Rosa Bucholle, *L'évolution poétique de R. Desnos* [Brussels: Académie royale de langue et littérature françaises, 1956], p.156.) The *de boue* repeats both the beginning ("born of dirt," i.e., clay, a new Adam), and a hypogram: *dormir debout* [to be sleepy enough to sleep standing up, fast asleep on his feet]. The raven details, for instance, cannot be mimetic; they are not even apt in context, they are simply a periphrastic hyperbole of the ideal raven (and, indirectly, exemplary blackness).

19. André Breton, "La Forêt dans la hache," in *Le Revolver à cheveux blancs* (1932).

20. Mallarmé, *Œuvres complètes,* Bibl. de la Pléiade, p.1489. There is a thicket of studies that try vainly to make sense of the sonnet at the mimetic level. Only a few have arrived at the perception of the *rien* significance (M.-J. Lefebve, "La Mise en abyme mallarméenne," *Synthèses* 258 [1967]: 81–85; Roger Dragonetti, "La Littérature et la lettre," *Lingua e Stile* 4 [1969]: 205–22; Ellen Burt, "Mallarmé's Sonnet en -yx," *Yale French Studies* 54 [1977]: 55–82). But they still leave much latitude to the reader's interpretation and concede too much to ambiguity. Both latitude and ambiguity, I believe, are avoided by the concept of the poem as derivative by expansion—conversion from a matrix.

21. On conversion, see pp.63–80.

22. But in a way nothing more than a transform of the formula that cancels the function of the home as symbol of social intercourse—the servant's response to a caller: "Monsieur n'y est pas" [Monsieur is not at home].

23. Mallarmé, *Œuvres,* p.1488.

24. The rhyme is difficult because /iks/ is an infrequent ending in French, but above all because the required alternation of feminine and masculine rhymes in a sonnet makes it necessary to find variants of /iks/ that do not end with a mute *-e.* The only possibility is *-ix* or *-yx* with the *x* voiced, and *that* narrows the choice down to learned words of Greek origin and spelling.

25. A model for another image of nothing: the empty mirror of the second tercet, empty of the reflection of a dead, therefore absent character.

26. A prose version entitled *Igitur* contains its own commentary in relatively straightforward French. Mallarmé himself (letter to Cazalis, Pléiade, pp.1489–90) discusses what he meant to say. But the only relevance of poetics

is to the text itself, not to the author's intention: good method demands that arguments be based on the poem alone, and this sonnet is quite self-sufficient. The sestet unfolds a description whose every detail cancels itself out: an open window, but described as *vacante,* "empty"; a light, but dying (*un or agonise*); a setting, but modified by *peut-être,* "maybe"; allegorical pictures, but on nonexistent myths; a mirror described as "framed forgetfulness." The only presence not cancelled is the *septuor* of *scintillations,* the Big Dipper; the musical term suggests that the constellation is also that of the sonnet's seven rhyme pairs: the only reality of the poem is its rhyming pattern.

27. For a very incomplete account of the tempest *ptyx* stirred up in scholarly teapots, see the Mondor and Jean-Aubry edition, Pléiade, pp.1490–91. Hugo's poem is the illustrious "Satyre," published eight years before our sonnet (line 19: an enumeration of sylvan gods leads to *Chrysis/Sylvain du Ptyx que l'homme appelle Janicule*). Hugo himself knew not of the alleged **ptyx,* "shell"; he first tried *phtyx* as an ad hoc coinage, to sound like ancient Greek with a vengeance (see *Légende des Siècles,* ed. Paul Berret [Paris: Hachette, 1922], vol. 2, pp.573, 576).

28. Cf. pp.12 and 17.

29. Athanasius Kircher, *Musurgia* (1662).

30. On overdetermination as a substitute for *effet de réel,* see Riffaterre 1970b, 1972a, 1973a; Hamon, 1977.

CHAPTER 2: SIGN PRODUCTION

1. See Eco 1976, pp.112 ff.

2. Hugo, *Chansons des Rues et des Bois,* Part I, Book VI, xvii, lines 38–40.

3. Conventional poetic forms can be interpreted conventionally so long as the corresponding esthetics survives. But a reader perceiving them from within another system uses a different hermeneutic metalanguage; in so doing he still reacts "correctly" to the same language as the original reader did: the text's unchanged language.

4. References: (1) *Contemplations* 2.19.21; (2) *Les Martyrs* (1809), vol. I, p.139; (3) *Le Temps retrouvé* (1922), p.848; (4) *Contemplations* 1.11.19–20; (5) *Ahasvérus* (1833), pp.259–60.

5. Batteux, *Les Beaux Arts* . . . , Part 1, chap. iii.

6. Father Daire's *Epithètes françoises* (Lyon: 1759). Most of these dictionaries are called *Gradus ad Parnassum.*

7. Benveniste posits a "distinction entre mots *autonomes,* fonctionnant comme constituants de phrase . . . , et mots *synnomes* qui ne peuvent entrer dans la phrase que joints à d'autres mots" (Benveniste 1966, p.124). Pursuing Benveniste's distinctions, we could say that the epithet (as meaningful, thus at the mimetic level) is autosemantic, but that in its poetic function (as significant, thus at the semiotic level) it is synsemantic.

8. Doric columns, Ionian, etc. The reference to Greek architecture is in itself a positive marker. On this theme, see Hermine B. Riffaterre, "L'Imagina-

tion livresque de Chateaubriand," *Revue belge de philologie et d'histoire*
50 (1972): 768–76.

9. Hugo, *Contemplations,* 2.3, lines 1–2, 10–12. Italics mine.

10. It is significant that Daire, in the *Gradus* mentioned above, lists the
following stock epithets under *chambrière* (chambermaid): *active, diligente,
industrieuse, prompte.* All of which are replaceable by *agile,* either with a
noun for "maid" or with a noun designating her metonymically in either tool
or house-appliance code: cf. *navettes* (3) and *fuseau* above.

11. Since the permanently poetic word stands for a hypogrammatic sen-
tence, we have to recognize that in literary discourse the *sentence can be a
sign,* whereas in everyday language, Benveniste shows, it cannot (Benveniste
1966, p.129).

12. Mallarmé, *Œuvres complètes* (Pléiade, 1951), p.45.

13. See Erik Michaelsson, "L'eau, centre de métaphores et de métamor-
phoses dans la littérature française de la première moitié du XVIIe. siècle,"
Orbis litterarum 14 (1959): 121–73; Jean Rousset, *L'Intérieur et l'extérieur*
(Paris: Corti, 1968), pp.199–235.

14. Favorable connotations, e.g., Hugo, *Contemplations,* "Magnitudo parvi,"
lines 560–69, where the sage's spiritual eye penetrates appearances: "[le voy-
ant] sent . . . son œil devenir éclatant. . . . Il regarde tant la nature Que la
nature a disparu! Car, des effets allant aux causes, L'œil perce et franchit le
miroir. . . . La matière tombe détruite Devant l'esprit aux yeux de lynx"
[(the seer) feels his eye becoming bright. He gazes so much at Nature, Nature
disappears! Moving from effect to cause, the eye pierces and passes through
the mirror. Matter falls into ruins before the lynx eyes of the mind]. The
connotations are clearly dictated by the presence of words acting as positive
markers (the brilliant gaze, the lynx eyes). As for unfavorable connotations,
we can eliminate at least the hypothesis of a cultural constant, an implied
reference to the quotation from Paul, 1 Cor. 13:12: the French do not know
about this *through a glass* business. For one thing, Paul is hardly ever quoted,
at least not this passage. For another, although the Latin Vulgate does in
fact say "*per* speculum," "through," the best-known French version (Le Maistre
de Sacy, 1667) has it "nous ne voyons maintenant que comme en un miroir, et
en des énigmes." Neither *through* nor *darkly* is to be found.

15. "Le Miroir et le monde," in *Sens, Destinée arbitraire* (Paris: Gallimard,
1975), p.212; the face in the mirror is destroyed at the same time ("La lèpre
marque le visage . . ."); the scars of a metaphorical leprosy correspond to the
peeling off of the silvering.

16. "La Sieste," in *Calixto* (Paris: Gallimard, 1962), p.46.

17. *Les Dessous d'une vie* (1926), in Eluard, *Œuvres complètes* (Pléiade,
1968, vol. I, p.201); Verlaine, *Jadis et naguère* (Pléiade, 1948, p.204); cf. Jules
Laforgue, *L'Imitation de Notre-Dame la Lune,* "Locutions des Pierrots," XI:
"déteins, Glace sans tain, Sur mon œil! qu'il soit tout atone"; Robert Desnos,
Mouchoirs au Nadir (*Domaine public;* Paris: Gallimard, 1953, p.173), "Vol de
mouette apparue dans le miroir sans tain," meaning a forgotten farewell
gesture with a waved white handkerchief.

18. "La Gamme," quoted in Guy Michaud, "Le thème du miroir dans le

symbolisme français," *Cahiers de l'Association internationale des études françaises* XI (1959): 207. Of course this phonetic and lexical dissonance, the very fact that it sounds ludicrous, is the icon of the moral anguish the poem is about.

19. Leiris, "Les Veilleurs de Londres," in *Failles* (1924–1934), *Haut-Mal* (Paris: Gallimard, 1969), p.117.

20. See chapter 3, pp.53–63.

21. Benjamin Péret, "Dernier malheur, dernière chance (fragment)," quoted in J. L. Bedouin, *La Poésie surréaliste* (Paris: Seghers, 1964), p.261.

22. Verlaine, *Poèmes saturniens;* cf. "Allégorie" in Verlaine, *Parallèlement.*

23. On the cliché as a component of literariness, see Riffaterre 1971; also Jenny 1972 and R. Amossy, E. Rosen, "Les clichés dans *Eugénie Grandet*," *Littérature* 25 (1977): 114–28.

24. I first sketched out this concept in Riffaterre 1970b, pp.417–18. The system is built around a lexeme, organized by the sememe, but unlike semantic fields (as conceived by Trier) it is a lexical reality; each of its components is associated with the others by well-defined syntactic relationships, and these are realized in the shape of clichés. The system differs from the isotopy in that it is structured: it has a syntax (cf. Rastier 1972). When the system is modified to designate the nucleus of another system, it functions as a special code: in Baudelaire's "La Géante," for instance, a woman is depicted in landscape code. (On the conversion of systems into code, see chapter 3, pp.66–70.) Synonyms do not have the same system.

25. My italics. Hugo, *Choses vues* (1851) (Paris: Imprimerie nationale), vol. I, p.67; Balzac, *Séraphîta,* ed. Bouteron (Bibl. de la Pléiade), vol. 10, p.493; *Massimilla Doni* (Pléiade), vol. 9, p.327 (the image stands for a voluptuous mistress, an abyss, because to yield to her seduction is to be unfaithful to another, and filled with flowers—literally made of flowers—because she is so magically attractive); Zola, *La Curée,* ed. Mitterand (Pléiade), vol. I, p.425; Saint-John Perse, *Exil* V (Bibl. de la Pléiade), p.131; Jean Tardieu, *Le fleuve caché,* "Fleurs et abîmes." (Note that the title itself here serves as a model. It is a variant of the theme snake-in-the-grass, or snake-in-a-bunch-of-flowers— that is, beauty as a snare, or beauty as danger, a matrix whose actualizations run the gamut from the melodramatic pathos of *femme fatale* to the philosophic equation of Beauty and Death.) Obviously, the landscape we are seeing here has nothing to do with the mimesis of reality. Neither the abyss inside the flower nor its thundering obeys the rules of verisimilitude or representational acceptability. For the "real" or "natural" metonymic contiguity of flower and abyss is substituted a metaphoric identification of one with the other. This is ungrammatical as mimesis, but grammatical as semiosis, that is, as an actualization of the matrix. This transformation from referential meaning to contextual (semiotic) significance is further pointed out by the equally ungrammatical variant *lait noir:* the polar metamorphosis of an exemplar of whiteness into a paragon of blackness is a metalinguistic commentary upon Beauty's deceptivity. Cf. Audiberti's *Race des hommes,* "la noirceur secrète du lait" [milk's secret blackness]; Aragon in "L'épingle stérilisée" (significantly an automatic-writing prose poem), "sous un arbre à lait dans

le pays où les hommes sont si noirs qu'on ne songerait pas à leur ouvrir la
poitrine pour en faire sortir du lait" [under a milk-tree in the country where
men are so black that you would never think of opening up their chests to
make the milk come out].

26. For example, Hugo writes in *Contemplations* (as the narrator picks a
flower from the brink of a sea-cliff to send to his beloved):

> . . . Pauvre fleur, du haut de cette cime
> Tu devais t'en aller dans cet immense abîme
> . . .
> Va mourir sur un cœur, abîme plus profond
> . . .
> Le ciel, qui te créa pour t'effeuiller dans l'onde,
> Te fit pour l'océan, je te donne à l'amour (V, xxiv).

Poor flower, from the crest of this peak you were fated to descend into
this immense abyss. Go die upon a heart, abyss of greater depth. Heaven
created you to shed your petals on the waves, Heaven made you for the
ocean, I give you to love.

Here *tu devais t'en aller, te fit pour l'océan,* are variants of *le ciel te créa
pour t'effeuiller,* which actualizes in floral code the matrix *born to die,* com-
monplace in pessimistic representations of man's fate.

27. Racine, *Athalie,* Act III, Scene 3.

28. *Histoire naturelle* (1749), quoted in P. Larousse, *Grand Dict. universel,*
s.v. *soupirail; Les Martyrs* (1809), book viii (Pléiade, vol. 2, p.233). A cliché
well illustrated in translations from the Greek and Latin: entrances to the
netherworld are called *soupiraux de l'Enfer.*

29. This hypothesis works just as well for words designating what is tra-
ditionally regarded as "naturally poetic": sunsets and sunrises, deep valleys
and lofty peaks (or green valleys and snowcapped peaks); fear and love and
death, etc.—in short, archetypes. I do not deny that such things do exist, or
that we have feelings about them, or that we build metaphysical constructs
around them, or that they readily lend themselves to symbolism. But I wonder
whether the poetic quality of sunrise and sunset has to do with primeval
emotions aroused by Nature's daily dramas, with the brilliant pageantry of
the spectacle, or whether this poetic flavor does not flow rather from the
dynamics of transformation, or change or exchange between polar opposites—
dark vs. *light,* *rise* vs. *fall,* and so forth. Again, it is true that large groups of
specialized words cluster around referents such as mountaintop and valley,
and are not likely to cluster about halfway stations along the slope. Certainly
there are such clusters around the words *noontide* and *midnight,* and none
for the early afternoon. But perhaps this unequal distribution is due not to
the fact that nothing poetic ever happens at 3:00 P.M., but to the ease of
opposing high noon to midnight, or even better, reconciling them despite
their opposition—whereas it is hard to find a workable polar opposite to
3:00 P.M. (3:00 A.M. will not do, in either reality or words). Again, anyone
speaking of mountaintops and valleys as poetic objects will necessarily op-

pose one to the other, and my two sets of adjectives (deep vs. lofty, green vs. white) do perhaps correspond to a reality, but they correspond above all to polarization.

30. *Poésie critique* (Paris: *NRF*, 1959) vol. 1, p.193. The equivalence between *appel, prière, cri,* and *regard* is overdetermined by the facile (but here implicit) paronomasia on *soupirail* and *soupir,* "sigh."

31. "Je reviens," in *Oubliés (1946), Poèmes* (Paris: *NRF* [1948]), p.264. The link between *soupirail* and *mur* is reinforced by a pseudomotivation: *l'éventail,* "hung on the wall like an art object," sounds and is spelled very much like *le ventail,* "the vent" a quasi-synonymic variation on *soupirail.*

32. Baudelaire, letter of 18 February 1860 (*Corr.,* vol. 3, p.40).

33. "Enfances," in *Illuminations.*

34. *L'Âne* (1873), line 1008.

35. At the expense, revealingly, of the mimesis. A *soupirail* has no window pane: this glass interference survives the conversion of the theme in the guise of the verb (*heurter*), which presupposes a barrier.

36. *Les Quatre vents de l'esprit,* 1.3.16.

37. The mechanical character of the opposition, its schematic simplicity, and its structural geometry are easily verifiable. If the sentence is generated not by derivation from *soupirail* but from *mur* or its equivalent, it produces a *soupirail* even though the phrase yielded is nonsensical: e.g., Leiris, *Le Point cardinal* (Paris: *NRF,* 1927), p.54: "les ais de la matière se resserrèrent encore sur moi, menaçant de transformer ma bouche en soupirail" [the building beams of matter tightened up on me still closer, threatening to turn my mouth into a *soupirail*].

38. See chapter 4.

CHAPTER 3: TEXT PRODUCTION

1. By *textual signs,* as we shall see in more detail later on, I mean signs standing for a whole text, that is, words that can be understood only insofar as they subsume a well-defined text either known to the reader or easy for him to reconstruct.

2. Théophile Gautier, *Histoire du romantisme,* chapter viii (Paris: Fasquelle, n.d.), p.71. The book is a collection of articles (this one is dated 1854) from Gautier's literary column—either reminiscences about other poets or commentaries on their work. These essays are invariably paraphrases, performing variations on themes selected from the poems: every one follows the rule of expansion. The portraits specifically are similar variations on stereotypes of the *poète* descriptive system(s).

3. *Histoire du romantisme,* pp.146–47, 151. Nerval, dead, is in the "world of elohim, of angels and sylphs . . . he was already familiar with."

4. Aristotle, *History of Animals,* 9, 13, already waxes literary on the subject.

5. As usual, the forms of the text oblige the reader to touch all the bases of preestablished themes and verbal commonplaces. In this particular instance, a comic form of the opposition is the distich in which a poet of the

1820s by the name of Loyson ("gosling") is lampooned thus: "even when he flies one remembers his legs"—a conversion of traditional praise for the mystic poet.

6. Cf. the proverbial "heureux comme un poisson dans l'eau" [happy as a fish in water] and "libre comme l'air" [free as air]. Add that levitation conventionally represents bliss ("il semblait ne pas toucher terre" [his feet didn't seem to touch the ground, he seemed to be walking on air]) or spiritual, supernatural beings.

7. Eluard, "Le Miroir d'un moment," in *Capitale de la Douleur* (1926).

8. The motivations of the narrative sequence, implicit before transformation, are made explicit by the descriptive discourse.

9. Jules Michelet, *La Montagne* (1868), Part I, chapter xii.

10. *Méduse* is a dual sign (which "jellyfish" is not—at least not in this context), because it was a mythological creature before it came to be an animal. The pressure of the animization paradigm significantly determines the "human" periphrasis "daughter of the sea" before her identification as a jellyfish.

11. Riffaterre 1971, pp.68–80.

12. A powerful *coincidentia oppositorum* in the semiotic system of eroticism and in the pornogram (on these see Steven Marcus, *The Other Victorians,* [New York: Basic Books, 1964]). This combination is one of the poem's givens (lines 2–4): "Elle n'avait gardé que ses bijoux sonores/Dont le riche attirail lui donnait l'air vainqueur/Qu'ont dans leurs jours heureux les esclaves des Mores" [she had not kept on anything save her ringing jewels/This rich attire gave her the conquering look/That the Moors' slaves have on their days of happy love]. (In context, the slaves of the Moors must be understood as the equivalent of harem or seraglio women.)

13. One more determinant here may be a very different crystal seat (where crystal results from a negativization of the seme *liquidity*), throne of the river nymphs in Vergil's *Georgica* 4, 350. (The traditional translation of *vitreus* is the embellished *crystal*.)

14. Of course this equivalence extends beyond the cases where the poem expands on its matrix through actual allegory, as in "Les Bijoux." Allegory is indeed a "visual" form of expansion. Whereas tropes in general are limited to the short phrase, allegory encompasses complex sentences. The eighteenth-century rhetorician Dumarsais had already noted that in this respect the allegory is akin to the extended metaphor (*Des Tropes,* Part II, chapter xii).

15. With the exceptions, of course, of sound effects, onomatopoeic words, and also popular etymologies, compound words in phrase form that appear to explain what they mean.

16. The literature of the sign-arbitrariness problem is enormous, since this has become a favorite *disputatio* in the true (sometimes this means the worst) scholastic tradition. See, for instance, Rudolf Engler, "Théorie et critique d'un principe saussurien: l'arbitraire du signe," *Cahiers Ferdinand de Saussure* 19 (1964): 5–65; 21 (1964): 25–32; and Gamkrelidze, 1974. On Cratylism, Genette 1976. See also *Poétique* 23 (1975).

17. It is of course quite logical that my hypothetical sentence should in

this particular instance echo Keats's *Pipe to the spirit ditties of no tone;* the line perfectly illustrates what I am trying to demonstrate, since the use of a lexicon referring to actual sounds as simultaneously themselves and their nonexistence, serves as interpretant for the *Grecian Urn*'s significance: the presence of an absence, the symbol as a monument (what is no longer, yet remains). Cf. Mallarmé's depiction of the patron saint of music in a stained-glass window: *musicienne du silence* (Mallarmé, "Sainte").

18. Saint-Amant, "Le Contemplateur" [1627], *Œuvres,* ed. Livet (Paris, 1855), vol. I, p.37.

19. Shelley, "The Cloud" (1820), lines 49–50.

20. Breton, "La mort rose," in *Le Revolver à cheveux blancs;* "Cours—les toutes," in *L'air de l'eau.*

21. See my commentary on Apollinaire's image of eyelashes as reeds, pp.97–99.

22. Paul Valéry, "Fragments du Narcisse," *Œuvres,* ed. Hytier (Paris: Bibl. de la Pléiade), vol. I, p.123.

23. Chateaubriand, *Génie du Christianisme,* Part IV, Bk. 1, chap. viii ("Les Rogations").

24. On dual signs, see pp.81–109.

25. Hugo, *Le Rhin* (1840), letter xx (Paris: Imprimerie nationale, n.d.), p.166. The italics are mine.

26. Rimbaud, "Les Poètes de sept ans"; "Accroupissements," in *Poésies.*

27. I am not thinking of open symbolism but of the established conventional system *(langage des fleurs)* set forth in many books for young ladies of the Victorian era. Under this system floral arrangements, equivalent to writing, were used to convey detailed, specific messages.

28. For a discussion of the whole sonnet as an expansion on *rien,* perhaps the ultimate in abstraction, see pp.16–19.

29. For the sake of comparison, consider this equally meliorative praise of the fingernail (but with the metonym staying where it belongs), Th. Gautier, *Spirite* (1866), chap. VII: "une main diaphane, aux doigts effilés, aux ongles luisants comme de l'onyx, dont le dos laissait transparaître quelques veines d'azur semblables à ces reflets bleuâtres irisant la pâte laiteuse de l'opale." [a diaphanous hand, with long thin fingers, fingernails shining like onyx, azure veins on the back like the pale blue iridescent reflections playing on an opal like milky china]. Cf. also Gautier, *Le Roman de la momie,* "Prologue."

30. Paul Eluard, *Donner à voir, Juste Milieu* (Pléiade), vol. I, p.926.

31. The reflexive form draws its generative power in the first place from its repetition of the title: the whole text functions as an embedding within an iterative statement of the matrix *(unis . . .* [text] *. . . nous nous unissons).*

32. An icon because the very repetitions resemble exactly the *nous nous* morpheme. This is very different from the symbolism the cave itself might have descriptively, as a narrow subterranean space, if the theme were treated according to the tradition Vergil initiated.

33. Eluard, *L'Amour la poésie* (1929), *Premièrement* vii (Pléiade), vol. I, pp.232, 1405.

34. Eluard, *Le lit la table,* "Chronique" (Pléiade), vol. I, p.1218.

35. Aragon, *Feu de joie* (1919), "Pierre fendre": the title itself presupposes *freeze* (until the stone splits open), just as *In Deserto* implies *Vox clamans* (see p.12); the context goes from *jours d'hiver to lèvres gercées.*

36. René Char, "Afin qu'il n'y soit rien changé" 6, in *Seuls demeurent* (*Fureur et mystère*, p.32).

37. *Tintin et les oranges bleues* (Paris: Casterman, 1965) (Album-film), p.4. "Dans ce petit paquet, on trouve ô surprise, une orange . . . une orange qui est bleue. C'est l'occasion pour le capitaine de philosopher:—Les oranges pour moi, elles sont oranges, et si une orange est bleue, vous me suivez bien, Tintin, si une orange est bleue, ce n'est plus une orange."

38. The Mandiargues quotation and others can be found in J. M. Adam 1976, pp.148–49—the latter also being responsible for the semanalytical caper. Onimus continues on this subject in his "Images d'Eluard," *Annales de la Faculté des Lettres d'Aix-en-Provence*, vol. 37, pp.131–48. See also Robert Champigny, *Le genre poétique* (Monte-Carlo: Editions Regain, 1963), pp. 148–49.

39. Cited, s.v. *cygne,* by Littré, who lists many others, now obsolete or forgotten (such as "il a autant de politesse qu'un crapaud de plumes"). We might add similar constructs that were not intended to be understood that way but are so understood now: e.g., Madame de Sévigné's imprudent dictum: "Racine passera comme le café" [Racine will soon go out of fashion, like coffee]. Cf. the nineteenth-century slang "Jésus qui chique" [Jesus chewing tobacco = no Jesus, therefore a *man* (only human)].

40. Raymond Queneau, *Le chien à la Mandoline*, p.82.

41. E.g., Paul Claudel in a meditation on the rainbow as metaphor: "en lui et par lui, l'extrême rouge combiné avec le vert, de même que le bleu combiné avec l'inverse orange, disparaissent dans l'unité du blanc" [deep red combined with green, just as blue combines with orange, its opposite, disappear into the unity of white], "Proposition sur la lumière," in *Connaissance de l'Est* (Œuvre poétique, Pléiade, p.101).

42. Which explains why conversion can work as a simplistic joke-mechanism, as in *you need it like a crevice in the cranium* (come across in a New York tabloid) or a risqué college-campus jest from the early forties, two variations on the matrix *he fell victim to unpredictable circumstances:* (1) where the converter is the capitalized initial of *Fate* (the capital being a significant emphasis, a philosophical symbol, a sign of Fate's inexorability): *he got fucked by the fickle finger of Fate;* and (2) where the converter is the initial of *Destiny: he got dingled by the dangling dong of Destiny.*

43. With the exception of conversion combining with expansion. See note 63, this chapter.

44. Lautréamont, *Chants de Maldoror,* ed. Walzer, Canto V (6) (Paris: Bibl. de la Pléiade), p.206. My italics.

45. First, *binarité,* especially conspicuous as the predicate of *incliner,* a verb that normally takes a concrete, physical predicate and excludes a conceptual one. Second, *rotule,* a Latinate form, hence scientific-looking, like *patella* as opposed to *kneecap.* This conversion, on the contrary, uses literary discourse, but with a twist in the case of "chant d'outre-tombe," where the trans-

formation is of course an allusion to Chateaubriand's *Mémoires d'Outre-Tombe*. Chateaubriand's compound coinage conforms to traditional esthetics and so would appear not to deny the dead the respect that is their due. On the contrary, the compound is quite fitting. Here is the twist: the conversion reverses the meaning Chateaubriand and everyone else gives the compound, "from beyond the grave," and it becomes "from this side of the grave." By using a word reserved for awesome messages from the next world, the text ludicrously depicts mourners serenading their dead listener.

46. Baudelaire, *Petits Poèmes en prose* (also known as *Le Spleen de Paris*), xxi, "Les Tentations."

47. Lexical collocations oppose *vieille mère* to *mère*, rather than to *jeune mère*, which is not a separate category but a hyperbolic variant of *mère*. *Vieille mère* and *mère* belong to two different descriptive systems that may be mutually exclusive, even though they correspond in reality to the same "maternity" referent. In the *vieille mère* system, for instance, the mother-child relationship of the *mère* system is inverted, for it is the child's turn to feed and protect the mother, or to abandon her. But where ingratitude is represented, as with the prodigal son, the child is linked rather to the father; *fils prodigue* is thus a subcategory of the *père* system. If the child dies, the mother shifts to an altogether different system, that of the *mater dolorosa*, etc. Such are the consequences of building the system with lexemes, with signifiers, rather than with referents. The relationship expressed in the Baudelaire poem could also be derived from a descriptive system of *famine*, "hunger."

48. Hugo, "La Vache," in *Les Voix intérieures*.

49. See Jauss 1974.

50. On the intrinsic valorization of the stanza and its pitch-setting for the whole sonnet, see the perceptive remarks of Victor Brombert, "Lyrisme et dépersonnalisation: l'exemple de Baudelaire (Spleen, LXXV)," *Romantisme* 6 (1973): 29–37.

51. It matters not whether it is dog or cat, since they are functionally equivalent. In fact, Baudelaire had a dog in his first draft of the sonnet. Whenever the descriptive system is used as the code for mimesis of contented or positive intimacy, the pet *actant* serves as metonym for the shelter. In statistical terms, which perhaps necessarily translate into terms of the reader's linguistic competence, the cat actualizes this function more often than the dog. Baudelaire calls the cat the pride of the home ("Les Chats"); in yet another sonnet he writes: "C'est l'esprit familier du lieu;/Il juge, il préside, il inspire/Toutes choses dans son empire" ("Le Chat"). It is in fact quite hard to find a literary description of home that does not conform to our descriptive system and does not employ the cat as ultimate symbol of inner peace; cf. Th. Gautier's representation of such a representation, in *Abécédaire du Salon de 1861* (Paris: Dentu, 1861), p.225: "là se pelotonne le chat de la maison,— de la maison tranquille,—. . . capable de comprendre et digne de partager ce bonheur paisible.—Le peintre a bien fait de ne pas oublier le chat dans cette poésie du foyer: le chat est l'esprit familier du logis, le *genius loci;* il

aime l'ordre, la propreté, le calme, tous les petits conforts d'un intérieur bien réglé. Où il se plaît, soyez sûr qu'un philosophe habite" [here the cat of the house curls up, the quiet house. The painter was well inspired not to forget the cat in this poem of the hearth, for the cat is the familiar spirit of the home, the *genius loci*. He loves order, cleanliness, quiet, every small comfort of a well-regulated household. You may be sure that the abode where he is happy is a philosopher's]. Inasmuch as the pet represents the master of the house, it is unlike the cricket, *le grillon du foyer*—another *genius loci,* true, but the cricket's function is to observe mankind from the outsider's vantage point, which is to say from an ironic or satiric angle: think of Jiminy Cricket's wry humor in the Disney cartoons.

52. Standard indeed: the sonnet's incipit, "Il est amer et doux, pendant les nuits d'hiver,/D'écouter près du feu qui palpite etc." [It is bittersweet of winter nights, beside the flickering fire, to listen etc.], parallels the stale lyric commonplaces, the cliché symbols the two soulmates wallow in during the first conversation between Madame Bovary and her future lover: "c'est comme moi, répliqua Léon; quelle meilleure chose, en effet, que d'être le soir au coin du feu avec un livre, pendant que le vent bat les carreaux, que la lampe brûle?" (Part II, chap. II).

53. Cros, "Le Buffet," in *Le Coffret de Santal,* ed. Forestier and Pia (Paris: J. J. Pauvert, 1964), pp.123–25 [it is just a piece of furniture made of inlaid wood, nothing more. But as soon as the highboy is closed, when sleep shuts the ears of intruders, when our thoughts and eyes are elsewhere, on something real, then girandoles go on inside, a chandelier lights up on an imaginary ceiling, etc.]

54. I cannot insist strongly enough upon the permanence of these verbal systems; it can make a modern detective novel look as if it were derived from a Baudelaire "source": Ian Fleming, *Live and Let Die,* chap. 7 (New York: Signet Books, 1954), p.49: "Between her hands, she faced the knave of hearts. Then the queen of spades. She held the two halves of the pack in her lap so that the two court cards looked at each other. She brought the two halves of the pack together until they kissed. Then she riffled the cards and shuffled them again."

55. This detail of the *vieille hydropique* curiously demonstrates the rigor of the negativizing process. The association between packs of cards and old ladies offers one thematic possibility (sometimes the old lady comes out of her own pack, as in Pushkin). Now *vieille* normally and tautologically generates adjectives like *maigre, ridée, parcheminée,* which are already negative: the conversion therefore reverses *maigre* into its contrary, and since the transform still has to be negative, *hydropique* is chosen—precluding as it does certain favorable connotations of plumpness. Not only because dropsy is a disease, but also because it is associated with habitual heavy drinking. The *vieille* is thereby turned into a variant of a type that goes back to classical antiquity; thus is woven into the text one more prefabricated, subconsciously familiar, and convincing component: the type of the *lena,* the old procuress of Greek and

Latin elegiac and erotic poetry, the bawd of sin whom old age should have made the ally of virtue. Racine's Œnone in *Phèdre* is the last explicit variant of this type, and Œnone's name means "drunkard".

56. André Breton, "Le Message automatique" (1933), in *Le Point du Jour* (Paris: NRF, 1970).

57. Alfred Jarry, "La Passion considérée comme course de côte," in *Spéculations* (1911) (*La Chandelle verte,* ed. M. Saillet, Le Livre de Poche, p.356).

58. André Breton, *Poisson soluble* (1924), 28, in *Manifestes du Surréalisme* (Paris: J. J. Pauvert, n.d.), p.121.

59. A dual sign of the hypogram-generating type, see pp.94–99.

60. Or to the transfer of the accident narrative from a conversion to another derivation: "les deux bolides blanc et vert, rouge et noir, fusionnèrent terriblement" [the two hot-rods, white and green, red and black, fused horribly with each other]. The two polarizing sentences *blanc-noir* and *vert-rouge,* which were ungrammatically distributed, are brought together again by the crash, thus tautologically ending the oxymoron and the story.

61. This description is overdetermined by the thematic structure of *fantastic architecture*: cf. my discussion of Julien Gracq's iceberg, note 25, chapter 4.

62. E.g., George Sand uses the same conversion as Desnos to emphasize the impossibility of the typical nineteenth-century dream dreamed by those obsessed with the desire to be elsewhere. The yearning for a geographic have-your-cake-and-eat-it-too is here the equivalent of the romantic quest theme. George Sand, *Lettres d'un voyageur,* x (Paris: Calmann Lévy, 1869), p.306: "Exigeante! lui dis-je, tu n'as pas trouvé le glacier assez blanc . . . Tu demandes les palmiers de l'Arabie-Heureuse sur la croupe du Mont-Blanc, et les crocodiles du Nil dans l'écume du Reichenbach. Tu voudrais voir voguer les flottes de Cléopâtre sur les ondes immobiles de la Mer de glace" [You *are* demanding! I said to her, the glacier was not white enough for you. . . . You want the palms of Arabia Felix on the brow of Mont Blanc and the crocodiles of the Nile in the foam of the Reichenbach Falls. You would like to see Cleopatra's fleet riding the moveless waves of the Sea of Ice].

63. The actualization may be only marking without permutation (since there is no external hypogram by opposition to which the text results). The markers will be identical with those of the matrix sentence; nevertheless they will attract attention because at first reading they will seem to be unmotivated with regard to the transforms they affect, as long as the latter are not yet understood as variants of the matrix.

64. See pages 48 ff.

65. I quote from the first version, as given in Antoine Adam's Bibl. de la Pléiade edition (Paris: NRF, 1972), pp.83–84. Other editors have preferred "Faim," a revised version that seems to have been a first step toward the simplified variant of *Saison en Enfer* (p.109). The revisions (pp.939–40) and the *Saison* variant are irrelevant to my purpose, which is to say either they do not contradict my interpretation, or else they support it.

66. R. G. Cohn, *The Poetry of Rimbaud* (Princeton University Press, 1973), p.216. He does try harder later on, resorting to facile and quite gratuitous psychoanalysis of the poem: *faim* leads to *mother,* and *Anne* is a woman, *ma*

has a capital *M*; all this must "support this feeling" that the refrain is about "sustenance through nursing"; *âne* and *Anne* echo *nanan,* "yumyum," like *banane, ananas,* etc. (p.217). This silliness is at least revealing in one way: like Bernard's explanations based on reference to the poet's biography, it testifies to the breakdown of the mimetic connection. Since the text fails to speak, we try to bypass it and get what we need from the author himself. A denial of the primacy of words. Of course the text is supposed to replace the writer, and no psychological laws can explain the peculiarity of an idiolect.

67. S. Bernard, ed.: Rimbaud, *Œuvres* (Paris: Garnier, 1960), p.442, fn. 1 and 5. *Coal* refers to the later version of line 6: "Le roc, les charbons, le fer."

68. Eluard, *Les Mains libres,* "Main et fruits." Eluard says the "dream," whereas in real life (or in referential communication) eating the uneatable is more like a nightmare.

69. Mallarmé, "L'Azur": S. Bernard is responsible for the rapprochement, but she is thinking of "Le Sonneur," a sonnet with similar content. The true formal parallelism, however, is in the other poem.

70. *Mémoires d'Outre-Tombe,* III, i, 3, 5: "les boulets roulaient leurs pains de fer au milieu des convives affamés." Cf. Robert Desnos, *Rrose Sélavy,* no. 15: "Perdue sur la mer sans fin, Rrose Sélavy mangera-t-elle du fer après avoir mangé ses mains?" and various confirmations of the image's consistency in automatic writing: e.g., iron and earth eaten in T. Tzara, *L'homme approximatif* (quoted in Hugnet, *Petite anthologie du Surréalisme,* p.133).

71. Tristan Corbière, "Rapsodie foraine," in *Les Amours jaunes;* Tristan Tzara, *L'Antitête.*

72. Nor does the play of binary opposition stop there. Magritte's stones in turn engender another contrary: bread into stone destroys the reference to real bread, then the loaves are suspended in mid-air so that heaviness into weightlessness destroys the reference to real stone.

73. It is not inconceivable that overdetermination has forged still another derivative link here: *dinn! dinn!* may also be the resonance of metallic hardness under the blows of a hammer; I remember a farcical TV show, *The Three Stooges,* where a famished character kept banging away on a friend's head with a loaf of hard bread. And Robert Desnos says that empty stomachs "tintaient tels des grelots" [tinkled like sleigh-bells] (*Corps et Biens,* quoted in R. Bucholle, *L'évolution poétique de R. Desnos,* Brussels, 1956, p.27).

74. Quoted in Ph. Audoin, *André Breton* (Paris: NRF, 1970), p.186.

75. It would appear that a morpheme such as a word ending (not necessarily a suffix) cannot be invested with a meaning independent of its function unless it is singled out, so to speak, by tautological derivation: cf. the punning rhyme in Hans Arp, *Jours effeuillés,* "Cuis-moi un tonnerre" (Paris: NRF, 1966), p.469: "Tire toutes tes langues aux roses./Donne tes langues aux doux rhinocé-roses" [Stick out all your tongues at the roses. Give your tongues to the sweet rhinoceroses] (this last a variant on the model of *donner sa langue au chat,* "give up," be unable to solve a riddle).

76. Maximal catachresis: it is not by chance that Eluard picks the *bouts d'air noir,* for instance, as an example of Rimbaud's most revolutionary boldness (*Premières vues anciennes,* Pléiade, vol. I, p.537).

CHAPTER 4: INTERPRETANTS

1. Peirce, 1.339. See also 5.484: "semiosis . . . is, or involves, a cooperation of three subjects, such as a sign, its object, and its interpretant, this tri-relative influence not being in any way resolvable into actions between pairs." The interpretant is not to be confused with the interpreter, such as the reader himself.

2. Here I adopt Umberto Eco's enlarged definition (Eco 1976, p.70): the interpretant may be the (real or apparent) equivalent sign-vehicle in another semiotic system (including translations or synonyms); or a definition in terms of the same semiotic system (this applies especially to the periphrasis, and more generally to any text produced by expansion); or the index pointing to a single object and implying an element of universal quantification; or an "established" connotation (for example, *dog* signifies *fidelity*).

3. Ronsard, *Amours* [1553], xli, ed. Laumonier (Paris: Société des textes français modernes), vol. 5, p.109; *Sonnets pour Hélène* [1578] II, liii (vol. I, p.321); Olivier de Magny, *Odes* [1559] (*Œuvres*, ed. Courbet, p.126). My italics. In other examples only the "unripe" meaning may be retained, by opposition to "mature" (e.g., Ronsard, *Amours* xviii, ed. Laumonier, vol. 4, p.21), but there is still the suggestion of viridity: "Un cœur ja mûr dans un sein verdelet."

4. Ariosto, *Orlando furioso*, Canto 7, 14. My translation. The Italian hypogram became such an eminently quotable verbal monument because, among other reasons, it contains two representations of the breast that are overdetermined: one by a polarizing derivation (combining two incompatible metaphors of the same tenor—the breast as natural fruit and yet an artifact); the other by its metonymic, indirect relation to an unspoken, unmentionable human body part of high sexual relevance, hence undescribable, forever taboo in the *blason* and love-lyric genres.

5. An extended or sustained metaphor is made up of one primary metaphor, a semantic given—usually acceptable, likely, convincing—and a string of derived or secondary metaphors whose vehicles are metonymic of the primary vehicle and whose tenors are metonymic of the primary tenor. See Riffaterre 1969 and a discussion of it in Dubois 1975.

6. Ronsard, *Amours* vi (Laumonier, vol. 4, p.10). Imitators of Ariosto found another solution: defusing the incompatibility by transferring the adjective to the other end of a periphrasis for *pome acerbe:* e.g., Pierre de Cornu, *Premier livre des Amours* [1583] xiv (ed. Blanchemain, Paris, 1870, p.8): "la verte jeunesse de l'arrondi contour de ton sein pommelé" [the green youth of the rounded contour of your apple-breast].

7. Some critics simply admire the boldness of the *gazons de lait* metaphor (Henri Weber, for instance, in *La Création poétique au XVIe siècle en France* [Paris: Nizet, 1955], p.288) without appearing to realize that the metaphor's power to unite two separate associative strings (breast and milk, breast as symbolic garden) stems from the dual appropriateness of the pun, as *verdelet* and as *vert de lait*. Others react by trying desperately to find for

gazon a meaning ("block") that will fit milk better and for which there is no evidence whatsoever: E. Huguet, *Dictionnaire de la langue française au XVIe siècle* (Paris: Didier, 1950), s.v. *gazon* (his examples are all obviously drawn from Ariosto). *Gazon,* like the German *Wasen* (the same etymology), has never meant anything but "grass," "grass-covered turf."

8. This is probably what happens even in Ariosto-conscious times if *verdelet* is omitted, as in the Magny quotations.

9. In other words, for a generative process coinciding with the genesis, the actual writing of the text, the reader's gap-filling is substituted as such a generative process.

10. Chateaubriand, *Mémoires d'Outre-Tombe,* Book IV, Part xi, chapter iii. The italics are his.

11. Here the plural would make *oublis* mean "forgetfulness," "(moments of) absentmindedness."

12. *Plaisir* as a moralistic term should be in the singular, as in *vendeuse de plaisir,* "prostitute." But the plural, while excluding the wrong meaning, aggravates the equivocation the moment the possibility of a double entendre is perceived, since pleasures are necessarily lower, more concrete, more inescapably carnal than Pleasure.

13. Mutually exclusive at the lexical level, *within* the word, even if they are equally desirable and relevant in the given descriptive or narrative environment, that is, even if they justify using the word twice in a poem written in everyday, cognitive language, so as to do separate justice to each of its two functions.

14. Hugo, *Contemplations,* VI, xxvi, "Ce que dit la bouche d'ombre," lines 654–56. The *mouth of darkness* belongs to a supernatural Being who reveals the meaning of the Universe to the beholder: hence Creation as two texts, one mimetic, one hermeneutic.

15. The valorization by the paradigm is independent of the subject matter, since it results from synonymic accumulation. The subject itself, like anything having to do with human suffering, and like horror stories, quickens our perception and eagerness to detect anything cryptic or terrifying in the description (what's going on? what are they doing to him? and the like). But, as in all good suspense stories, the text never fully satisfies this curiosity.

16. The personification would permit visualization as a kind of allegory, but involved here is the extreme specificity required (Hugo is alluding to the torture he describes more exactly in another poem, *Légende des Siècles,* "Sultan Mourad": you squeeze the victim between boards and saw right through the whole sandwich, like the magician slicing up the lady inside the box). This increases the distance between the sentence's difficulty, which leads the reader to content himself with vague impressions, the "feel" of the textual connotations, and the detailed picture that a history of man's cruelty to man could theoretically provide.

17. Leiris, "Ecumes de la Havane," ii, *Haut-Mal* (Paris: NRF), Coll. Poésie, p.239.

18. Idiolectic because *château d'eau* as used by Leiris has no currency in other texts. It is a case of *hapax* homonymy.

19. André Breton, *Oubliés,* "Je reviens" [I'm back, or Home again], *Signe ascendant* (NRF, 1968), p.120.

20. This turn of phrase is not unknown in English (*tower of strength,* etc.), but in French the first noun is that of an animate being. The examples quoted are clichés, but new instances still flow from the same structure: e.g., this parodic derivation in Eluard's *L'amour la poésie,* XI, "un coq de panique jaillit" [a rooster of panic bursts forth].

21. It must be clear that Breton's griffin is not a metaphor, for there is no connection with a literal meaning of *griffin: griffin* is only the adjective, as it were, modifying *transparence* with a "suddenness" seme. There is the temptation to perceive it as a metaphor: we might recognize at least a similarity of situation in T. S. Eliot's London fog as a big cat: "The yellow fog that rubs its back upon the windowpanes, / The yellow smoke that rubs its muzzle on the windowpanes / Licked its tongue into the corners of the evening" ("The Love Song of J. Alfred Prufrock," 15). Somewhere in the human psyche there may even be a tendency to fantasize sudden intrusions from the outside world as faces against the windowpane. This natural fear will then be a factor in overdetermination. But technically the image derives from *poil* (the more readily for the reason just given) and *poil* from the "other meaning" of *lustrer.*

22. Wiping away steam or mist is a recurrent image in Breton. He uses it to describe the gradual and difficult uncovering of a reality beyond (a surreality), of a suspected truth behind a screen, more especially a smokescreen (a cloud of steam), behind appearances (e.g., *L'Amour fou,* pp.99–102). In such a context it may not be so strange that the revelation is metaphorized by the griffin as a supernatural or esoteric Jack-in-the-Box.

23. Ponge, *Douze petits écrits,* in *Tome premier* (Paris: NRF, 1965), p.14. The Latin is from Suetonius's *Life of Nero,* xlix, 1.

24. Instead of getting a "neologism" effect, that reader may respond as to an "original" image, that is, he may perceive the novelty of associations that make the sign dual through a rationalization: he will react to its dual reference by upgrading it on a scale of value judgments. Reading Julien Gracq's metaphor *burg de cristal* [crystal castle] he will see it against the background of *iceberg,* while at the same time perceiving it as an original image (with the archaic flavor conferred by *burg*). As an image it refers to a rich text of traditional representations of ice and the marvels of the winter world or the Polar landscape. As a pun on or translation of *iceberg* it is both appropriate itself and a stylistic rejuvenation of the word ("La Barrière de Ross," *Liberté grande*):

> c'était l'heure où le froid brusque du soir détache de la banquise ces burgs de cristal qui croulent dans une poussière de glace avec le bruit de l'éclatement d'un monde, et retournent sous la volute cyclopéenne d'une vague bleue un ventre de paquebot gercé d'algues sombres

> this was the hour when the sudden chill of evening breaks off from the ice floe those crystal castles that crumble into a dustcloud of ice with the

boom of a universe exploding, and beneath the giant curl of a blue wave
roll up an ocean-liner's underbelly cracked with dark seaweed

Iceberg is technical. Our hidden neologism/apparent archaism is felt as a
phrase circling around a simpler word in a display of rhetorical pomp and
circumstance, lining up two tropes for one word, instead of just two words for
one: a simile (*burg*) and a hyperbole (*cristal*). The latter is the conventional
metaphorical embellishment of *ice* in classical French, in addition to being
the perfectly ordinary noun for ordinary crystal in everyday language. Fur-
ther, *burg* replaces *château* or *palais* because it is morphologically and pho-
netically the form closest to *berg* in French. But even such closeness would
not trigger the true pun were it not for the fact that one theme of travel lit-
erature is the description of weirdly shaped icebergs as exotic or dream cha-
teaux. It is a variant of the *natural architecture* theme.

But then fantastic architecture provides two secondary chains of associa-
tion. One determines the selection of *burg* (if we set aside the pun): ruined
Gothic Rhineland castles (for which French reserves this borrowing from
German) have been, from romanticism on, fantasy settings of choice. Another
chain determines *crystal,* apart from the semic analogy between *cristal* and
glace: for one of the fantastic architecture motifs is the crystal castle, a rhe-
torical adynaton as well as a fantasm. There are many examples of the hold
this adynaton has on artists' minds, from the crystal haunts of fairies and
mermaids to the Crystal Palace of Victorian London. The conversion of *ice-
berg* expels the word from the text, but the expansion derived from it as a
matrix only displaces its literal translation or metonym, the word *glace*. This
latter serves to qualify the cloud of dust arising from the avalanche and thus
maintains descriptive verisimilitude and insures the reader's interpretation of
burg as a metaphor. But *poussière,* "dust," is nonetheless an outgrowth of
cristal, for by virtue of the polarization of crystal as beauty and crystal as
fragility, from the French baroque era on, the cliché has pulverized *cristal,*
reduced it to *poudre* or *poussière*. And finally, the effect of the repressed
matrix is felt in the description of the upturned iceberg as a ship's hull
covered with strips of seaweed. Instead of strips we have chaps or cracks:
gercé reintroduces the iceberg into a text built upon the latency of the ap-
propriate word for *ice*.

25. On lexical blends, or portmanteau words, of the type Lewis Carroll made
popular (e.g., *bread-and-butterfly*), see Souriau 1965; also Jacques Chaurand,
"Des croisements aux mots-valises," *Le français moderne* 45 (1977): 4–15.

26. First because the new suffix defines the class of words it provides end-
ings for, and since many of them suggest confused noises or shapes (like
gazouillis, "twittering" of birds, *gribouillis,* "scribbling," "doodling"), the
suffix itself may function as a marker of a "swarming" seme. Second, the
suffix shift makes the reader conscious of the radical as a separate entity, and
this makes it seem to belong to a class of words ending in *-ouille*. None of
these has anything but pejorative, unpleasant connotations (except for
mouiller, "wet," "moisten," and *houille,* "coal"): pejorative as with *rouille,*
"rust," or *souiller,* "to soil"; vulgar as with *couilles,* "balls," or disgusting as

with *pouille,* "lice" (in *chanter pouilles,* "insult," a compound based on *pou,* "louse").

27. Claudel, "Développement de l'église," in *Art poétique* (*Œuvre poétique,* Bibliothèque de la Pléiade, pp.211–14).

28. Apollinaire, *Poèmes à Madeleine,* "Le deuxième poème secret," verses 20–21.

29. In the paradigm of words for aquatic plants, indeed, *roseau* has a meliorative marker, and hence shares the same positive connotation as the whole system's kernel word. This connotation is the more compelling for the reader because *roseau* is opposable to *jonc,* "rush," which belongs strictly to the style of realistic genres or to texts generated by negative conversion. For example, this, from a Germain Nouveau parody of Jean Richepin's poems about beggars, "La ballade du méchant poète" (1876): "Mon père était un loup dans les forêts / Ma mère fut une chienne aux crins flaves / Et j'ai grandi dans les joncs des marais" [My father was a wolf in the forest / My mother was a bitch with yellow hair / And I grew up in the rushes of the marsh]. Or again, from Lautréamont's *Maldoror* III, 5, "route ténébreuse à travers les eaux stagnantes et les humides joncs de la mare où, recouvert de brouillards, bleuit et mugit le crime" [Dark road across the stagnant waters and the damp rushes where, swathed in fog, Crime turns blue and howls]. Jules Laforgue, master of irony, parodies love poetry by switching from clear to stagnant water and from reed to rush in "Locutions des Pierrots" (*Notre-Dame la Lune*): "Les mares de vos yeux aux joncs de cils" [the ponds of your eyes with their bulrushy lashes]. Hence the phrase *cils roseaux* converts an abstract statement into a descriptive piece, the equivalent of *beautiful eyelashes.*

30. The lover gazes at his own reflection in the eyes of his beloved—a visual image of reciprocal love, a *topos* exemplified in all Occidental literatures. In French it begins with Ronsard, who has a poem that (like our Apollinaire piece) mixes water and war imagery, comparing the eyes to lakes, the eyebrows to bows, the lady's glances to arrows (ed. Laumonier, vol. 2, p.164), and goes on to Michel Leiris, *Mots sans mémoire,* p.103, who speaks of "l'eau paisible de l'œil" [the still water of the eye].

31. So solidly established is this system that the metonymy linking *cil* and *roseau* can operate in reverse, with *roseau* as the word to be metaphorized— as in these lines where Mallarmé describes a delicate Chinese painting of "Un lac, . . . Un clair croissant . . . , Non loin de trois grands cils d'émeraude, roseaux" ("Las de l'amer repos . . . ," lines 25–28) [A lake, a clear crescent moon, not far from three great emerald eyelashes, reeds]. To trace fully the determinant associative chains, I should have to analyze the whole poem, not just these verses. But I can at least point out that, of the various metaphors for "eyelash" in love poetry (soldiers watching the lover, arrows ready to pierce his heart, etc.), "reeds" was here further determined by the matrix for the whole poem: *to me you are everything*—first actualized through an animal model, then, thanks to a polarizing derivation, through a vegetable one: "Je pense à toi ma panthère bien panthère oui puisque tu es pour moi tout ce qui est animé/Mais panthère que dis-je non tu es Pan lui-même sous son aspect femelle . . . Qu'ai-je à faire autre chose que chanter aujourd'hui

cette adorable végétation de l'univers que tu es Madeleine" [I am thinking of you my panther really panther yes because you are for me everything that is alive/But panther what am I saying no you are Pan himself in his female form . . . What else have I to do but sing today of the divine vegetation of the universe that you are Madeleine]. Consequently the poem emphasizes the hairy parts of the body.

32. I need not go on to *penseurs penchés,* since it is more a paronomastic determination than a semantic one, on the model of the proverbial *voleur volé* [the robber robbed], which has many variants, such as Aragon's title *Persécuteur persécuté* [persecutor persecuted], or Prévert's parody of poetic justice: *l'empailleur empaillé* [the taxidermist stuffed]; plus a pun on *penser/ pencher,* which brings us back to the lover anxiously trying to read the enigma in a pair of female eyes. The pun on *penser/pencher* [think/lean over] is the more tempting because one of the clichés for serious-thinking-about is *se pencher sur (une question, un problème, son passé).* Cf. Max Jacob, *Le Phanérogame,* p.108: *roseau à penchants* [reed with penchants].

33. Oft quoted and oftener parodied: for instance, Prévert, *Paroles,* p.49: *roseau bien-pensant* [a reed with sound ideas, *bien-pensant* being the satirical cliché for conservative, conformist Roman Catholics]. Similarly, the phrase *roseaux jaseurs* is probably a cliché: I find *roseau qui jase* in Laforgue, *Notre-Dame la Lune* (vol. I, p.205), and there seems to be a tradition that the soft murmuring of reeds goes well with love scenes, e.g., "la susurration des roseaux inclinés sur notre passage," in Chateaubriand's "Cynthia" love monologue, *Mémoires d'Outre-Tombe,* ed. Levaillant, Edition du Centenaire (Paris: Flammarion), vol. 4, pp.284–85. Ovid's metamorphosis of Syrinx (her name means the "pipes of Pan") into a reed (*Metamorphoses,* Book 1, lines 687–711, exp. 707–708) already fuses the love theme with the narrative rationalization of (or expansion on) the singing reed cliché.

34. Its code, that is, the nature of the poem's idiolectic conventions, its lexicon, etc.: e.g., Queneau's "Héraldique" (see pp.169–76). A statement of topic may at the same time identify the code, especially where the topic designated is an object standing for something else: Verlaine's "Le Rossignol" tells us that the poem so named is about a nightingale, but the nightingale also generates a *bird* code, which serves to depict human thoughts and feelings (see pp.37–39).

35. *Ivanhoe,* chap. viii: "His suit of armour was formed of steel, richly inlaid with gold, and the device of his shield was a young oak-tree pulled up by the roots, with the Spanish word *Desdichado* signifying Disinherited."

36. Hugo, *Chansons des rues et des bois* [1865] I,II,ii (see other texts quoted by R. Journet and Guy Robert, *Notes sur les Chansons* [Paris: Les Belles-Lettres, 1973], p.96).

37. These are the details critics try to explain by allusions to the poet's personal experiences: which is, of course, only a way of excusing an inability to translate ungrammaticalities or mere obscurities by pleading pardonable lack of biographical knowledge, facts lost through no fault of the critic's. Some real adventure of Rimbaud's is discovered behind the whole story: the first stanza is an Italian affair; the *Sabines de banlieue* who help him forget

his frustrations are London prostitutes, since we know from Verlaine's letters that there were hookers in London and that Rimbaud knew of their availability when he was there. I am faithfully quoting Suzanne Bernard, authoritative editor of Rimbaud's *Œuvres* (Garnier, 1960), p.530, fn. 1, p.531, fn. 5.

38. Overdetermined by a polarization exemplified in Pascal's oft-quoted maxim: *qui veut faire l'ange fait la bête.*

39. Add Mallarmé, *Vers de circonstances,* xxviii (Pléiade, p.155), and "Sonnets" II "A.M." (ibid., p.177), and "Moi, sylphe de ce froid plafond" [I, sylph of this cold ceiling] in "Surgi de la croupe . . ." (ibid., p.74), the birdcode equivalent of the *page blanche* theme of frustration. The cancellation of the skyward-flight symbolism obviously corresponds to a structure, since it crosses linguistic borders. E.g., Anthony Trollope, *The Warden,* chap. VI: "see how the archdeacon, speechless in his agony, deposits on the board his cards, and looks to heaven or to the ceiling for support."

40. Heine, *Atta Troll,* Caput XXV, stanzas 16–17. Cf. Charles Cros, "Intérieur," ed. Pia and Forestier, p.316.

41. Robert G. Cohn, *Rimbaud* (Princeton University Press, 1974), p.379. Cf. Jules Laforgue's grotesque hags (*Derniers vers,* V, "Pétition"): "Vénus étalées et découvrant vos gencives . . . et bâillant des aisselles" [Venuses spread out, baring your gums and showing your gaping armpits].

42. We may assume that the jackass's *membrum virile* is a *grief,* "grievance," because of sexual frustration suffered during the night ("Tout se fit ombre et aquarium ardent," however obscure, is an obvious allusion to nocturnal sex: its very obscurity acts upon us like the dots or omissions in the novels of more prudish times, when hot episodes were evaded). The parodic note of *Sabines* (they make the same gesture in David's 1799 painting *Sabines*) is reinforced by *banlieue;* the word for an urban periphery that is neither city nor country was pejorative in Rimbaud's day, connoting as it does the mediocre.

43. Hugo, *Promontorium Somnii* (Paris: Imprimerie nationale, 1937), p.316.

44. Queneau, *Le Chien à la Mandoline* (Paris: NRF, 1965), p.83.

45. A comic device frequent in Queneau. Cf. *Chien,* p.120, *icizoula* (ici ou là); 121, *un zoizeau* (un oiseau); 126, *ici-zè-là* (ici et là), etc. First, it satirizes illiteracy or semiliteracy, a sure-fire hit in a country obsessed with words, where the State (ever since the Académie française) has never ceased its efforts to regulate even language, and where correct pronunciation and spelling are still status symbols.

46. There is also the passing shadow of another vulgarity: the various readers on whom I have tried out the text's effect, and I myself, all understand instinctively: "the abyss that swallows everything up," until they are set right by line 8, which explains that *tout* is the subject, in inverted word order the first time around. But this initial interpretation—quite natural, since it is a tautological reading—assumes *qu'* to stand for *qui,* subject (instead of *que,* predicate), in which case the elision of *-i* is decidedly colloquial.

47. When the romantics started their campaign against the neglect or destruction of historic monuments, *badigeonner* became an obsession, especially in travel stories. The word seems to sum up the sin of painting over the em-

blems of the past, and so silencing the language of the stones. In addition, the other two groups in which *passer* can be used with paint or color as predicate are *passer à la chaux, badigeonner* again, *passer au bleu,* a colloquialism for "make disappear" if the subject is a conjuror, or "filch" if he is a pickpocket.

48. The same type as *bull in a china shop* rewritten as *China in the bull shop,* a joke on the admission of Communist China to the United Nations.

49. Lautréamont tops the Greek *exemplum* of the philosopher who died laughing when he saw a donkey eating the figs prepared for his own dinner (*Chants de Maldoror,* Canto iv [37]). Unquestionably there is something tempting in these interversions, some power over the imagination, since Eluard and Breton's *Dictionnaire abrégé du Surréalisme* (1938) picks precisely this example for the *possible* entry (the "possible universes"), and Eluard quotes it again among "the images that obsess him and make him admit to himself that nothing is beyond comprehension" (*L'Evidence poétique* [1937] 15 [Pléiade], vol. I, p.1490).

50. Michel Leiris, *Glossaire j'y serre mes gloses* [1939], s.v. *limon* (the title of the collection is another example, with the lexical given's inverted syllables expanded into a sentence).

51. E.g., *Le Chien à la Mandoline,* "Souvenir": "j'y suis tout *pressé comme en caque hareng* et sardine en boîte," a reversal of the proverbial *serré comme hareng en caque* [packed like herring in a barrel]. Note that *pressé* is also a reversal of *serré.*

52. Psalms 41:8. The quotation, always in Latin, was until recently part of the French sociolect; it still appears in *Petit Larousse*'s pink pages listing useful quotations.

53. One of the most "official" monuments of the sociolect, hallowed by the teaching of literature in the public schools: Lamartine, *Harmonies poétiques et religieuses,* II, ii, "L'Occident." The tautology (everything dashing into the cosmic void, also called *tout*) parallels *abyssus abyssum,* as well as the tautology or circularity of lines 7–9, and the suggestion that the abyss in turn is inside its victim (*tout* as part of *toutou*).

54. The more obvious jokes keep in step with the more serious developments: *mézou* comes just in time to balance the reader's awareness that *passer* stands for "mortality." *Toutou* coincides with the climax, and also underscores *tout:* setting two extreme poles of a paradigm in opposition to each other is tantamount to representing the whole paradigm. Oppose the elephant to the fly (*moucheron*) or the flea (*puce*)—a common French conceit—and you sum up the entire animal class. In our text the most ordinary, the most domestic animal (*chien*) and the most supernatural together form a class that seems to encompass all Creation. Changing *chien* into *toutou* polarizes the opposition and enlarges the compass.

55. That would be the case with Gautier's "In Deserto," a poem I use to demonstrate another point (see pp.12–13). Or we might say that, since "In Deserto" is significant both as a complete syntagm (or even as a lexeme) and as an incomplete quotation, it should fall into a category intermediate be-

tween the text-sign interpretant and the textual interpretant. But it seems to me this would complicate things too much while applying to relatively few poems.

56. Or, in a different formulation, the pretransformation version and its transform, sharing the same matrix.

57. Dated 1946, now in Francis Ponge, *Le Grand Recueil*, vol. 2: *Méthodes* (NRF, 1961), pp.200–202. In this and other poems, the interplay between hypogram and derivation is signalled by ungrammaticalities so distributed as to cause the component texts to mirror one another, thus creating a closed verbal universe, or the illusion of it, stemming from the reciprocal referentiality among the texts. In such a case the text can have no other purpose than to demonstrate showily that it is self-sufficient, that it is an end unto itself (on textual self-sufficiency, see Riffaterre 1973c). This is all the more striking because in writing about his poetic principles, Ponge states his aim: he strives for a rounded, objective representation of things. This aim he calls a bias toward reality—*le parti-pris des choses*. All he does, however, is construct complexes of interconnecting descriptive systems, with semantic or formal parallelisms that do indeed give the reader a strong sense of actual representation—whereas it is all in fact an affair of highly visible overdetermination: *parti-pris des choses*, but as Ponge himself says: *compte tenu des mots* (see Genette 1976, especially pp.377–81).

58. On the grammar of descriptive poetry, especially didactic poetry, see Riffaterre 1972a.

59. The poet indeed represents himself as a writer experimenting with various ways of telling what we all see. The poem's "voice" speaks in the first person plural, but that simply implies he is speaking for others as well, that he is discussing a common experience. For the sake of brevity, let us say: the poet.

60. We find typical miraculous infringements in the poems European romantics (Shelley among others) devoted to the sensitive plant, an animated flower straddling the vegetable and animal kingdoms. Even Ponge, affecting to discountenance an exemplary shunting from one natural kingdom to another, yields a little later to the pressure of the genre's basic structure with his own image. In extolling the crystal's hardness and transparency, you can achieve an image of perfection by merely transferring these two semes onto a scale of values. Instead, Ponge chooses to turn the semes into markers of liquidity and minerality, making an impossible union of incompatibles out of their coincidence in crystal: "Oui, voilà donc enfin avec les qualités de la pierre celles du fluide coordonnées!" [Yes, here at long last the properties of stone and those of liquid, coordinated!]—a powerful polarizing derivation that tempted Proust before Ponge. The former uses it in his celebrated description of bottles left to cool in the Vivonne River, with a protracted play on solid crystal within liquid crystal.

61. Here is my translation of the whole paragraph, quoted on page 110: [even modern mineralogists may sometimes lapse into this flower cliché without really believing it, probably because of their natural bent toward a classical imagery. It is obviously our raison d'être, as poets, if we have one,

to try to give them, as well as the general public, a distaste for such images.] The conventional praise starts out with a triple quotation: Ponge quoting Littré quoting Fontenelle quoting Tournefort; these three levels of precedent-invoking function together as one iconic sign that the literary text is a latticework of other texts.

62. The title "Golden Verse," alludes to Pythagorean tradition, which in turn motivates a reverie on an animistic cosmos, and on symbolic correspondences.

63. It is a law of the *epigraph* that it tells us what is essential in the work of art by a double detour: saying it through another author, and letting it out in the guise of some trivial detail apparently unconnected with the subject, or through a seemingly superficial lexical similarity. On top of the epigraph's role as interpretant here—as central to the poem as can be, of course —there is another connection, perhaps the ghost of one, yet a formal echo, since Rimbaud seems to be correcting an error made by Haüy and Tournefort. They say that stone flowers are in hiding. Rimbaud replies, "No, it is the stones that are hiding; the flowers are looking."

CHAPTER 5: TEXTUAL SEMIOTICS

1. On intertextuality, see Kristeva 1969, p.255, also pp.191, 195; Philippe Sollers: in *Théorie d'ensemble* (Paris: Seuil, 1968), pp.75, 324. The most recent contribution to the study of intertextuality: issue 27 (1976) of *Poétique,* especially Laurent Jenny, "La stratégie de la forme," pp.257–81.

2. Aragon, quoted in Delas and Filliolet 1973, p.167. Cf. Max Jacob, *Le Cornet à Dés* [1916], Préface (Paris: Stock), p.16: "Une page en prose n'est pas un poème en prose, quand bien même elle encadrerait deux ou trois trouvailles" [a page in prose is not a prose poem, even if it should enclose a couple of felicitous images].

3. E. A. Poe, *The Poetic Principle,* ed. H. Allen, *The Complete Tales and Poems* (New York: The Modern Library, 1938), p.889.

4. For such a matrix-representing word to become a generator something must call it to the reader's attention as exceptional and "loaded." Its use as a title, for instance, will do the trick, or its underscoring by a semantic incompatibility with its context, like *splendeur* in *splendeur de la lune,* which I shall be discussing later.

5. Compared with the many prose poems whose outlandish departures from ordinary language usurp the function of verse, this poem is so simple, even flat, that some will refuse to grant it any poetic quality. A questionable attitude, for Eluard himself found it important enough to rewrite and include in his last collection of poems: *Œuvres complètes,* ed. Dumas and Scheler, Bibl. de la Pléiade, vol. I, pp.926 and 1551, which gives the 1939 version (first published in *Donner à voir*). I use the later version as revised by Eluard in 1951, a year before his death (*Choix de poèmes,* NRF, p.213). There is a long commentary on it by the French linguist Mounin (Mounin 1969, pp.279–82), another indication of the poem's pregnant efficacy. On Eluard's prose poem, see Jean Breton's brief remarks, *Europe* 525 (1973): 120–25.

6. E.g., Robert Desnos, "Les espaces du sommeil" (*Domaine public,* p.96): "Dans la nuit passent les trains et les bateaux et le mirage des pays où il fait jour. Les derniers souffles du crépuscule et les premiers frissons de l'aube./Il y a toi./Un air de piano, un éclat de voix./Une porte claque. Une horloge. /Et pas seulement les êtres et les choses et les bruits matériels./Mais encore moi" [In the night trains are passing and boats and the mirage of countries where it is light. The last breathings of dusk and the first shivers of dawn. There is you. A piano tune, a voice raised. A door slams. A clock. And not only human beings and things and noises made by things—but me, too . . .]. See other instances: Jean Tardieu, *Le Fleuve caché,* p.41; Julien Gracq, *Liberté grande,* pp.52, 77 (cf. p.107); Hélène Cixous, *Tombe,* p.15.

7. The generating power of the diminutive is demonstrated by this nonsense sequence in an automatic-writing text of Eluard's: "L'ironie est une chose, le scarabée *rossignolet* en est une autre. Je préfère *l'épuisette* à prendre les animaux féroces . . ." (*Les Dessous d'une vie,* "Anguille de praline," Pléiade, vol. I, p.207, cf. p.1387). My italics. Eluard was quite conscious of the connotations of diminutives, especially the corny ones: "Quelques-uns des mots qui jusqu'ici m'étaient mystérieusement INTERDITS" (1937) [some of the words that until now have been mysteriously forbidden to me] (Pléiade, vol. 1, p.694); "Le mot *maisonnette*/On le trouve souvent dans les annonces des journaux dans les chansons" [the word *maisonnette*/You often find it in newspaper ads and in popular songs].

8. See, on the contrary, a novelist's version of a similar scene, but spread out through a motivated, context-bound narrative (the similarity of details, or of their function, strikingly demonstrates how a descriptive system can pattern different texts identically): George Eliot, *Daniel Deronda* (1876) VIII, chap. 61 (ed. Barbara Hardy, Penguin Books, p.799): "Mirah slipped away to her own room. . . . If the angels once supposed to watch the toilet of women had entered the little chamber with her and let her shut the door behind them, they would only have seen her take off her hat, sit down and press her hands against her temples as if she had suddenly reflected that her head ached; then rise to dash cold water on her eyes and brow and hair till her backward curls were full of crystal beads, while she had dried her brow and looked out like a freshly-opened flower from among the dewy tresses of the woodland; then give deep sighs of relief, and, putting on her little slippers, sit still after that action for a couple of minutes, which seemed to her so long, so full of things to come, that she rose with an air of recollection, and went down to make tea." Cf. Aragon, *Anicet* (Gallimard, 1921), chap. vii, p.104. On the kettle as a metonym of the "happy home": Robert Desnos, "Identité des images" (*Domaine public,* p.138).

9. Claudel, *Connaissance de l'Est* (1900), first published in 1898 (*Œuvre poétique,* ed. St. Fumet, Pléiade, p.65). For lovers of perhaps too-easy parallelism, see a Claudel verse wherein the moon is seen in its normal moonlit stereotypes: "Luna perfecta," *Poésies diverses* (Pléiade, p.865).

10. Francis Ponge, *Nouveau Recueil,* pp.141–42.

11. Claudel, *Accompagnements,* "Paul Verlaine" (*L'Œuvre en prose,* ed. J. Petit and Ch. Galpérine, Pléiade, p.491). The Claudel image is *not* co-

extensive with his text; but it is most formally generated by the topic. Verlaine was born in *Ardennes,* and *Ardennes* generates *ardoise; ardoise* in turn activates the theme of geology as the archival storehouse of Nature, and this makes the contemplation of geological evidence a Book-of-Nature subgenre.

12. *Les Regrets* (1558), sonnet xxxi. Such is the power of polarization that the same *rapprochement* occurred to Claudel, who cites the same line of Du Bellay's.

13. A careful distinction between humor and irony may not be entirely superfluous. Both involve the comic, and humor can be sharp, perhaps even aggressive. Irony, however, has two levels of meaning, one contradicting the other (for instance, *you must be very pleased with yourself* spoken to a person responsible for a disaster). Humor has not two such levels. Humor is a form— a bizarre or twisted one—and in many respects most purely exemplifies the conversion process.

14. *Le Grand Recueil, 3, Pièces* (NRF, 1961), pp.62–63. The poem is dated 1939. Ponge is one of the writers who have made systematic use of humor in their work. See Riffaterre 1974d.

15. The first of the three volumes has a more assertively traditional title: *Lyres.* But within a context of constant attacks upon lyricism (again in the second volume with a jarringly technical title: *Méthodes*), a *lyre* is hardly more than a pun on *lire* [read].

16. "Formation d'un abcès poétique." Needless to say, the joke of the title further points up the meaning of the substitution in *Tome premier* (NRF, 1965), pp.343ff., especially 348–69 (cf. p.359, a commentary on generating a poem by destroying its conventions). The mimesis of the unfinished is, however, an icon of the artifact as the product of painstaking corrections (cf. Ponge's description of Braque's sketches: "une suite de tentatives, d'erreurs tranquillement compensées, corrigées," *Grand Recueil,* I, p.87, and his play on *dessin, dessein,* and *design*).

17. If we had nothing left but *Le téléphone,* we might conceivably expect a lyric version of one of those playlets inspired by the invention when it was new, by the prospects of conflict it offered, despite and because of the physical remoteness between the speakers—partings of the ways, threats of suicide made on the phone, pathos of the helpless witness, and so on. This is the sort of suspense Cocteau is still exploiting in *La Voix humaine,* hardly nine years before our poem. These potentialities are cancelled by *appareil,* which limits *téléphone* to its mechanical-gadget meaning, at least until we perceive retroactively that this meaning has been destroyed by *du.*

18. E.g., humorous effects at the lexical level, such as [5] *y pendante,* an unmotivated archaism combined with an allusion to legalistic phrases such as *y appendu.* Or the mock hyperbole [13] *perfore.* The exaggeration does not diminish appropriateness: *perforer* is overdetermined, since it is equally linked by stereotypes to sounds (*son perçant*), to the ear (*perforer le tympan*), and to wounds (*perforer l'abdomen, un abcès,* etc.). This is Ponge's characteristic manner: his descriptive poetry is not based upon direct mimesis, but upon an accumulation of verbal stereotypes. The reader gets the feeling that the description is accurate not because he can check it against reality, but because

the description is couched in familiar, time-tested language, hallowed commonplaces.

19. Another example of humor giving a text its structure is "La Pompe lyrique" (also dated 1939), the poem immediately following. This proximity is not a matter of chance, since *pompe* is the second definition of *appareil* in Littré. In this respect, each poem is the reciprocal intertext to the other. First, this relationship is one of the signs pointing to the fact that in neither title does the significant noun mean what it seems to mean. Second, the pairing of the two texts despite the difference in topics is further indication that they must be performed as formal exercises. *Lyrique* in the title forces the reader to select from the two *pompe* homonyms the one that means *pomp* rather than the one that means *pump*: "lyrical pomp" is the more likely, being within the context of other titles such as the metaphorical "La Robe des Choses," or the allusive "Symphonie pastorale," or "Ode inachevée à la Boue." It announces something like a ceremonial celebration of the self, a bit similar to Verlaine's *Liturgies intimes*. But the reader soon discovers that the text is in fact referring to a pump. Worse still, this pump is the vacuum cleaner on wheels employed in French towns not so long ago to empty out cesspools. This distasteful subject is treated periphrastically in highflown style, with all the adjectival emoting and exclaiming that Ponge dismisses in his critical writings as so much romantic poppycock. Although the title is totally deceptive if read referentially, and would be taken as a joke in bad taste anywhere else, it is perfectly accurate as an index to this poem's significance, since the whole text is derived from it. The adjective *lyrique* generates a lyrical text. The noun *pompe* generates a periphrastic, riddle-type text alluding to the unmentionable subject that is incompatible with and therefore satirical of the first subject (the allusion is a transform of a description that good taste demands be omitted from social exchanges; in a conversation, for instance, the transform would be a single noun or a demonstrative adjective: *that* pump; in literature, however, the graphic description forbidden by the rules of society may by the very fact of those rules become a feature of subgenres like the French Naturalist novel). The poem is thus the interplay of two texts, one modeled upon lyric poetry, the other upon a pornogram, the first overwhelming the second even while being undermined by it. The effect of this unresolved conflict is comic. Because its only visible motivation is the title, both pun and oxymoron, the nature of this comicality must appear to be verbal: this is humor. Its function, however, is to stress comically a content that in another style would be stressed seriously. The second text is generated as a challenge to or as an intentional antiphrasis of the first. The lyrical style is only the expansion into a whole text of a short, noncommittal periphrasis like *you-know-what,* whose function is to block out the pornogram. The pun on *pompe,* as explicated within the body of the poem, suggests that the poetry of the self is nothing but a sublimation of more excremental complexes. All this arising from a back-and-forth confrontation between the two meanings of *pompe,* each alternating as the matrix of the other. What is relevant to the text is not the title's referential meaning but its form, the hidden incompatibility between *pompe* and *lyrique,* doubletalk we catch on to by a double-take. The significance of the poem lies not

in what it depicts but rather in the destruction of a literary genre—a metalinguistic praxis.

20. The effect is not unlike what a modern reader, unforewarned, may experience when confronted by *écorchés,* those ancient anatomical engravings wherein what was felt to be an offensive dissection of the body was toned down by draping the skeleton or opened-up corpse in some sort of garment and giving him the more decent posture of a statue.

21. It is also a rewrite in the passive voice of ² *une crustace se décroche.* The parallelism between the two nonsensical utterances functions exactly like the parallelisms typical of poetic discourse.

22. In fact its equivalent in common expressions like *prendre l'appareil* or the cliché used in answering: *X à l'appareil.*

23. As listed in Littré, so often quoted by Ponge as the tool he used in probing *l'épaisseur sémantique des mots* (*Proêmes, Tome premier,* p.200), e.g., *Tome premier,* pp.278–83, also *Entretiens de F. Ponge avec Philippe Sollers* (Gallimard-Seuil, 1970), pp.46–47. The *appareil* entry reads: "S.m. 1⁰ Disposition de ce qui a grandeur ou pompe. Appareil de guerre. Appareil de fête . . . 2⁰ Pompe, magnificence . . . 4⁰ Assemblage de pièces . . . propres à une opération . . ."

24. *Quelques médaillons et portraits en pied,* Bibl. de la Pléiade, p.499.

25. It is explicitly mentioned in 5 and 11. This heaviness is also part of our everyday experience when we can dial without making the telephone case slide, without having to hold it steady. This comfortable sense of convenience is exploited with a slight distortion by Ponge in 11: he affects to think that this practical convenience is in itself reason enough for using a telephone—another type of humor, a play on content rather than on words.

26. *Implicit* rather than outer or external intertext, or hypogram. *Implication* fits the phenomenon to a T, since the term covers the intertext both when actually identified, and when only implied by the text but nowhere to be found except within the forever inaccessible psyche of the author.

27. The implicit intertext must therefore be carefully distinguished from R. Barthes's concept of intertext (e.g., Barthes 1973, pp.58–59), which proclaims the reader's freedom to associate texts at random, as dictated by his culture or personal idiosyncrasies—a response by definition personal, shared with others only by chance: this is hardly the disciplined reading the text in its structured entirety demands of the reader; it hardly gives the text a physiognomy readers *must* agree on.

28. Mallarmé, *Œuvres complètes,* ed. H. Mondor & Jean-Aubry (Bibl. de la Pléiade, 1951), pp.470–71.

29. Jarry, *Gestes et opinions du docteur Faustroll, pata-physicien,* xxvi, *Œuvres complètes,* ed. M. Arrivé (Pléiade), vol. I, pp.699–700. Confirming the *homard-crustace* equivalence, the text verifies that *homard* automatically generates tautological representations of hard shell: "il se cuirassait d'une carapace dure" [it was putting on its hard-shell armor].

30. Coining a noun from an adjective by dropping the adjectival ending is no new procedure, but it always looks novel, as if it were inverting the more natural derivation of adjective from noun. Cf., on the model *espace/*

spacieux, grâce/gracieux, Michel Deguy's coinage from *fallacieux* to state an abstract concept that is expressed by the adjective only in concrete instances: "nous pouvons dissocier, pris au fallace de la chronologie, . . . deux moments . . ." *Tombeau de Du Bellay* (NRF, 1973), p.70.

31. Some indices suggest that the word *homard* has comic connotations as well. To wit, the turn-of-the-century catch phrase *En voulez-vous, des-z-homards* —so catchy indeed that it soon became an automatic nonsense retort, applicable to all contexts, in lowbrow spoken humor. Cf. also Alfred Jarry's choice of *homard* for his parody: "Une boîte de corned-beef, enchaînée comme une lorgnette, Vit passer un homard qui lui ressemblait fraternellement . . . ," etc.

32. "Texte sur l'électricité" (1945) (*Grand Recueil*, I, pp.176–77; cf. p.179); "et quand je dis qu'il (l'homme) a su perfectionner son outillage, le plus simple est de le comparer à ces arthropodes, . . . Voyez par exemple homards et crevettes. N'est-il pas merveilleux d'admirer leurs cuirasses et leurs appareils d'estime et de détection, de combat et d'appréhension? Et pourtant! Sans doute n'est-il pas très commode de ne pouvoir jamais quitter sa cuirasse, ni aucune de ses armes, ni aucun de ses appareils, et de toujours devoir vivre avec cet attirail sur le dos. Que dis-je! non seulement sur le dos, mais intimement mêlé à sa chair, et donc à son psychisme, et donc vous faisant devenir entièrement autre, vous faisant devenir cuirassé, périscope, etc. . . . [on *périscope* applied to man's eyes, see *Tome premier*, p.238]. Voilà l'avatar, qui, par merveille, se trouve à l'homme épargné. *Qu'est-ce que l'homme! C'est un homard qui pourrait laisser sa carapace au vestiaire*, son périscope, et ses étaux, et ses cannes à pêche. . . . j'ai fait intervenir à chaque instant la notion de vestiaire, celle de hangar, d'atelier, de placard. C'est qu'en effet, avec des outils que l'on peut quitter, il faut bien quelque endroit pour les ranger, et lorsqu'on reste nu, quelque maison, *caverne* ou palace, pour s'y abriter au besoin. Et c'est ainsi que l'homme, dès les premiers temps, a dû se loger, non seulement pour établir le nid de sa compagne et de sa progéniture, mais pour ranger ses membres détachables . . ." (my italics) [and when I say that Man knew how to improve his tools, the simplest way is to compare him with these arthropods. Take lobsters and shrimps, for instance. Isn't it marvelous to see their admirable armor and their devices for exploration and detection, for combat and capture? And still! It is probably not very convenient never to be able to get out of your suit of armor or drop any of your weapons or tools, to have to live with all that gear forever on your back. What am I saying! not only on your back but intimately mixed in with your flesh, therefore into your psyche, turning you into something entirely different, a dreadnaught, a periscope. This is the avatar that Man, by a miracle, was spared. *What is man! A lobster who was able to leave his shell with the hat-check girl . . .* I am always dragging in the idea of the checkroom, the toolshed, the workshop, the closet. That is because, if you have tools you can lay aside, you have to have some place to put them, and when you are left naked, you have to have some house, a *cave*, or a grand hotel, for shelter when you need it. That is why Man, from the beginning, has had to find lodging, not only to build a nest for his companion and his children, but to store away his detachable limbs].

33. This is no more farfetched than *homelette,* in the slang of the nineties, for a mouse of a man (Ch. Virmaître, *Dictionnaire d'Argot fin-de-siècle,* [Paris: Charles, 1894]). Ponge's text quoted in note 32 realizes the model by means of a pun: "Qu'est-ce que l'homme? c'est un homard qui pourrait . . ."). Cf. *La Rage de l'expression,* "Notes prises pour un oiseau" (1938), *Tome premier,* p.275: "L'oiseau trouve son confort dans ses plumes. *Il est comme un homme* qui ne se séparerait pas de son édredon et de ses oreillers de plume" (my italics) [The bird finds his comfort in his feathers. It is like a man who refused to part with his eiderdown quilt or his feather pillows]. Another text of Jarry's, "Le Homard du capitaine" ("Spéculations" in *La Chandelle verte,* ed. Maurice Saillet [Paris: Le livre de poche, 1969], pp.57–58), contained in a collection of grotesque tales written for *La Revue blanche* in 1901, attributes to a lobster various risqué gestures and intents, making him a salacious henchman to his master. The text first describes the lobster as a mechanical iron hand: this suggests that the *homard* descriptive system facilitates such shifts from the mimesis of the crustacean to that of the mechanical contraption (cf. note 29 and again *Grand Recueil,* II, 193). Then the text veers toward a play on *homard* as a sort of *homme.* A periphrasis skirting both phallus and castration shows the lobster acting out sexual symbols for a man whose right hand has been cut off: "le homard a *commis le délit,* poussé uniquement par sa *sensualité naturelle,* entraînant derrière soi l'*innocent membre* du vétéran" (my italics) [the lobster committed the crime, driven solely by his natural sensuality, dragging behind him the veteran's innocent limb] (a pun here, since *membre* in the singular may be any limb, but is perhaps first of all the *membrum virile*).

34. See pp.138 ff. on scrambling.

35. Cf. *Proêmes,* I, "Un rocher": "De jour en jour la somme *de ce que je n'ai pas encore dit* . . . porte ombrage à la signification pour autrui de la moindre parole que j'essaye alors de dire. Car, pour exprimer aucune nouvelle impression . . . , je me réfère . . . à tout ce que je n'ai encore si peu que ce soit exprimé" (*Tome premier* [NRF, 1965], p.167; text dated 1928, italics are Ponge's) [more and more every day, the sum total of what I have not yet said casts its shadow over the meaning for others of the slightest thing I try to say. For to express any new impression, I refer myself back to everything that I have not yet been able to express even a little].

36. André Breton, *Poisson soluble,* text 27. On this text, Laurent Jenny, "La Surréalité et ses signes narratifs," *Poétique* 16 (1973): 499–520, especially pp.500–501, 515 ff. (cf. Kristeva 1969, pp.227 ff.).

37. One of the cardinal rules of literary fantasy is that verisimilitude must be respected, however extraordinary the tale told. Otherwise we have the *merveilleux,* a representation of the supernatural that fits into no literary genre.

38. A more frequent form is *c'est le dindon de la farce,* but the version I use is authentic and figures in the title of a fable by the eighteenth-century fabulist Florian.

39. André Breton, Paul Eluard, and René Char, in *Ralentir travaux,* "Page blanche" [Slow. Men at work, "Blank Page"]. As part of the surrealist challenge

to the ideological assumption that poetry is an experiment in humanity or the direct lyrical expression of the poet's personality and inner life, these poems are a collective creation. One participant writes down a phrase. The next writes down whatever pops into his head, inspired by this roll of the dice. The initial model that gets the sequence going ("le jeûne des vampires") is a phrase provided by Eluard; Breton produces the associative series derived from it. The model is the more effective because the phrase looks to be a joke like *un lion à jeun* [a lion before breakfast, on an empty stomach]. The following stanza confirms that I am not reading too much into the phrase: a second given, introducing a new development in the text, is described as a *seconde [proposition] un peu moins bête* [a little less silly] than the first, our *jeûne*.

40. *Soif du sang* is obviously a partial periphrastic equivalent of *vampire*. A riddle whose solution is *vampire* would include *soif du sang* in its definition questions (Who slakes his thirst with blood?). So that the text is indeed the transform of one word, and its every verbal feature brings us back to that one word; this makes for the formal unity or cohesiveness that empirical, evaluative, or normative criticism has always assumed is characteristic of a verbal "monument." The first step of the derivation, *aura pour conséquence,* linking the initial given and the model, can be read at two levels: the narrative level, where it seems to be recounting the fateful aftermath of a true horror story, and the metalinguistic level, where the author comments upon his application of the rule of the game described above. Like any double-track sequence, this is a form of overdetermination, but one observed perhaps mostly in automatic-writing poems that proclaim the formal interplay of their components. Reflecting the way the poem was born, *aura pour conséquence* is the icon of the text's genesis.

41. A metaphor supported by tradition with such groups as "thirst for knowledge." "Thirst for blood" *as a group* is metaphoric of "fanaticism," "cruelty," "aggressiveness in pursuit," etc., according to context.

42. A deserted, therefore dangerous, neighborhood, within a thematic network of urban blight, is the only possible interpretation of *endroits déserts,* which in the singular might still permit of a more general interpretation like "wasteland."

43. The reader, by the way, is not at liberty to try to correct or ignore this non sequitur, for the explicit assertion is made that all this refers to a logical chain of events (*aura pour conséquence*); the semantic incompatibilities of literary texts are not to be solved or palliated.

44. *Chants de Maldoror,* Canto 3, stanza 1 (*Œuvres complètes,* ed. P. O. Walzer [Pléiade, 1970], p.136). Significantly, Alexis Lykiard, in his impressive translation (New York: Apollo Editions, 1973), shies away from unacceptable tautology (p.90), though he is usually faithful to every quirk of Lautréamont's language.

45. Not quite. If *verrou* really is part of the mimesis of jail, the padlock (*cadenas*) belongs rather to the inglorious locks on flimsier doors, like those of toolsheds, and has no prison pathos. Paradoxically, however, the adjective here (or the corresponding verb) functions as hyperbolic of locking up, re-

gardless of who or what is padlocked where; hence it belongs to our descriptive system as well.

46. *Maldoror* 5, 4 (p.199).

47. And yet it may, inasmuch as the hypogrammatic (inter)text is only an intermediate stage between the reader and the descriptive system from which it was initially derived. Thus a reader ignorant of that particular (inter)text may perceive the text he is reading as an indirect play on that system. An unsophisticated, incomplete reading, that, but not a "wrong" one.

48. *Moires* (Paris: Mercure de France, 1962), "Larmes d'octobre! ou bien honte d'automne . . ." (p.76). The effect of this scrambling and our certainty that it has been correctly perceived are reinforced by the next poem in the collection, "Portrait" (p.77), which contains an unscrambled quotation from the same Baudelaire verse: "l'homme vieux . . . usé par l'image / Déconcerté depuis longtemps 'comme le roi / D'un pays pluvieux' blasé de ses débauches." A case of double intertextuality, between Jouve and Baudelaire, and between Jouve and Jouve.

49. *Blessure intime, plus mort même que vieux,* refer, of course, to Baudelaire's "Rien . . . Ne distrait plus le front de ce cruel malade . . . , de ce jeune squelette, . . . ce cadavre hébété."

50. Even these personal symbolisms, to be sure, are borrowed from the sociolect's repertory of themes and motifs, but their application to the text remains a highly individual affair, the reader's effort to come to terms with seeming nonsense.

51. *Le Sanglot de la Terre,* "Sieste éternelle."

52. Retroactive reading may get rid of the inconsistency, because a return to the sick afternoon of the first stanza calls up verbal associations that fit dizziness to waltzing. In common French parlance, and in quite a few literary passages as well, a cliché uses the dance metaphor to describe a spell of vertigo: everything around the sufferer seems to be dancing (in English they would more likely be swimming). See for instance the dance of the inanimate in the mimesis of hallucination (the text contains *danse, encensoirs, tourner,* and *extase*) in Balzac, *Jésus-Christ en Flandre* (Pléiade), vol. 9, pp.262–63.

53. This is applying a general rule of style: in any paradigm of synonyms, antonyms, or metonyms, the word with the smallest lexical distribution or collocability is used as a hyperbolic substitute for any word of that same paradigm. *Encensoir* is a rare form; its root, the word for incense, is also sparsely distributed, fitting as it does circumstances and contexts much more limited and particularized than other perfume names.

54. This last is later made explicit in the Baudelaire poem by lines like: "Le violon frémit comme un cœur qu'on afflige / . . . Un cœur tendre, qui hait le néant vaste et noir, / Du passé lumineux recueille tout vestige! / . . . Ton souvenir en moi luit comme un ostensoir" [the violin quivers like a heart being made to suffer . . . A tender heart that hates the vast black void, a heart that gathers up and clings to every vestige of a luminous past . . . Your memory shines within me like a monstrance].

55. Two representative examples will suffice: Shelley, "The Triumph of Life": "All flowers . . . Swinging their censers in the element, / With orient

incense lit by the new ray, / Burned slow and inconsumably, and sent / Their odorous sighs up to the smiling air"; and Théophile Gautier, *Mademoiselle de Maupin,* chap. iv: "de larges fleurs étrangères balançaient leurs urnes sous mon balcon comme pour m'encenser."

56. There is evidence that Mallarmé's creative procedure was to start with simple statements and then belabor them to obscurity with involved periphrases, private allusions, systematic inaccuracies of vocabulary, choice of unusual words, contorted syntax, phrases that flout both the rules of ordinary language and the conventions of traditional literary language—all forms displaying the artifact. (A first and somewhat different version of this analysis of obscurity was published in *The Georgia Review.*)

57. Jeffrey Mehlman, "Entre psychanalyse et psychocritique," *Poétique* 3 (1970): 365–85.

58. Charles Mauron, *Mallarmé l'obscur* (Paris: J. Corti, 1968), pp.30–32, 54–56, 73. Also Ch. Mauron, *Introduction à la psychanalyse de Mallarmé* (Neuchatel: La Baconnière, 1950), pp.13–14. Philippe Sollers builds his text on the Mauron metalinguistic intertext: *je t'apporte l'enfant d'une nuit d'inhumé* (*H* [Paris: Seuil, 1974], p.158).

59. Flaubert, *Madame Bovary,* Part I, chapter V.

60. Vergil, *Georgics,* III, 12.

61. A transformation from abstract to figurative sign. Cf. Alfred Jarry, *Œuvres complètes,* ed. Arrivé (Pléiade), vol. I, pp.704–705, a two-page expansion on *ha ha.*

62. J.-B. Rousseau, *Epigrammes* III, xviii. Or from the author of *Vie de Bohème,* to vary the menu a bit, this irony of Murger's at the expense of those "authors who want the birth of their last born mentioned (in the literary columns). These people forget that criticism does not enter the stillborn in its birth records." Henri Murger, *Propos de ville et propos de théâtre* (Paris: Michel Lévy, 1869), p.155.

63. Herrick, *The Hesperides,* DCXXVI.

64. Gautier, "Sonnet-Dédicace," *Un Douzain de Sonnets;* Molière, *Les Femmes savantes* III.i; D. Saurat, *V. Hugo et les dieux du peuple* (Paris: La Colombe, 1948), p.248.

65. The bird is central to the poem; it therefore appears only through metonyms—the hole in the doughnut (see p.17).

66. See chapter 3, pp.48–49. Cf. Baudelaire's *Albatros,* a symbol of the poet, whose giant wings hinder him from walking.

67. Cf. Hugo, *Contemplations,* 6.21, "Spes": *le coq à la voix sibylline.*

68. Mallarmé, "Crayonné au théâtre," *Œuvres complètes* (Pléiade), p.312.

69. *Variations,* "Le livre, instrument spirituel," in *Œuvres complètes,* p.379.

70. *La Musique et les lettres, Œuvres complètes,* p.648.

71. *Variations sur un sujet,* "L'action restreinte," *Œuvres complètes,* p.370.

72. "Le dieu Richard Wagner irradiant un sacre / Mal tu par l'encre même en sanglots sibyllins" (*Œuvres complètes,* p.71).

73. On the *milk-black* polarization, see note 25 of chapter 2.

CONCLUSION

1. It is therefore the form of unlimited semiosis peculiar to poetry, first brought to light by C. S. Peirce. The final interpretant is not a *habit* (his term, 4.536), but the stylistically guaranteed physical permanence, the "monumentality" of the poem in which a given idiolect is encoded.

Bibliography

No attempt has been made to offer a comprehensive bibliography of poetics, let alone of semantic theory or general semiotics. Only such works have been listed as I have found in one way or another suggestive and serviceable to my specific purposes. Not included are studies of individual poems or particular literary problems without general applicability, but these are referred to in the notes.

Adam, Jean-Michel.
  1976. *Linguistique et discours littéraire. Théorie et pratique des textes.* Paris: Larousse.
Arrivé, Michel.
  1973. Pour une théorie des textes poly-isotopiques. *Langages* 31: 53–63.
Barthes, Roland.
  1964. Eléments de sémiologie. *Communications* 4: 91–135.
  1970. *S/Z.* Paris: Seuil.
  1973. *Le Plaisir du Texte.* Paris: Seuil.
Benveniste, Emile.
  1966. *Problèmes de linguistique générale.* Paris: Gallimard. Volume I.
Bouasiz, Charles, ed.
  1973. *Essais de la théorie du texte.* Paris: Galilée.
Brooke-Rose, Christine.
  1976. *A Structural Analysis of Pound's "Usura Canto." Jakobson's Method Extended and Applied to Free Verse.* The Hague: Mouton.
Charles, Michel.
  1977. *Rhétorique de la lecture.* Paris: Seuil.
Cohen, Jean.
  1966. *Structure du langage poétique.* Paris: Flammarion.
  1970. Théorie de la figure. *Communications* 16: 3–25.
Coppay, Frank L.
  1977. The Internal Analysis of Compression in Poetry. *Style* 11: 19–38.
Coquet, Jean-Claude.
  1973. *Sémiotique littéraire.* Tours: Mame.
Culler, Jonathan.
  1975. *Structuralist Poetics.* Ithaca: Cornell University Press.
Delas, Daniel, and Filliolet, Jacques.
  1973. *Linguistique et poétique.* Paris: Larousse.
Dubois, Philippe.

1975. La Métaphore filée et le fonctionnement du texte. *Le français moderne* 43: 202–13.

Dupont-Roc, Roselyne, and Lallot, Jean.
   1974. La Syrinx. *Poétique* 18: 176–93.

Eaton, Trevor.
   1966. *The Semantics of Literature*. The Hague: Mouton.

Eco, Umberto.
   1975. Peirce and Contemporary Semantics. *Versus* 15: 49–72.
   1976. *A Theory of Semiotics*. Bloomington: Indiana University Press.

Fish, Stanley E.
   1970. Literature in the Reader: Affective Stylistics. *New Literary History* 2: 123–62. Reprinted in *Self-Consuming Artifacts*. Berkeley: University of California Press, 1972.
   1973. How Ordinary is Ordinary Language? *New Literary History* 5: 41–54.

Fowler, Roger.
   1969. On the Interpretation of Nonsense Strings. *Journal of Linguistics* 5: 75–83.
   1975. Language and the Reader. In *Style and Structure in Literature*, ed. R. Fowler, pp.79–122. Ithaca: Cornell University Press.

François, Frédéric.
   1971. Du sens des énoncés contradictoires. *La linguistique* 7: 21–33.

Gamkrelidze, Thomas V.
   1974. The Problem of "l'arbitraire du signe." *Language* 50: 102–10.

Genette, Gérard.
   1966, 1969, 1972. *Figures* I, II, III. Paris: Seuil.
   1976. *Mimologiques. Voyages en Cratylie*. Paris: Seuil.

Greenlee, Douglas.
   1973. *Peirce's Concept of Sign*. The Hague: Mouton.

Greimas, Algirdas Julien.
   1970. *Du Sens*. Paris: Seuil.
   1972. *Essais de Sémiotique poétique*. Paris: Larousse.

Groupe μ.
   1970. *Rhétorique générale*. Paris: Larousse.
   1977. *Rhétorique de la poésie*. Brussels: Complexe.

Guymon, Wayne.
   1975. An Exercise in Semantic Analysis. *Journal of Literary Semantics* 4: 73–91.

Hamon, Philippe.
   1972. "Qu'est-ce qu'une description?" *Poétique* 12: 465–85.
   1977. "Texte littéraire et métalanguage." *Poétique* 31: 261–84.

Hardt, Manfred.
   1976. *Poetik und Semiotik. Das Zeichensystem der Dichtung*. Tuebingen: Max Niemeyer.

Hendricks, William O.
   1974. *Essays on Semiolinguistics and Verbal Art*. The Hague: Mouton.

Hirsch, E. D., Jr.
   1967. *Validity in Interpretation*. New Haven: Yale University Press.

Hjelmslev, Louis.

1961. *Prolegomena to a Theory of Language.* Madison: University of Wisconsin Press. (The original was published in 1943.)

Ihwe, Jens.

1970. Kompetenz und Performanz in der Literaturtheorie. In *Text, Bedeutung, Aesthetik,* ed. Siegfried J. Schmidt. Munich: Bayerischer Schulbuch Verlag.

Ikegami, Y.

1965. Semantic Changes in Poetic Words. *Linguistics* 19: 64–79.

Iser, Wolfgang.

1974. *The Implied Reader.* Baltimore: The Johns Hopkins University Press.

Jakobson, Roman.

1973. *Questions de Poétique.* Paris: Seuil.

Jauss, Hans-Robert.

1974. La Douceur du foyer: The Lyric of the Year 1857 as a Pattern for the Communication of Social Norms. *Romanic Review* 65: 201–29.

Jenny, Laurent.

1972. Structure et fonctions du cliché. *Poétique* 12: 495–517.

1976. La Stratégie de la forme. *Poétique* 27: 257–81.

Johnson, Anthony L.

1977. Anagrammatism in Poetry: Theoretical Preliminaries. *PTL* 2: 89–118.

Kibédi Varga, A.

1963. *Les Constantes du Poème.* The Hague: Van Goor.

Kristeva, Julia.

1969. *Sèméiotikè: Recherches pour une sémanalyse.* Paris: Seuil.

1974. *La Révolution du langage poétique.* Paris: Seuil.

1977. *Polylogue.* Paris: Seuil.

Lefebve, Maurice-Jean.

1971. *Structure du discours de la poésie et du récit.* Neuchâtel: La Baconnière.

Levin, Samuel R.

1962. *Linguistic Structures in Poetry.* The Hague: Mouton.

1965. Internal and External Deviation in Poetry. *Word* 21: 225–37.

1971. The Analysis of Compression in Poetry. *Foundations of Language* 7: 38–55.

Lotman, Yuri.

1973. *La Structure du texte artistique.* Traduit sous la direction d'H. Meschonnic. Paris: Gallimard.

1976. *Analysis of the Poetic Text.* Translated by D. Barton Johnson. Ann Arbor: Ardis.

Lyotard, Jean-François.

1971. *Discours, figure.* Paris: Klincksieck.

Meschonnic, Henri.

1970, 1973. *Pour la Poétique* [I] II, III. Paris: NRF.

Molino, Jean.

1971. La Connotation. *La Linguistique* 7: 5–30.

Mounin, Georges.

1969. *La Communication poétique.* Paris: NRF.

Nowottny, Winifred.

1965. *The Language Poets Use.* London: The Athlone Press.

Peirce, Charles Sanders.

1931–1958. *Collected Papers.* Cambridge: Harvard University Press. (Because these papers are spread over such a long period, references in the text are to volume and paragraph numbers rather than dates and pages.)

Petöfi, János.

1970. On the Structural Analysis and Typology of Poetic Images. In *Studies in Syntax and Semantics,* F. Kiefer, ed., pp.187–230. Dordrecht: D. Reidel.

Polish Academy of Sciences.

1961. *Poetics Poetyka Poètika.* Warsaw: Państwowe Wydawnictwo Naukowe.

Rastier, François.

1972. Systématique des isotopies. In Greimas 1972, pp.80–105.

Ricœur, Paul.

1975. *La Métaphore vive.* Paris: Seuil.

Riffaterre, Michael.

1969. La Métaphore filée dans la poésie surréaliste. *Langue française* 3: 46–60.

1970a. The Stylistic Approach to Literary History. *New Literary History* 2: 39–55. Reprinted in *New Directions in Literary History,* ed. Ralph Cohen, pp.147–64. London: Routledge and Kegan Paul, 1974.

1970b. Le Poème comme représentation. *Poétique* 4: 401–18.

1971a. *Essais de Stylistique structurale.* Paris: Flammarion.

1971b. L'Explication des faits littéraires. In *L'Enseignement de la littérature,* ed. S. Doubrovsky and Tzv. Todorov, pp.331–55, 366–97. Paris: Plon.

1972a. Système d'un genre descriptif. *Poétique* 9: 15–30.

1972b. Dynamisme des mots: les poèmes en prose de Julien Gracq. *L'Herne* 20: 152–64.

1973a. Interpretation and Descriptive Poetry: A Reading of Wordsworth's Yew-Trees. *New Literary History* 4: 229–56.

1973b. Poétique du néologisme. *CAIEF* 25: 59–76, 328–39.

1973c. The Self-sufficient Text. *Diacritics* 3: 39–45.

1974a. Decadent Features in Maeterlinck's Poetry. *Language and Style* 7: 3–19.

1974b. Paragram and Significance. *Sémiotexte* 1: 72–87.

1974c. Semantic Incompatibilities in Automatic Writing. In *About French Poetry from Dada to Tel Quel,* ed. Mary Ann Caws, pp.223–41. Detroit: Wayne State University Press.

1975. Francis Ponge's Poetics of Humor. *Books Abroad* 48: 703–706.

1977. Ponge tautologique, ou le fonctionnement du texte. In *Ponge inventeur et classique,* ed. Philippe Bonnefis and Pierre Oster, pp.66–84, 85–90. Paris: 10/18.

1979. *La Production du texte.* Paris: Seuil.

Ruwet, Nicolas.
   1972. *Langage, musique, poésie.* Paris: Seuil.
Scholes, Robert.
   1974. *Structuralism in Literature.* New Haven: Yale University Press.
Sebeok, Thomas A.
   1975. Six Species of Signs: Some Propositions and Strictures. *Semiotica*
       13, 3: 233–60.
Segre, Cesare.
   1975. *Semiotics and Literary Criticism.* The Hague: Mouton.
Shapiro, Michael.
   1976. Deux paralogismes de la poétique. In Todorov 1976, pp.423–39.
Skalmowski, Wojciech.
   1970. On the Notion of Subcode in Semiotics. In *Sign, Language, Culture,*
       ed. R. Jakobson et al., pp.57–63. The Hague: Mouton.
Smith, Barbara Herrnstein.
   1970. *Poetic Closure.* Chicago: The University of Chicago Press.
Souriau, Etienne.
   1965. Sur l'esthétique des mots et des langages forgés. *Revue d'esthétique*
       18: 19–48.
Starobinski, Jean.
   1971. *Les mots sous les mots. Les anagrammes de F. de Saussure.* Paris:
       NRF.
Steinberg, Danny D., and Jakobovits, Leon A., eds.
   1971. *Semantics: An Interdisciplinary Reader in Philosophy, Linguistics
       and Psychology.* Cambridge: Cambridge University Press.
Todorov, Tzvetan.
   1973a. *Qu'est-ce que le structuralisme?* 2. *Poétique* (second, revised edition).
       Paris: Seuil.
   1973b. Analyse du discours: l'exemple des devinettes. *Journal de Psycho-
       logie normale et pathologique* 70: 135–55.
   1976. (ed.). Le discours de la poésie. *Poétique* 28: 385–510.
   1977. *Théories du Symbole.* Paris: Seuil.
Van Dijk, Teun A.
   1972. *Some Aspects of Text Grammars. A Study in Theoretical Linguistics
       and Poetics.* The Hague: Mouton.
   1973. Modèles génératifs en théorie littéraire. In Bouasiz 1973, pp.79–99.
Van Dijk, Teun A., and Petöfi, János S., eds.
   1975. Theory of Metaphor. *Poetics* 14–15: 131–363.
Warning, Rainer, ed.
   1975. *Rezeptionsaesthetik.* Munich: Wilhelm Fink.
Weinreich, Uriel.
   1966. Explorations in Semantic Theory. In *Current Trends in Linguistics,*
       vol. III, *Theoretical Foundations,* ed. Thomas A. Sebeok, pp.395–477.
       The Hague: Mouton.
Weinrich, Harald.
   1976. *Sprache in Texten.* Stuttgart: Ernst Klett.
Wetherill, P. M.

1974. *The Literary Text.* Berkeley: University of California Press.
Wierzbicka, Anna.
    1970. Descriptions or Quotations. In *Sign, Language, Culture,* ed. R. Jakobson et al., pp.627–44. The Hague: Mouton.
Wiggins, David.
    1971. On Sentence-Sense, Word-Sense and Difference of Word-Sense. Towards a Philosophical Theory of Dictionaries. In Steinberg and Jakobovits 1971, pp.14–34, 35–47 (discussion by Wm. P. Alston), 48–52 (Wiggins's reply).

Index

Numbers in parentheses are note numbers.

Actualization, *19*, *22*, 24, 25–26, 31, 39, 45–46, 48, 52, 68, 73, 75, 82, 91, 98, 109, 117–18, 119, 121–22, 133, 134, 137, 139, 143, 164, 172 (25), 175(8), *180(63)*
Adynaton, 48, 80, 185(24)
Allais, Alphonse, 14, 169(17)
Allegory, 50, 53, 67, 153, 160, *175(14)*
Allusion. *See* Quotation
Ambiguity, 2, 90, 165, 169(20). *See also* Equivocal
Amplificatio, 49, 51, 55
Anaphora, 63, 141
Apollinaire, Guillaume, 97–99, 109
Appropriateness, Aptness, 37, 95, 98, 107, *109*, *114*, 122, 130, 133, *138*, 143, 146, *165*, 182(7), 193–94(18)
Aragon, Louis, 116, 172 (25), 187(32), 192 (8)
Arbitrariness, *21*, *54*, 137
Archetype, 173–74(29)
Ariosto, 83, 85
Arp, Hans, 181(75)
Artifact, 14, 65, 74, 116–17, *124*, 137, 150, 164, 200(56)
Associative sequences, 11, 86, 88, 95, 182(7), 185(24)
Audiberti, Jacques, 172(25)
Automatic writing, 36, *70–75*, *139–43*, 192(7)

Balzac, Honoré de, 40, 41–42, 199 (52)
Baudelaire, Charles, 4, 13, 23–25, 44, 51–53, 65–66, 67–70, 75, 92, 121, 145, 147–49, 160, 172(24)
Banville, Théodore de, 160
Beginning. *See* Model
Béranger, Pierre-Jean de, 140
Blason, 77, 78, *82*, 98, *128–29*, 132
Breton, André, 15–16, 44, 55–56, 70–72,

80, 93–94, 108, 139–41, 141–43, 160, 184(22), 189 (49)

Cancellation, 15, 17, 18–19, 43, 66, 68, 121, 124, 126–27, 129, 170(26)
Capital. *See* Graphemic level
Catachresis, 16, *19–21*, 59, 75, 80, 93, 94, 117, 123, *124–38*, 164, *165*, 181(76), 191(63)
Char, René, 141–43
Chateaubriand, François-René de, 43, 57, 79, 86–89, 153, 187(33)
Class, Classeme, 23, 28, 52, 185(26), 189(54)
Claudel, Paul, 95–97, 119–20, 122, 177(41)
Clausula, 11–12, 60, 70, 75, 104, 131–32, 180(60)
Cliché, 11, 18, 22, 25, 33, 37, *39–42*, 52, 55, 60, 63, 66, 67, 71–72, 78–79, 90, *94*, 99, 118, 119, 123, 140, *141–43*, 153, 165, 193–94 (18), 199(52)
Cocteau, Jean, 44, 162, 193(17)
Code, 7, 10, 36, 38, 50, 51, *54*, 59, 65, *66*, 70, 81, 83, 88, 98, 100, 102, *105–109*, 114, 120, *125*, 135, 136, 157, 159, 162, 171(10), *172(24)*, 173(26), 178(51), 187(34)
Cognitive language. *See* Nonliterary language
Collocation, 42, 66, 86
Comic, 104, 135, 194(19)
Commonplace. *See* Cliché
Compensation, 113
Competence: linguistic, *5*, 39, 91, 139, 165, 178(51); literary, *5*, 136, 144–45
Conceit, 85, 124, 189(54)
Connotation, 8, 26, 32, 65, 95, 102, 104, 112, 134, 148, 149, 164, 171 (14), 182(2), 183(16), 185–86(26), 196(31)

Constant (formal), 116–17, 120, 124, 138
Content, 64, 195(25)
Context, 33, 42, 48, 53, 72, *89*, 97, 134, 146, 153, 167(4), 192(8)
Convention(al), 22, 23, 27, 39, 42, 65, 81, 97, 111, 124, 127, 129, 131, 143, 170(3), 176(27), 185 (24)
Conversion, 10, 11, 15, 17, 22, 38, 45, 47, 57, 58, 60, *63–80*, 84, 99, 101, 102, 103, 117, 139, 154, 174(35), 177(42), 177–78 (45), 179(55), 185(24), 193(13)
Converter. *See* Model
Corbière, Tristan, 79, 124
Cros, Charles, 179(53)
Crux. *See* Obscurity

Decoding. *See* Reading
Decoding control. *See* Restrictive reading
Dedicatory epistle, 154–57
Deguy, Michel, 196(30)
Deictic function, 12, 31, 109, 134, *137–38*, 161, 194 (19)
Derivation, 20, 21, 26, 66, 69, 73, 91, 93–94, 97, 104, *117*, *119*, *121–22*, 129, 159. *See also* Polarization, Tautology
Description, Descriptive, 6, 19, 49, 53, 57, 99, 128, 144, 157, 159–60, 176(32), 193–94(18)
Descriptive system, 22, 31, 35, 36, *39–40*, *42–46*, 63–64, 65, *66–70*, 75, 83, 84, 98, 115, 122, 129, 130, 139, 143, 144, 150, 153, *172*(24), 174(2), 178(47), 179(54), 190(57), 192(8)
Desnos, Robert, 15, 33–34, 72–75, 171 (17), 181 (73), 192(6)
Detail (descriptive), 6, 66, 70, 87, 103, 119, 152
Detour. *See* Catachresis
Didactic poetry, 111, 128
Difficult decoding. *See* Obscurity
Diminutive. *See* Suffix
Displacement, 11, 19, 31, 36, 37–39, 52, 113, 134, 139, 151, *185*(24)
"Doughnut," *13*, 17, 113, 123–24, 137, 185(24), 200(65)
Dual sign, 57, 62, 71, 73–74, *81*, *86–91*, *91–94*, *94–99*, *99–105*, *105–109*, 165
Du Bellay, Joachim, 123

Eliot, George, 192(8)
Eliot, T. S., 184(21)
Ellipsis. *See* Gaps
Eluard, Paul, 3–4, 13, 17, 34, 49, 60–63, 78, 117–19, 124, 141–43, 181(76), 189 (49), 192(7)

Embedding, 22, 51, 70, 143, 159, 165, 168 (16), 176(31)
Encoding, 155
Entailing, *5*, 86, 87
Epigraph, 110, *113*, *191*(63)
Epithet (stock), *27–31*, 170(7)
Equivalence, 17–18, *19*, 27, 41, 43, 47, *81*, 87, 112, *114*, 116, 119, 164, 166, 168(16)
Equivocal, 85, *86*, 87, 88, 91, 94, *108–109*, 165, 183(12), 183(18)
Esthetic(s), 1, 115, 119, 132, 137
Ethos, 30, 98, 111, 129. *See also* Genre
Exemplariness, *21*, 24–25, 27, 29, 30, *43*, 73, 78, 89, 169(18)
Exemplum. See Cliché
Expansion, 12, 22, *47–63*, *75–80*, 91, 97, 100, 101, 102, 107, 112, 115, 121, *124*, 130, 141, 164, 174(2), 175(14), 182 (2), 185(24), 194(19), 200(61)
Explicit. *See* Actualization

Figurative sign, 3, 27, 36, 45, *53–63*, 122, 154, 200(61)
Filtering, 102, 160
Form, 11, 13, 15, 18, 19, 20, 64, 89, 115, 124, 125, 128, 148, 154, *164*, 193(11)
Function, 89, 178(51)

Game. *See* Ritual
Gap, Gap-filling, 12, 13, *40*, 91, 109, 147, 148–49, 151, 165, 183(9), 189(55)
Gautier, Théophile, 6–13, 15, 47–49, 59, 75, 156, 176 (29), 178–79(51), 189(55), 200(55)
Generating, 48-49, 51, 53, 70, 91, 94, 108, 112, 157, 179(55), 194(19). *See also* Derivation
Generator, 21, 42, 45, 85, 116, 124, 191 (4). *See also* Matrix
Genesis of the text, 72, 144, 183(9), 198 (40)
Genre, 65, 71, 77, 83, 98, 100, 111, 115, *116–24*, 129, 132, 140, *150–63*, 190(60), 191(63), 193(11), 194–95 (19). *See also* Blason, Dedicatory epistle, Didactic poetry
Given (semantic). *See* Matrix, Model
Gracq, Julien, 184–85(24)
Graphemic factors, 88, 109, 177(42)
Gratuitousness, 94, 99, 133. *See also* Rationalization

Harmony. *See* Textuality
Herrick, Robert, 155–56
Homonym. *See* Equivocal

Homophony, 86, 89
Hugo, Victor, 18–19, 26–27, 40, 45–46, 57–58, 89–91, 121, 157–59, 171(14)
Humor, 56, 122, *124–38*, 193(13)
Hyperbole, 79, 97, 129, 131, *148*, 149, 169(18), 185(24), 198(45), 199(53). *See also* Exemplariness
Hypogram, 11, *12–13*, 22, *23*, 24–25, *26–46*, 53, 64, 65, 71, 72, 73, 81, 85, 92, *94–99*, 102, *110*, 111, 115, 135, 138, 139, 142, 143, *145*, 157–59, 165, *168–69(16)*, 171(11), 190(57), 195(26), 199 (47)

Icon, 12, 20, 49, 54, 61, 97, 108, 131, 135, 137, *150*, 172(18), 176(32), 191(61), 198 (40)
Idiolect, 21, 23, 35, 65, 81, 84, 88, 90, 93, 128, 131, 133, 134, 167 (4), 167(5), 181 (66), 201(1)
Image, *143–44*
Implicit, 39, 44, 52, 113, 117, 119, 136, *147*, *195(26)*
Incompatibility (semantic), 10, *13*, 55, *56*, 72, 85, 95, 119, 129, 142, 159–60, 191(4), 194(19), *198(43)*
Incompleteness. *See* Gap
Index. *See* Deictic function
Indirection, 1-2, *19*, 59, 98
Intention, 46, *150*, *155*, 170(26)
Interpretant, *46*, 74, *81–114*, 115, 176 (17), *182(2)*, 190 (55), 191(63)
Interpretation. *See* Rationalization, Reading
Intertext, 31, 74, 79, 86, 88, *91*, 92, 94, 99–100, 123, 127, 165, 179(54), 194(19), *195(27)*, 199(47)
Intertextuality, 11, 42, 69, *82–86*, 95, 100, 103, 106–108, *109–10*, 114, 115, *119*, *124*, *124–38*, *138–50*, 160, *165*, 194 (19), 199(48)
Invariant, 3, 42, 55, 74, 75, 76, 87, 104, 117, 155
Inversion, 107–108, 139, 146, 189(49, 50, 51)
Irony, 65, 193(13)
Isotopy, 172 (24)

Jacob, Max, 187(32), 191(2)
Jarry, Alfred, 13, 71, 135–37, 196(31), 197(33)
Joke, 13–15, 16, 105, 106, 125, 128, 177 (42), 198(39)
Jouve, Pierre-Jean, 144–45

Keats, John, 121, 176(17)
Key word. *See* Matrix, Nuclear word
Kircher, Athanasius, 20–21

Laforgue, Jules, 125, 145–49, 171(17), 186(29), 187(33), 188(41)
Lamartine, Alphonse de, 108
Latency. *See* "Doughnut"
Lautréamont, 64–65, 108, 125, 143–44, 186(29)
Leiris, Michel, 35–36, 91–93, 108, 175 (37), 186(30), 189(50)
Lexical factors. *See* Word
Linearity, 12, *143*
Literariness, 3, *13*, 15, 22, 23, 28, 44, 63, 64–65, 74, *84*, *85–86*, 124, *137–38*, 148, *150*
Littré, Emile, 177(39), 191(61), 194(19)

Mallarmé, Stéphane, 15–19, 60, 79, 81, 125, 133, 134–37, 150–63, 176(17), 186 (31), 188(39)
Marker, 12, 22, 26, 27, 29, 32, 36, 37, 39, 44–45, 54, *64*, 65, *66*, 68, 70, 84, 99, 103, 117, 118, 127, 140, 180(63), 186 (29), 190(60)
Matrix, 6, 12, *13*, *19–21*, 23, *48*, 52, 54, 56, 57, 59, 61, *63*, 75, 78, 84, *97*, 98, *100*, 103, 107, 111, 117, *119*, 128, 136, 138, 159, *165*, 168(16), 172(25), 176(31), 185(24), 186(31)
Meaning, *1–3*, 5, 71–72, *81*, 100, 124, 184 (21)
Meliorative marker. *See* Valorization
Metalanguage, 54, 72, *138*, 170(3), 172 (25), 195(19), 198(40), 200(58)
Metaphor, 1, 2, 4, 10, 35–36, *39*, 41, 47, 49, 53, 60, 61, 65, 72, 73, 74, 83, 90, 91–92, 98, 122, *123*, 124, 129, 130, 133–34, 136, *143*, 147, 155, 158, 175 (14), *182(5)*, 184 (21)
Metonym, Metonymy, 1, 2, 7, 32, *39*, 49, 52, *58–63*, 65, 68, 78, 89, 98, 104, 113, 120, 122, *123*, 135, 140, 142, 144, 149, 163, 172(25), 176(29), 182(4), 200(65)
Michelet, Jules, 49–50, 75
Microcontext, 52, 129. *See also* Context
Milosz, O. V. de L., 34–35
Mimesis, 2–3, *4–6*, 7, 13–14, 18, 19, *21*, 23, 29–30, 49, 55, 61, 62, 68, 88, 111, 115, 121, *124*, 128, 143, 154, 161, 166, 168(14), 169 (20), 174(35), 181(66)
Model, 13, 17, *19–21*, 24, 39, 42, 48, 49, 50, *51*, 52, 57, 62, 70, 73, 81, 85, 87, 108, 110, 111, 126, 136, 138, 142, 172 (25), 177(42), 181(75), 186(31), 198(39)

Molière, 156
Monumentality, 20, *21–22*, 26, 198(40), 201(1)
Morphological factors, 89, 95, *117*, 122, 134, 135, 176(32), *181 (75)*
Motivation, 153, 175(8)

Narrative, 49, 53, 73, 99, *133*, 140, 151, 157, 175(8), 187(34), 192(8), 198(40)
Negation (sign permutation), 54–58, 119, 125, 127, *135*, 175(13)
Negative (pejorative). *See* Valorization
Neologism, *26–27*, *95–97*, 131, 134, 135–37, *184–85* (24)
Nerval, Gérard de, 100–101
Nodal point, 86, 87, 90, 92, 95, 96, 108, 153, 155
Nonliterary language, 75, 92, 114, 115, *164*, 183(13)
Nonsense, 2, 10–11, 16, 29–30, 36, 79, 93, 124, 130, 134, *135–37*, *139*, 140–41, *143*, 145
Nouveau, Germain, 186(29)
Nuclear word, 24, 25–26, 31–32, *39*, 48, *66*, 92, 144, 169(16), 172(24)

Obscurity, 13, 16, 84, 109, 115, 121, *139*, 145–46, 149, *150–63*, 183(16), 188(42)
Opposition (polar), 17, 25, 43–44, 53, 68, 69, 72, 74, 78, 110, 112, 113, 119, 138, 173(29), 175(37), 181(72), 186 (29)
Overdetermination, 11, *21–22*, *23–25*, 37, 53, 69, 74, 84, 88, 98, 107, *117*, *132*, 134, 153, 190(57), 193(18), 198(40)
Oxymoron, 11, 17, 41, 63, 111, 133, 161, 180(60)

Palimpsest, 86
Paradigm, 3–4, 8, 19, 20, 21, 34, 50, 56, 59, 78, *89*, 90, 91, 95, 96, 131, 138, 144, 183(15), 186(29), *189(54)*, *199 (53)*
Paragram. *See* Hypogram
Parody, 71, 93, 105, 108, 109, 127, 137, 139, 186(29), 188(42)
Paronomasia, 18, 21, 63, 135, 174(30), 187(32)
Paul, St., 171(14)
Pejorative marker. *See* Valorization
Péret, Benjamin, 14, *36–37*
Periphrasis 4, *19*, 31, 47, 64, 100, 113, 124, 129, 154, 175(10), *182(2)*, 194 (19), 198(40)
Poe, Edgar Allan, 74
Poem, 2, 21, 127–28, 131–32, 138. *See also* Text

Poetic discourse, 1, 3, 13, *19*, 21, 47, 53, *54*, 72, 109, 116, 138, *166*
Polarization, 6, 17, 41–42, *43–44*, 46, 52, 53, 66, 69, 72, 73, 78, 79, 93, 130, 132, *174(29)*, 182(4), 185(24), 186(31), 189 (54), 190(60), 193(12)
Polysemy, 90
Ponge, Francis, 94–95, 110–14, 122–24, 124–38
Portmanteau word, 95–97. *See also* Neologism
Positivization. *See* Valorization
Presupposition, 5, *25–31*, 53, 55, 69, 81, 86, 104, 124, 126, 142, 149, 168 (16)
Prévert, Jacques, 187(33)
Proairesis, 52
Prose poem, 70, 95–97, *116–24*, *124–38*
Pun, 21, 24, 81, *82–86*, 95, 105, 112, 113, 122, 128, 131–32, 141, *164*, *182(7)*, 185 (24), 187(32), 197(33)

Queneau, Raymond, 105–109
Quotation, 12, 63, 85, 95, 98, 99, 108, *109*, *110*, 116, 123, *134*, 139, *145–50*, 189(55), 191(62), 194(19)

Racine, Jean, 11, 41, 180(55)
Rationalization, 13, 16, 18–19, 35, 46, 62, 73, 76, 83, 85, 92, 115, 122, 124, 131, 145, 146, 164, 184 (24), 185(26), 187(37)
Reader, 2, 4–5, *12*, 16, 19, 22, 26, 28, 51, 55, 60–61, *63*, 75, 78, 84, *94*, *115–63*, *164–66*, *168(14)*, 168(16), *199(47)*
Reading, 1, *1–6*, 46, 138, 159, 160, *164–66*, 180(63), 188(46): correct, 74, *149*, 154, 199(47); hermeneutic, *5–6*, 12–13, *81*, 137–38, *145*, *168(13)*, 170(3), *198* (40); restrictive, 12, 21–22, 90–91, 109, *124–38*, *147*, *150*, *165*, 190(57), 195(27), 198(43). *See also* Retroactive reading
Ready-made, 116
Realism, 7, 9, 66, 67, 88, 160, 186(29)
Referent, 2, *5*, 6, 29, 54, 66, 73, 75, 79, 97, 121, 122, *130*, *137*, 142, *143*, *150*, 168(14), 173(29), 178 (47), 181(72), *190* (57)
Refrain, 77, 140–41
Repetition, 3–4, *49*, *51*, 61, 67, 88–89, 97, 102, 105, 107, *108–109*, 127, 144, 149, 165, 176(31)
Repression, 103, 113, 151, 185(24). *See also* Displacement, "Doughnut"
Retroactive reading, *5–6*, *9*, 12, 51, 68, 70, 72, 76, 81, 85, 90–91, 94, 109, 128, 132, 139, 165–66, 193(17), 199(52)

Riddle, 194(19)
Rimbaud, Arthur, 45, 58–59, 76–80, 101–105, 113, 118, 120–21, 191(63)
Ritual (the text as a verbal), 71, 108, 128, 132, 138, 140, 164
Ronsard, Pierre de, 82–86, 114, 153, 186 (30)
Rousseau, Jean-Baptiste, 155

Saint-Amant, 54–55
Saint-John Perse, 40–41
Sand, George, 180(62)
Scott, Walter, 100
Scrambling, 36, *138–50, 139*, 153, 159, 165, 199(48)
Self-sufficiency of the text, 124, 131–32, 170(26)
Semantic(s), 2, 37, 44, 91, 120, 134, 136, 140, 148, 155, 168(16), *172(24)*
Seme, 11, 22, 24, *25*, *31–39, 39*, 48, 52, 53, 54, 62, 75, 76, 79, 92, 96, 118, 133, 154, 175(13), 184(21), 185 (26), 190(60)
Sememe, *26*, 53, 78, 83, 96, 172(24)
Semiosis, *4, 6*, 8–10, 11, *13*, 14, 15, 52, 55, 60, 71, 88, 97, 115, 130, 138, 141, *166*, 172(25), *182(1)*, 201(1)
Semiotic(s), 4, 22, 72–74, 103, 116–24, 143, 146, 157, 162
Shakespeare, William, 101–104
Shelley, Percy Bysshe, 55, 190(60), 199 (55)
Sign, 3, 4, *11–12*, *23–46*, 47, 53–63, 87, *139*, 140, 164, *165*, 167(5), 168(14), 261 (11). *See also* Arbitrariness, Dual sign, Equivocal, Figurative sign, Textual sign
Significance, 2, 4, *6*, 10, *11–13*, 17, *19*, *22, 23*, 38, 42, *46*, 55, 57, 65, 68, 70–71, 80, *81*, 86, 99–100, 105, 107, 109, *115*, *117*, *118*, *124*, *143*, 144, 145, *149–50*, 163, *166*
Simile, 8–9, 52, 62–63, 185(24)
Sociolect, 30, 54, 97, 102, 104, 145, 161, 189(52), 189 (53), 199(50)
Sollers, Philippe, 200(58)
Sound symbolism, 175(15), 181(73)
Spoonerism, 108
Stereotype. *See* Cliché
Structural decoding. *See* Reading (hermeneutic)
Structure, *13*, *19*, 39, 44, *46*, 56, 63, 99, 150, 159, 166, 169(16), 188(39)
Style, Stylistic, 15, 23, 39, 47, 48, 52, 58, 59, 69, 73, 117, 127, 134, 139, 143, 154, 164, 184(24), 199(53), 201(1)
Substitute. *See* Transform

Suffix, 27, 30, 80, 84, 95, 135, 136, 181 (75), *185(26)*, 192(7)
Superimposition. *See* Hypogram
Surrealism, 70, 94, 124, 139–43
Syllepsis, 81
Symbol, 8, 10, 33, 38, 46, 53, 65, 99, 145, 147, 161, 176(32)
Synonym, 172 (24)
Syntax, 47, *89*, 129, 143, 144, 146, 159, 189(55)

Tautology, 3, 26–27, 54, 78, 85, 179(55), 180(60), 181(75), 188(46), 189(53), 195 (29), 198(44)
Tenor. *See* Metaphor
Text, 2, 3, *4, 6*, 11, *19*, 22, 45, *47–80*, 85, 94, 114, 118, 127–28, 137, 144, 164, *191(61)*
Textual sign, 36, 47, *70–75*, *109–14*, 121, *139*, 165, 175(1), 190 (55)
Textuality, 2, 20, 42, 51, 64, 66, 70, *109*, 114, 122, 131, *139*, 198(40)
Theme, 15, 36, *39*, 43, 45, 49, 56, 67, 68, 72, *90*, 96, 117–19, 121, 128, *141*, 146, 160, 180(61), 185(24), 188(39)
Title, *11–12*, 58, 67, 72, 77, 78, 80, *99–105*, *105–109*, 117, 121, 126, 127, *131*, 133, *154–55*, 172(25), 176(31)
Topos, 84, 186(30)
Transcoding, 36, 51, 81, *143*, 160, 162, 185(24), 188(39)
Transform, 21, 37, 39, 70, 72, 73, 107, 131, 133, 152, 169(23), 180(63), 194(19), 199(53)
Transformation, 11, *51*, 52, 55, 155, 161, 173(29), 190(56)
Tzara, Tristan, 79, 181(70)

Unacceptability, 139, 147–48, 160
Ungrammaticality, 2, 3, *4, 5–6*, 11, *13*, 21, 26, *42*, 55, *59*, 61, *62–63*, 70, 82, 85, 88, *89*, 94, 95, 97, 115, *123*, 128, 131, *136–37*, *165–66*, 190(57)
Unity. *See* Textuality
Usage. *See* Nonliterary language

Valéry, Paul, 56–57
Valorization, 90, 178(50), 183(15): meliorative, 11, 29, 31, 52–53, 64, 78, 84, 98, 111, 170(8), 171(14), 186(29); pejorative, 32, 34–36, 39, 45, 58, 59, 63, 78, 95, 102, 161, 179 (55)